Mind station

ASHISH BERI

NewDelhi • London

BLUEROSE PUBLISHERS
India | U.K.

Copyright © Ashish Beri 2025

All rights reserved by author. No part of this publication may be reproduced, stored in a retrieval system or transmitted in any form or by any means, electronic, mechanical, photocopying, recording or otherwise, without the prior permission of the author. Although every precaution has been taken to verify the accuracy of the information contained herein, the publisher assumes no responsibility for any errors or omissions. No liability is assumed for damages that may result from the use of information contained within.

BlueRose Publishers takes no responsibility for any damages, losses, or liabilities that may arise from the use or misuse of the information, products, or services provided in this publication.

For permissions requests or inquiries regarding this publication, please contact:

BLUEROSE PUBLISHERS
www.BlueRoseONE.com
info@bluerosepublishers.com
+91 8882 898 898
+4407342408967

ISBN: 978-93-6783-748-1

Cover design: Yash Singhal
Typesetting: Namrata Saini

First Edition: April 2025

Dedication

My book is dedicated to that divine power who had created circumstances so that I can fulfill my dream, and to my family which had always stand with me during difficult times.

Introducing My Self

I was born to parents who along with their families migrated from Pakistan after partition of India in 1947, my father offered his services to armed forces during 1971 Indo-Pak war. I put my first step on this mother earth on 1st October 1969, did my schooling from Central School and completed my graduation in 1991 from University of Allahabad with subjects English Literature, Economics & Education. We used to live in different cantonments due to my father's association with armed forces, he was avid reader and encourage whole family to read by subscribing magazines & newspapers, since childhood I had dream of joining Indian Military Academy, but got rejected by Services Selection Board due to an injury during SSB interview at Bhopal on 4th December 1992 and joined corporate sector in February 1994 to earn my livelihood.

I got married to my classmate on 25th February of 1994 and have one wonderful son who is presently working with British Telecom at their Gurugram office in Cyber Hub. Since childhood I had always believed that every individual should maintain its class & level irrespective of position or economical status, and lead a meaningful life which is the most precious gift of nature.

After having joined corporate sector February 1994, and spend approximately 13 years in industry and 13 years in an education set-up, during those 26 years I have seen many ups & downs from failures to injury and overcome them with the help of strength only which I have inherited from my parents and that is sheer courage which does not allow me to lose sight of my goal, which was to give my best while writing this book.

What prompted me to write this book? What is the reason or inspiration behind this book or I have written this just to showcase my knowledge? There was always a hidden desire in the corner of my heart for writing something which is totally genuine in nature and true. After taking career break in April 2021 (during covid times), Idea of converting my experiences and thoughts into a book comes to my mind, Before conceptualizing this book I have not published a single paper, it is my first attempt to express my thoughts, there is an incident which motivated to write or devise concepts role specific, it was summer time in 1979, when I was approximately ten years of age, and was mostly interested in reading articles, sports news, current affairs etc., but I could not understand few topics such as spiritualism and economy , one day when my father came back from office in the evening, I asked him about the same, he told me that "it's not for the person of your age, you will understand when you grow up" , then as a child I suggested him that above every article it should be mentioned for which age group it is written, to avoid wastage of time and energy he gave me a smile and kept himself busy in some house hold work.

My love with books continued from short stories to novels, world war stories, self help books & autobiographies, during my career transition from industry to a higher education set-up in the second half of my career, I got a chance to teach students general management and personality development topics, during that period of life I decided to write a book on soft skills and personality enhancement.

In the beginning of this project only one thing was in my mind that my book should be totally different from books presently available on the above topics. After spending more than 27 years in corporate and education sector, I came to understand that all the actions and emotions are not applicable to all the positions or roles at same point of time, one action may be applicable for one position, same action may be applicable to other position at other point of time. this can be understood by the example,

Emotional understanding for a blue collared team member is totally different for a white collared one, every role requires some specific qualities to execute it responsibilities or in other words things will be much better if manage ourselves and team members in accordance with the role assigned.

Some thing about book;

My book contains role specific requirement on the topics, **1) Know thy self, 2) My mind is my best friend, 3) Personality, 4) Lead your ship, 5) De-Stressing, 6) Time Awareness, 7) Building a winning team, 8) Attitude, 9) Communication and 10) Emotional Understanding.** These four roles are **Student, team member, team leader and leader**, out of the above four position I have experience of first three roles, what ever I have written in the book is personally experienced by me in one form or the other, I avoid preaching any thing which I can't practice.

My Motto in life is "Everybody cannot do everything, but everybody can do some thing".

I am very much sure that readers from all walks of corporate sector will be benefited from this book and come to know about few concepts for the first time. My motive will be fulfilled and serve my purpose of sharing my ideas and experience through this book if some of the readers got benefited by using these ideas for managing affairs of their personal and professional life.

In this book I have tried to explain every topic or concept by giving example and creating scenarios, some new concepts you will come across such as instead of 'Time Saving', I have devised new concept of 'Time Generating', instead of 'Emotional Intelligence' you will know a new concept of 'Emotional Understanding'. I have crafted a new word 'Trichual' in place of mutual, mutual as we all know that is used for action between two individuals, but in a corporate set-up there are three separate identities, I, we (team) and organization, to move ahead of 'mutual' we have to see things from the point of view of 'Trichual'.

I am not exaggerating but I am very much sure that this book will definitely benefit all the four pillars of society **Student, team member, team leader and leader of the organization** and help them to act as per their assigned specific role.

All of us are executing our assigned roles and responsibilities with the best of our abilities, but with the changing times some gaps keep on surfacing, in order to know those gaps and fill them to realise our goals, we can take the help of this book, which has approximately 375 pages covering ten topics.

In my views this extraordinary book is created by an ordinary person, ordinary person in the sense that I have not worked in any fortune 500 organisation, or executed my responsibilities as CEO in any reputed institution or ever topped in my class, but after having worked for around 27 years I was clearly able to point out if I have acted in a better manner or improved myself, I would have definitely reached higher ladder of my career.

Recommendations

After having read this book, in short, I can say that this is beneficial to every pillar of mankind i.e. from student to corporate team member irrespective of which society or country she or he is from.

This book has universal appeal across the boundaries.

Maj. (Retd.) Saras C. Tripathi.

This book offers a compelling insight into the motivation and purpose behind its creation. It captures a personal journey from childhood curiosity to corporate and academic experiences, shaping a deep understanding of soft skills and leadership. The originality of the book shines through concepts like "Time Generation" and "Trichual." Its structured approach, role-specific applications, and practical scenarios make it a valuable resource for both professionals and students. Overall, it stands as a thought-provoking and practical guide to self-improvement and leadership.

Prof. Vineeta Dutta Roy

"A cornucopia of well-reasoned, insightful analysis of how growth of an individual leads to corporate growth and economic well being."

Vijay Emmanuel
Founder & CEO
Cinnamon Wealth Pvt. Ltd.

Contents

Know thyself and team 1

Mind is My Best Friend 43

Attitude 77

Communication 114

Emotional Understanding, Stability & Sensibility 156

Lead Your Dhip 199

Personality 242

De-Stressing 277

Building a Winning Team 309

Time Awareness 353

Know thyself and team

Knowing yourself is the beginning of all wisdom; Aristotle.

Knowing self is one of the prime requirements for a professional to be successful in respective domain, not only in the domain but also to lead team in a better way, knowing self is a learning experience and must to move in right direction which requires adequate time, relentless effort, and positive intentions by removing the status quo, shake ourselves and leave the comfort zone. There is only one obstacle in knowing self and that is **self-deception**, there is a say which states that 10% of human being deceives others whereas 90% of human beings deceive themselves, we must introspect and avoid wilful blinding of self. A person who really wants to know self for betterment has to take first step by accepting the responsibility of its present condition and avoid blaming others, blaming others thwarts our ability to see as we are and we avoid seeing our true selves. After having understood above one has to act accordingly for bringing required changes as nothing in life changes until we change ourselves.

If a student, a team member, a team leader, or a leader wants to excel in their personal & professional roles, they must do one thing for sure that is '**know thy self**'. When we meet some body, we are interested in knowing about him or her in detail, similarly we must meet ourselves daily which is very important to know who we are. What we want in our life? We have to know ourselves in order to know others, knowing each other is the basic of understanding. 'Knowing thy self' is also known as personal quotient (PQ) with the help of which, we can improve upon our emotional understanding (EU) and intelligence quotient (IQ) by filling the existing gaps.

We must know thy self to know our limitations, weaknesses and strengths so that we can work on them, rise above our ego and exceed our limitations. We are the best creature of nature and have to make balance between our desires and ground realities of life, in order to have peace with self we must understand the whole process of thoughts, feelings and actions which requires great deal of maturity and awareness to move towards a state of bliss.

We expect people to accept our demands and restrictions, when they do not dance to our tune, we maintain distance with them by creating a wall of difference, we have to love and understand people as they are. Best thing in our life happens when we start discovering and guiding self to know our limitations and how to overcome them to realise our full potential, which is the ultimate goal of every human being.

Discovery of qualities and abilities in our team members keeps us in tune with time, whereas lack of discovery in others leads to stagnation like still water. When we are angry or miserable, we believe someone else needs to be fixed, but when we are sick it is we who need the medication. We need to know our weaknesses, strengths and qualities to play a particular role, to be successful in different roles we need different qualities and approach. Let us discuss them one by one.

Scenario; Rahul was returning from head office, in his bag there was an envelope containing promotion letter as head of north zone (operations), he looks back at his career spanning over twenty years, as trainee in his first job, there after he moved to department head and now in the same organisation he is promoted as head (operations).

He started self-analysing and his entire career flashed in front of his eyes in slow motion when he joined his first organisation as trainee, he reached HR department for joining formalities and met department head Mr. Bajaj for introductory orientation who asked one question. Tell me young man how you will execute your responsibilities as trainee? I replied by saying that "I will know about my colleagues, seniors & department and follow their instructions". Mr. Bajaj said "My dear young man it is good to know others, but in the process, you must know thyself to be successful in life and career. Mr. Bajaj told me about four points which an individual must look around i.e., positive, negative, plus and minus then he explained all the four points by giving **example of a car, positive point can align with top gear, negative point as brakes, plus point as neutral gear and minus point as flat tyre.** Throughout his life Rahul remember the words of Mr. Bajaj and follow the advice received on the very first day of his career, today with promotion letter in his bag he gave million thanks to Mr. Bajaj by joining his both hands in gratitude.

Know thyself and team

Knowing thyself for Leader; Rakesh receives an e-mail from his head office in which he was given additional responsibilities to look after another branch which handles business for dealing in sugar trading, whereas till now Rakesh has exposure to business related to printing papers only while driving back to his residence after day's work, He was thinking about the reasons for assigning additional responsibilities in spite of availability of many other experienced and senior team members, he started counting some qualities which he know about self. One of them is combination of smart and hard work, second is honesty is still the best policy and last but not the least teamwork can take you to the highest level, he was very happy & satisfied for being part of this organization since last five years and top management also relied upon him due to these qualities.

It is very important for a leader to introspect to move from title based leadership to attitude based leadership and is expected to take responsibility of all the activities going on in organisation and should have proficiency & exposure to every managerial activity, but most of the times it has been found that no individual is complete there is always a room for learning and a gap to be filled for better results and to practice choice based leadership, a head of organisation has to move one step further i.e. from merely managing team to leading the team, introspection means knowing the strength and weaknesses of self, this can be done only once the strength & weaknesses are on drawing board for redesigning, a leader who is interested in executing his responsibility in diligent manner make continuous efforts to know thyself.

Top Gear (Positive); Achievement oriented; as soon as you turn your car key, to do list start flashing in front of your eyes, every day is a fresh beginning, leaving your weak thoughts behind you feel happy by executing required tasks, waiting for another task to be added and completed with great deal of enthusiasm. A leader's job is to discover the best for organisation and take it to the next level. Achievement oriented leader is always full of positive energy by accepting new challenges as stepping stones towards organisational and professional excellence. An achievement-oriented leader motivates whole team and team also wants to follow the footprints & examples set by its leader. Having top gear **(Strength)** is very much required for a leader who is symbol and represents the organisation.

Scenario; Ashok's team is participating in annual quiz competition organised by **quality control department** of organisation and won runners-up trophy in the quality circle competition, but Ashok is not satisfied with the performance of his team as he wants to pick winners trophy in the next competition, so he decided to act early by forming team, budget allocations, providing extra facilities and resources required for winning, for Ashok a win is a win whether it is small or big.

Why Ashok wants his team to win **Quality Circle** competition? Just not to have more feather in his cap, along with winning he want his team to be involved in more meaningful activity, as he is a firm believer in producing quality products, by this quiz competition he wants youngster to know about the benefit of producing quality product and negative side of not doing so, he always emphasis upon and communicate his team that poor quality products will endanger the very existence of our organisation by throwing us out of competition.

Brake (Negative); Over-Analysis oriented; You analyse situation or demand to unrealistic length, even it might result in the obsoleteness of demand, even it is very important for a department or an individual team member, it may be demand for a new software or ergonomic furniture for team members. As a leader my job is to overcome the weakness in the interest of organisation and team members, doing too much analysis while taking small decisions, or spending too much time on the matters which do not require time in proportion to their importance, it has been observed that too much analysis is mostly done on the matters which are not related to self. A leader must not involve self in deciding petty things for which he or organisation is not directly affected. Every individual had brakes **(Weaknesses)** in his personal and professional lives, identifying, acknowledging and working smart & hard to remove these brakes will increase the speed of organisation, team and self.

Scenario; Ashok's board of management has approved the purchase of ergonomically designed office furniture to save time and increase productivity, as team members are repeatedly taking medical leaves due to neck & spine problems, it was decided to provide ergonomically designed furniture to all team members, expenditure to which was much less than cost of losing manpower & manhours. Procurement has to be finalised within one months' time, but due to extra cautiousness and to much analysis Ashok has not been able to finalise the purchase of furniture as deadline is getting near.

One more point to be noted down that Ashok was no where being an expert or specialist in ergonomics, after being reminded about the purchase of furniture, Ashok set aside his analysis and handover the task to a committee comprising of Purchase Manager, Finance Manager and an Ergonomic Expert (hired from outside) which ultimately completed the task by the second deadline.

Neutral Gear (plus); Flexible approach is required when you see new opportunity for growth as your adaptability quotient has wide range which can prove that you are not far behind your competitors in terms of attitude or hard work. There comes a time in every organisation or in the life of a professional when she or he has to leave aside personal vendetta by start thinking in the interest of organisation, be it involving those team members who are in the eyes of management are not efficient or it may be including those who have not taken your side in a conflict. Neutral approach brings clarity in taking decisions with strength.

When there is a dark cloud of confusion, put yourself in neutral gear, neither forward nor backward, taking nobody's side only the interest of organisation in mind. Having neutral gear **(Opportunity)** in the professional basket of a leader is a boon for self and for the team as well, a neutral gear is that peaceful situation which helps a leader to take decisions which have long lasting impact on organisation & team.

Scenario; Ashok received an instruction from his board of directors to form a team to counter false information campaign spread in social media by their competitors, for this Ashok has to include Ranjeet in his team, whom Ashok don't like a bit personally, but in the interest of the organisation Ranjeet was also included in team and assigned important role as well, because Ranjeet is well known for his expertise in social media and is looking after digital marketing campaign of new product to be launched next month. Ashok and Ranjeet had some altercation during their last meeting in the presence of senior board members. Ashok kept aside his differences by giving Ranjeet important role in the team. This decision of Ashok as CEO bore fruit as Ranjeet's team was more than successful in handling the maligned campaign of their competitors. The decision of Ashok has set the example and well rewarded for remaining in **neutral gear** at the time of decision making

Flat Tyre (Minus); As leader of an organisation, one has to daily encounter some unforeseen incidents or situation which one has not planned for and has to find time from your planned schedule for these unannounced activities, it could be sudden breakdown of assembly line, one of your important team members putting up papers for greener pastures or the project you were sure of winning but could not. Dealing with unplanned activity makes you feel like a flat tyre, unable to move forward or backward and remaining in a confused state of mind, which situation to deal with, or in other words you feel discomfort while dealing with complex situations simultaneously you are happy to take one situation one time.

For **example,** if you have to prepare a report regarding setting up of new branch office in other city, suddenly a mail popped up in your box intimating you about preparation of annual report. Knowing one's flat tyre **(Threat)** is very beneficial for a leader as it will help him or her to repair it fast and move ahead, any ignorance shown in this matter will have very negative effect on the personal and professional front.

Scenario; Ashok was preparing annual report for board meeting, suddenly he receives a call from secretary reminding of two important upcoming events to take place this week, first is inspection of fire department's audit and second one is meeting of internal productivity council. On hearing this Ashok become perplexed and could not apply himself to any one task, this is Ashok's flat tyre which he has to change to move forward otherwise he will be struck in the middle and all his positive points won't be counted. Ashok become confused and could not decide which one is important, which job is time bound or which could be postponed, he was so confused that for an hour his productivity comes to stand still.

Then he decides to call his deputy and seek help, his deputy clarified the situation by telling him that fire department's inspection is regulatory requirement whose 'NOC' is very much required to continue the operations and could not be postponed, whereas annual report preparation is internal matter and board of members can be requested for extended new deadline. In this way Ashok was able to repair his flat tyre with the help of his deputy and move forward.

Developing qualities for and by a Leader; When we are discussing role specific qualities for each & every role from leader to student, there are few qualities a leader must develop to lead the team successfully and keep the flag of organisation flying high. These qualities if developed will make a leader's path easy. Let us discuss those qualities one by one.

Bulldozer; As a leader one needs to develop and discover the qualities like a bulldozer i.e. ability & intention to remove obstacles for the smooth functioning of organisation, paving way for better team functioning, always looking for doing the things right i.e. identifying the hinderances, finding an amicable solution and try to implement it with full force, even if it makes some important team members unhappy, if it is in the favour of team and organisation it has to be implemented without fail, a bulldozer will do it any way, whether it is terminating a toxic employee or modifying a policy which is being misused by few team members. A bulldozer will get rid of a toxic employee who might be instrumental in getting the latest project but in whose eyes he is the only one important and other team members are mediocre, they all are supposed to follow him and dance to his tune which makes others feel bad, but before removing a toxic employee a leader will make sure that there is well trained replacement is on the cards and ready to take charge to avoid any gap in the performance of the team.

A leader will bulldoze any policy change which is done to benefit the upper layer of the organization, during tough times of any organisation cutting down the benefits of lower-level employees is always the first choice and another cost cutting measure which is adopted is terminating the services of 'weak' employees but not of inefficient employees, a bulldozer does not only smoothen the way but also obstruct the way of a problem which is coming to harm the interest of the organisation. It stands in the way of any projectile which is fired to dislodge the team or organisation. It is necessary for the leader to discover these qualities not only in self, but also in other team members to continue the legacy of bulldozer, one can identify a young bulldozer by behaviour and standing for the right, a young bulldozer can be identified by its sad behaviour if any thing wrong or unjust happened to a team mate, that's all s/he can do at this point of time.

Binocular; A leader must develop and discover binocular instinct, as we all know that with the help of binocular we can see beyond our limit of naked eyes and very far, we can see what is coming towards us or how far we can take our team, in other words we extend our vision beyond normal boundaries, In practical and professional words we can see what our competitors are doing, what will be the life cycle of our product, how much budget is required to remain ahead of competitors, if we are behind what steps need to be taken to win the race of excellence or to remain in neck to neck healthy fight with competitors. We have to discover not only our strengths but our weaknesses also which will make us realise that we are using 20th century solutions to solve the problems of 21st century. Binocular instinct will help us to remove the obstructions of short 'sightedness' and take us towards 'farsightedness'.

Scenario; One of the best examples of farsightedness I have come across in my life is about the chief of the Indian contingent which summited the mount Everest in May 1965, Indian Government wanted to honour head of the contingent with 'Arjuna' award, as he had led the expedition successfully, but he out rightly rejected the proposal, in his reply he informed the government authorities that "I will accept award only if all the members of the team is awarded "Arjuna award", With this binocular instinct 'chief of contingent' was able to keep his team together for the rest of life, the team went on to celebrate fifty years of togetherness, which was possible only due to binocular instinct. Imagine what would have happened if chief had accepted and walked away with the award, there will be no glory for other team members, by his binocular instinct chief was able to spread the glory & pride in the life of every team member of the expedition.

Electrode; An electrode is a metallic rod which has both ends, i.e. positive and negative, no equipment can be run without proper fitment of electrode and will work only if we connect the right end to its place in that equipment, similarly a leader is expected to discover the electrode like qualities and should be able to infuse positive current & energy in organisation and simultaneously ready with negative current & energy to infuse it if required, As we all know that positive current & charge is required to lift the organisation upward and for making efforts to make it better and move forward but at the same time negative energy & charge is also required to safeguard the interest of the organisation.

From inside it may be taking tough decision regarding an efficient but toxic team member, who is making other team members survival difficult or implementing a policy which is in the larger interest of the organisation and in tune with the time for better future of organisation, it really requires negative side of the electrode to absorb the shock, stand tall & still. Now it must have been clearly established that we as a leader must posses the both side of the electrode as having single side does not serve our purpose to be a successful leader. Secondly, we must discover the same within our team members, educate & expose them about the benefits of having negative current or charge as well and how & when to use it.

Inverter; As a leader when ever a need or requirement arises team members will come to leader, what will happen if a leader is not able to fulfil their need for completing a professional process, we feel guilty and some times blame those who demands these resources, but they are not so experienced or can take decision as a competent authority,

Now the qualities of inverter comes into picture, as we all know that inverter provides us uninterrupted power supply in case of **'power'** failure, which saves systems from crashing, as a leader we must inclined towards qualities of inverter, an experienced & matured leader must fully understand the process by identifying the weak links which can disturb the whole process, these precious resources of team and organisation could be in the form of human assets, finances or important machines, hardware or software. It is the duty of leader to visualise the possible breakdown or failure of the process by doing mock tests & drills.

Scenario; This could be understood by traditional **example** of not so qualified but educated housewives in the form of our grandmothers and mothers, during those times bank facility was not in the reach of every household, but during any emergency, be it a sudden announcement of marriage in family or business requirements, our grandfather and father look towards our grandmother and wife, who never let them down, it could be understood by another domestic example, what we learn from our 'inverter' father, we all used to have water pumping machines which helps us getting water to our second floor house it was called 'tullu', once our tullu pump broke down, we have to buy another pump, first thing my father did was to get that broke down pump repaired and keep it well oiled ready to be used in next emergency requirement.

Although it was difficult to bear the expenses to buy new pump and getting the older one repaired at the same time, now what a leader has to do if it wants to create a back up plan to fill the sudden loss of human assets. S/he is expected to take active interest in the hierarchy along with HR department by always having standbys to fill in the gap. Normally in an organisation only the required or a smaller number of manpower is provided, an inverter leader always finds the way to have one or two extra hands which can be used at the time of emergency.

Know thyself and team

Knowing thyself for Team Leader; A team leader needs to introspect about qualities they posses for leading the team and those qualities which are to be added for moving to next level, when a team leader decides to introspect leading to successfully handling the team and open to correction if required, this introspection when reach final stage will be of immense importance for self and other team members as well.

Top Gear (positive); A team leader must have quality of an actor, an actor starts taking action as soon as she or he listen the words light, camera, action from the mouth of director, as an actor you are ready to take action once a decision is taken, you know action is the key to keep you and your team moving even if there is little doubt about it, for example; if a decision is made to procure better raw material to improve quality of the product you start searching for the best material available nearby without wasting any time.

A top gear team leader is very important for every organisation, besides setting the tone and speed for the team, she or he sets the example to be followed by young mind and professionals who are new to the team. Knowing about one's top gear is very beneficial to and spreading it honestly with selfless intention among colleagues is beneficial for organisation as well and is very helpful for seniors to allocate important tasks and projects with confidence.

Scenario; As soon as **Harish's** senior say's light, action & camera he is charged up by started taking action without wasting a single minute, Harish very well understands the importance of immediate action on the decision taken, yesterday he receives a go ahead to execute the recruitment process for newly formed department, which includes hiring a placement agency, giving ad in newspapers, developing job description for all the vacant positions, s/he very well understands that human assets are the most valuable, modifiable and responsible for the make or break of any organisation and aware that competitors are also vouching for best professionals, so, he don't want to make any delay in the process to remain ahead of competitors.

Brake (negative); Once you take charge you do not hesitate to impose your line of action on your team members or while moving towards goal you face constructive criticism, even you do not listen to a team member who is expert in this matter. Every team leader is responsible for the best results a team can produce, but sometimes in overenthusiasm some of the team leaders go irresponsibly far, where they want to do every activity by them selves due to one reason or the other and are also unaware that this practice is pulling the team backward, because other team members when not allowed to utilise their expertise, suffers from feeling of uselessness and loses motivation to be part of team, doing everything by self for a team leader may be short term approach but in long term this approach will alienate from team and found standing alone at the time when she or he needed it most. This philosophy of 'solo acting' is **weakness** for team leaders, which needs to be overcome and corrected as soon as it is identified in **trichual** interest of self, team and organisation.

Scenario; Harish is team leader (Marketing) of ASG corporation which is manufacturing agriculture related product, ASG corporation has developed a new improvised device which they think will be very successful and increase their profits many times, Harish was given the responsibility to start preparation for the launch of new product as soon as he received the instructions from his Head office to finalise the date for new product which is meant for rural market, harish decided to launch it in the month of March.

During one of the launch meetings a senior & experienced team member suggested that we should launch our product in the last week of April, because in the month of April rural population will have more cash in hand after the seasonal harvest, as per this senior and experienced team member timing is equally important in the launch of any product. But Harish did not pay any attention to the advice of this experienced team member and went ahead with his plan of **'solo acting'** which resulted in partial failure of product launch and not generating the expected revenue. Harish after this incident understood the participation of whole team in decision making by taking care next time and every time.

Neutral Gear (plus); A team leader is bridge between top management and team, every team leader should pass on the good deeds of team to higher authority and management with positive intention & purpose, this positive action of team leader will bore fruits beyond imagination by creating an atmosphere of mutual trust, which is the most desirable action required to complete this cycle of give and take. with the good communication skill any one can turn a challenge into **opportunity,** Good communication skill can turn a negative situation into a positive one and an unproductive activity can be turn into a productive one, it all depends on what you say, how you say and when you say, timing is very important in communication, as words expressed at appropriate time have double effect and we should not leave any opportunity to learn how to communicate effectively for the **trichual** benefit of self, team and organisation, Now you understand the most important component which keeps a team together is communication, it is communication which brings an idea into reality.

Scenario: Harish who joined this organisation as a trainee twelve years back rose to the post of team leader (marketing) due to one of his qualities and that is his communication skills which is one of the best among team leaders, whether it is formal or informal, during movement in corridor nobody can go unnoticed or any miss call not called back. One of the examples of communication he sets was during difficult hours of covid -19 due to which whole world was suffering. He kept his staff motivated and able to convince the top management to minimize the downsizing process, make sure that salary of middle and lower level does not take a cut due to financial constraints.

Most important point of his communication was in the form of warning that this type of situation may be reoccurring so its better to save money, avoid unnecessary expenditure and always have the bank balance to sustain one year without regular income. Third point he communicated was equally important, he declared that if any team member is laid off due to ongoing crisis s/he will be the first preference to join back after normalisation of conditions. Harish was able to create an atmosphere of trust between top management and team members, those who were laid off were also communicated the difficult condition with sincerity and make them aware of the circumstances which has forced the organisation to take tough and unpleasant decisions.

Flat Tyre (Minus); A team leader while leading a team might become overfriendly with some team members or establish social & family relations with some of the them, all these actions make a team member emotionally weak. As a team leader it is very necessary and important to keep personal & professional life separate, as captain of the team, team leader's job is to get the allotted task completed in time, failing which a real **threat** is clearly visible and the very existence of team is in danger. To keep the team intact a team leader must follow the policy of treating every team member equally, follow the standard operating procedure and do not hesitate to direct firmly.

Scenario: Harish was sitting in his office, thinking about the project 'Z' to be delivered to its client on schedule, but actually he was really worried about the input to be delivered by Rakesh, he is not sure whether Rakesh is serious enough to provide support to execute the project or not as he was late in submission of input during last project also, but Harish did not say anything to avoid confrontation as Rakesh is from same city and both families become very close and celebrate festivals with each other, but Harish has to intervene at one point of time in the interest of organisation and team, if Harish does not deal firmly with Rakesh other team members might start doubting his capability to lead and allegation of favouritism starts moving around. A team leader must handle this **threat** amicably to avoid the situation turning ugly.

Developing the qualities required for a team leader; A team leader requires some specific qualities in addition to those which s/he is already possessing. These qualities will help a team leader to further enhanced area of impression, these qualities not only help the team leader but also infects other team members being exposed to new unconventional topics and situations.

Historian; You must be wondering what is the role of history in a dynamic setup, for most of the people what is gone is gone, let us forget and move ahead but one has to remember history to move ahead in future, remembering history helps in taking appropriate & correct decisions with the context of a particular situation, a historian will go back in flash back and try to sum-up what were the circumstances then and what was the outcome of that decision, what will be the effect of decision in present situation only a historian team leader can go back in to history to decide about the future, as his experience tells him that history is never obsolete and it is very well a part of present and future, or in other words history, present & future are interconnected and popup at appropriate time for betterment of trichual. A team leader must remember that history will help to take correct decision for and in the future. A historian will be able to remove so many problems by keeping in context every situation. This could be understood by following scenario.

Scenario; While working with my previous institution I came across this type of situation not once but twice. One of our team members whose father has just retired from paramilitary services and wanted to do some social service voluntarily, so my team member requested HR head that his father will give volunteer services to the organization, but Administration-head who was associated with the organization since last twenty-five years, refused. When other members enquired about the reason behind his refusal, He sited one incident when he faced humiliation in spite of doing good, it was six years back when almost same scenario happens as one of the team members approached admin head for permission of voluntary services for his retired father, permission was granted, during this time two more team member approached administration department to accommodate their fathers for voluntary services, Admin-head refused the permission as organisation cannot accommodate team member's retired parents for voluntary services, to avoid the allegation of biasness from those whose parents were not given permission to do volunteer service, but this time Admin head was able to take correct decision by keeping history in mind with respect to same incident.

Scenario 2; Our organisation selected a professional whose expertise was very much required for project which was expected to last for five years, but he was asking for remuneration much more than our existing team members, our historian HR head told me that we have to be very careful while taking final decision, he reminds me what happens when we have appointed one specialist on higher remuneration without taking our present team member into confidence resulted in two key members of project leaving the organisation, this time our historian HR head wanted to take into confidence the other team members before taking any decision, now it is very much clear from scenarios discussed above which shows us the importance of historian in self and team members as well.

Gardener; What a gardener does? A gardener look for qualities in each one of the plants & trees in garden, s/he knows when it will bear fruit or flower and understand what are the conditions required for full blossom, s/he is matured enough to distinguish between the different plants of same category which will bear fruit and which will not, a gardener also find out which plant is creating trouble for other plants, which plant is obstructing sunlight of other plants or in other words which plant is consuming other plants water and manure, which plant deserve better care to flourish. Which part of the garden (organization) requires beautification (diversification). Gardener looks for those qualities in team members which others can not see, a gardener is interested in discovering many flowers & fruits in one plant by regularly doing experiments or exposing the plants to various different and trying conditions, making it more fruitful for team & plant for itself.

A gardener loves all his plants despite of different shape or size, some of the plants or branches might have thorn on it but all are given equal attention and looked after to make garden a beautiful place. All the plants and trees are given their due requirement of water, sunlight and manure till they don't harm others. When a team leader discovers the qualities of a gardener in self, team also discovers some hidden qualities, they know that what condition or ground is required to make those qualities beneficial for the team and individual it self.

Sometimes a gardener will restrict water and manure supply to few plants so that they can find their own way by extending & digging their roots deeper, (putting it's team member to difficult and different conditions for their upliftment and growth), a team leader with gardener's quality will spend extra time to mentor/coach, a pro-acative team member will look forward to its team leader for requirement of any professional training in the interest of team and self, gardener team leader will go extra length to make budgetary arrangements for the same. In other words, a gardener team leader is happiest when his team member is growing horizontally or vertically, simultaneously a gardener will provide every possible help to a team member who is unable to meet goals or struggling to execute assigned professional responsibility, s/he will spend extra time to find out the reason behind a struggling team member and if possible, will extend all sort of help to remove shortcomings or reason behind under-performance.

Proposer; Proposer can be defined as an individual who is filled with ideas and does not hesitate to put forward it during meetings and discussions and is confident that what ever has in its mind will bring better results, s/he will try to propose a simple solution for a difficult problem and will have its hands up during a meeting by suggesting to highest authority an improved or better option, saving team from herd mentality.

But how a proposer comes into picture or why a proposer is confident about proposals, because s/he has the habit of thinking and imagining betterment in every circumstances & condition, s/he is exercising every moment for improved condition, what if this road would have been designed better, it would have saved many liters of fuel and what if redlight have been placed at this point would have been clearly visible to drivers, what if this dustbin has been little bigger so that housekeeper does not have to clear it after every two hours saving time, energy and resources (garbage bags), what if we could change the direction or design of this piece of furniture will result in saving office space, or if we could place water cooler or coffee dispenser at this place will help team members save time, a proposers mind is always had its lights on in public place or at work,

Scenario; A proposer is attending a meeting to cut cost and curtail extra expenditure, during first step of cost cutting all members have voted in favor of discontinuing the transport services provided to its employees, A proposer will suggest that we should start with discontinuation of transport services for morning shift only, transport services for evening shift should continue as usual, because for female team members its unsafe and difficult to get public transport during evening & night shift. A proposer is always interested in bringing permanent change but at adequate speed. It's the responsibility of organization & leader to encourage proposers in team to bring clarity, a small suggestion accepted might bring the desired change, secondly when proposals are accepted by higher management other team members are also encouraged to participate in the process, one very important thing a team leader who has discovered proposer in his team, may assigned a task to work on the particular situation for brain storming it for better outcome.

Magnet; What does a magnet do? It remains static and all other particles having iron ore are attracted towards it, wants to be in its sphere or with it or like it, Similarly a team leader should develop magnet like qualities to attract and motivate other team members to develop qualities of magnet by developing and maintaining the properties which attracts other team members, magnet in the team has solution to most of the problems, if cannot solve a problem things are cooled by the patient hearing of the matter, listening is one of the fine qualities which a magnet posses, magnet while attracting does not discriminate between known and unknown.

Scenario; A new joiner was standing on shop floor little bit perplexed; everybody will avoid her because if they will ask what happened? They have to give time and if it is with in their radius they have to provide solution as well, but a magnet will not hesitate to ask, spend time and provide solution as well and is confident of their friends as its friends know that what ever matter we will discuss with magnet will remain up to magnet only will not use it in his favor during weakest of time, Magnet is interested in making new bonds with in and outside its team, for the sake of maintaining bonds a magnet will spend some valuable time and resources to bring confidence into those who are attracted towards him or her to make this bond long-lasting, sometimes a magnet might lose few things in the process , but it don't changes track or back walk because a magnet is firm believer in attracting. Having few magnets in team will help in keeping the team together, as during any problem before heading towards final authority 'magnet' is the first stop which gives them right advice and prevent any loss to team and organization, a magnet can be best utilized to make new team members comfortable. In short, we can say "A magnet will shine brighter and brighter when utilized frequently".

Knowing thyself for Team Member; A team member is backbone on which head & heart of every organisation stands, so it's very necessary for this back bone to remain straight with strength and keep growing by considering self as future leader and taking steps in the right direction for realising dreams, It is one of the basic requirements for a team member to know about self, as s/he might have own strength in the form of being energetic, positive approach and problem-solving qualities (positive), but may not be good at team management, patience and giving (negative), a team member can take steps to make his strengths more result oriented and remove its weaknesses, s/he can use energy and time available for the purpose (plus), a team member is normally in the third stage of hierarchy and has to devote lot of time in keeping balance between personal and professional life which demands lot of energy & resources, this may offset an individual's plan for improvement and biggest obstacle is resistance to change (minus). Let us discuss those plus and minuses in brief.

Top Gear (Positive); A team member who is just new to corporate set up must posses the quality of an improver, an improver has the **strength** to introspect, embrace the areas of learning and overcome those roadblocks by using the available resources, a team member should realistically examines potential and must know where s/he stands, with a very insightful observation while executing any task s/he must tend to find better procedure to execute the same and find every possibility to implement that improvement, not only improvement in process but in improving self and others as well, a s/he have firm belief that small improvements lead to big changes. This quality differentiates an improver from other team members, after some times other team members will also follow by mentioning an improver as example.

Scenario; Akhilesh has joined as trainee three years back in the sales department of a multinational company, since the beginning of college time he is interested in making some improvement in current status of every activity or make things more useful and better. During his instinct as trainee, he came across one such incident in which final product could not be delivered on time due to non-availability of one key component, he started finding new source & vendor to procure the same, to avoid the dependency on one supplier. Finding and suggesting a new supplier has not been very easy. It requires go-ahead from seniors, lot of ifs and buts created by already established vendor, quality testing of new component and price variation has to be handled properly, it was not easy for seniors to digest that a team member having only three years of experience is taking initiative of introducing an additional vendor for key component, but with over the time everything settles down making Akhilesh a satisfied professional as he was well praised by other team members for taking initiative in the interest of organisation.

Brake (Negative); When we are young and lacks experience & practical knowledge, we want to look for perfection in every activity, tend to count every second to execute the things as per operating manuals and books, but things are little bit different from the description of books. Operating manuals are written assuming the perfect conditions where as conditions on the floor is totally different in terms of weather, atmosphere, working conditions and above all human resources, but when as a perfectionist we try to execute things as per operating manual, looking for perfection in every activity we do it by adopting rigidness and leaving flexibility far behind, we are inviting **weakness,** creating hurdles for self and team. To get rid of this weakness one has to adopt and understand that we can achieve near perfection but not perfection. It is very important for an individual team member to embrace the rule of flexibility and execute the task with its help.

Scenario; Akhilesh wants to do everything with perfection as he is looking after distribution of product and was interested in every second counts as distribution of product involves a process which is mainly handled by human beings, if any consignment got delay due to a reason which is well beyond the control of his team it may be mechanical fault of production unit, any logistics or transportation problem in reaching destination. Akhilesh loses his cool and become very stressful resulting in the poor relationship with team members.

Akhilesh has to understand that by creating a negative atmosphere he is further pulling the efficiency of his team members down. When words reach senior management, they counselled Akhilesh by telling him that there is no harm in trying to reach for perfection, but there are certain situations when one has to think and handle carefully, especially when he is dealing with human beings. Second thing which was conveyed to keep the moral of the Akhilesh at higher level that what ever step you have taken were intended to benefit the organisation and there was no personal interest. Akhilesh understood the situation by accepting the changed scenario with positive attitude.

Neutral Gear (Plus); Best thing a team member can do in the beginning of career is to remain focussed to the assigned task amid chaos of department & profession by remaining in touch with the inner voice which makes more noise and pulls the attention of a professional in different directions, we as young team member has some pre-conceived notions about job, working atmosphere and getting the satisfaction out of it, which we have read or listened in social media or heard from our relatives & friends, but every organisation is different from other in terms of culture & working atmosphere, when a team member joins an organisation, lot of thoughts keeps on moving in mind giving rise to inner voices, depending on the meeting the expectations s/he has imagined, this gives the **opportunity** to a team member to learn how to keep calm, remaining focussed and improves efficiency by avoiding any disturbance in schedule. One must understand & know the steps to be taken to reach the desired destination and chosen career path.

Scenario; From the day one of the joining this company Akhilesh charted out his career path as his goal was to reach the highest level of the ladder not only professionally but personally as well, to realise his dream he has taken admission in diploma course through correspondence in sales of fast-moving consumer products, started watching personal grooming and etiquettes videos on YouTube. Due to some family and personal reasons he could not pursue regular course, but his desire and ambitions were like any other young professional. He was very happy on being selected for on the job training by a reputed company of his choice. During his tenure with the company, he was reminded many times by his colleagues about his educational qualification which was through correspondence and not a regular one, but his seniors never made any difference while assigning tasks, Akhilesh also have to remove some pre-conceived notion about job and working atmosphere, he adjusted well by constantly telling self about the **opportunity** he got in spite of his professional qualification being through correspondence. He focussed himself by negotiating and silencing inner & external voices creating turbulence, and aligned self to right track by adjusting & accepting imperfect conditions.

Flat Tyre (Minus); Every team member is combination of positive & negative qualities, but it is human tendency that we are aware of our positive qualities and vocal about it at every possible platform available. There is one more side of us which is negative one, our negative aspect if not controlled may turn out to be a **threat,** which can offset the effect of many good deeds in few moments, it is so powerful that it can bring down laurels and reputation of an individual, team or organisation which were earned over a period of years. To remain on right track a team member must identify 'Flat Tyre' and replace it with stepney as soon as possible.

Scenario; Akhilesh is an important team member of designing department of a multinational organisation engaged in manufacturing premium cars, like every human being he also had his flat tyre, His flat tyre is his inability to control his personal likes & dislikes during formal & informal meetings & gatherings, it is something which he has inherited and comes naturally to him because of his wealthy family background, he is very proud of coming from metro city and convent educated, he consider other team members coming from small towns as inferior, his notion of being superior to everybody results in poor inter-personal relationship with in team and some times it was reflected in conversation with his seniors as well, this flat tyre which has become integral part of his personality, like every **threat** it was bound to bounce back by permanently impacting the career of Akhilesh.

During an official meeting, Akhilesh could not control self and lost cool on one of his team members, who has not agreed to his suggestion, this matter was reported to top management and discipline inquiry was initiated against Akhilesh, in the report submitted by fact finding committee Akhilesh was found guilty of misbehaviour, in addition to this Human Resources department also quoted three more incidents in which Akhilesh has shown arrogance to his team members. In this way a threat has overtaken all good aspects of a professional, but Akhilesh learned a lot by this incident and promised self to remove this threat from his professional life by giving equal importance & respect to all colleagues irrespective of their social or financial backgrounds.

Developing Qualities required for a Team Member; There are certain qualities which a team member must develop to be in good books of team leader and self, these qualities will help a team member to become an important part of team and will be liked by colleagues as well. Let us discuss them one by one in brief.

Explainer; As a team member what one should do to keep floating, as one has to explain so many things to others and self as well, for a young and not so matured professional, only explaining will give the correct solution by removing doubts & confusion, an explainer will always be required by team as valued member because s/he is able to resolve difficult conditions coming out of any mis-communication, an explainer loves to talk with other team members or ready to address the team informally to avoid any demotivating factor taking over which might have arises due to one reason or the other, an explainer will redefine official or unofficial communication in the interest of the team and self, and will always act as pacifying agent, s/he not only clears a mis-communication but can explain correct version of an official communication.

Scenario; When explainer receives an official communication for working in night shift s/he explains to self that it is part of duty, someone has to do it, if it is me its better although my personal & family life will be disturbed a little but it is only for some specific period, not for whole career, again he will pacify self that some of his friends are doing it for last few months. I must accept this order with positive mind set.

Similarly a pacifying agent will sooth other team members as well, one of his teammates was issued warning letter for regularly reporting late for office, which makes this team member upset, while discussing the matter with the friend, explainer tells him that there is nothing personal in this warning and it is our responsibility to report for duty on time which helps our organization to function properly and is in the interest of all of us, furthering the discussion explainer will ask this team member what will happen if all of us started coming late. This lengthy discussion bore fruit and remove doubts of team member, an explainer will turn a communication into case study or story as per the need of the time.

Connector; A connector is very important asset in a professional setup, as s/he is connected to everybody in the organization, irrespective of its domain or department, connector would like to have good relationship with all other team members whom s/he might have met only once in connection with professional or personal reasons, a connector working in planning department will have good relationship with team members in purchase department or HR department, s/he will accept and offer a cup of tea when visited officially or unofficially, note down birthdays of all those and wish them too with promptness. Why a connector is a precious part of any machinery? A connector connects two parts of a machine even if it has to bear a cut or being heated, a sense of giving is always there, as s/he is always willing to give in the interest of team to avoid any strife, connector is solely interested in keeping working atmosphere healthy & positive, s/he don't like much argument for petty things, when an argument is taking place out side its department a connector consider its responsibility to diffuse the situation by connecting two opposite parties on a common ground, s/he consider it sheer waste of energy in imposing own point of view on others, as a matured person and futurist professional s/he knows that these type of tactics might work for shorter span, but in the longer interest of team it is of no use. An individual team member with connecting qualities is matured enough to leave small things for bigger gain, s/he understands that every team member comes from different backgrounds and it is very natural for them to have different point of views or some times ego also comes in between to accept a common platform. A cool-headed connector exhibits h/her qualities to save time and introduce new type of functioning which takes from competition to co-operation, which is one step forward in a team's play.

Scenario; Our team was planning to go for a short trip on this weekend to a nearby place, team zeroed in on two options one was Rishikesh and the second was Shimla, team got divided into two groups each pressing for different destination here comes the role of connector, connector new that if nobody bends lot of time & energy will be wasted in argument, connector in one team decided to gave up in favor of team by accepting 'Shimla' as destination for short trip even though connector has already been to 'Shimla' last summer, anybody else would have continued arguing by spending time & energy for a destination which is new for them but a connector will compromise and adjust to avoid confrontation. A connector will happily do other's work if it is in favor of team or saving the reputation of organization for example, a connector will happily take substitution classes in the absence of regular faculty to avoid any disturbance.

Winner; Why a winner is required to be part of team members group? What does a winner do for team, a winner is always looking for bringing out best in team and always have yardstick & benchmark ready to be met, why benchmark or yardstick, because a winner wants to win and do better than other teams, s/he does not register for race merely for the sake of participation or competing, s/he had all the data of previous performance standard and start preparation keeping in view those standards.

Discovery of winner in a team will lead to professional uprising because a winner sets high standard of performance which is a must for a team and an organization to grow. A winner can be seen preparing for upcoming event or competition in advance not only for self but s/he is able to persuade other team members to exceed their limits and able to visualize what is in store for them in near future or what should be done to make a better future, a winner in a team member brings out best in every other team member as s/he introduce them to their strong points and what improvement is required to keep our team ahead, now the question arises is an organization is always on competition mode there are seldom three or four competitions annually, but for a winner daily activity is a competition which gives satisfaction or is daily dose for living, for a winner doing small things in a beautiful manner is winning daily.

Weighing scale; What does weighing scale do? it displays the same digit if same weight is put on it by anybody i.e., means s/he will not tilt in unfavorable mode just by seeing a particular designation or a heavy weight, a team member having weighing scale qualities is a 'kilo-class' team member, should be recognized and given its due place, weighing scale team member treats every one with equal respect and is mostly in control of self, h/her reaction to a particular situation is consistent, a weighing scale category team member is very dependable because for him a task is a task whether it's conveyed by head of department or similar level team member, s/he will execute it with same amount of zeal & sincerity, one can depend on weighing scale team member in case if s/he needs to report to office one hour early for official reason, s/he will come without anybody's instruction this time and every time, balancing act here also means not doing any body's favor, let the right action prevail.

When a weighing scale is present in a team, other team members feel safe and secure, which is very much required for smooth & efficient functioning of a team. What is the best time when one can utilize the qualities & abilities of weighing scale or can be put to best use in the interest of team & organization? That time is when organization is going through change or rough patch, because during change management weighing-scale is the one who can help a team to remain stable during these turbulent times, it is like leading disaster management team during a cyclone, which can not stop a cyclone but can minimize the damage by using life saving skills. Now it must be clear that how much important it is to discover and retain the weighing-scale in favor of organization & team. Weighing scale does not make much sound about the actions s/he takes, as a proud member of team s/he silently keep tilting conditions in organization's favor for smooth functioning or transition.

Knowing thyself for Students; Students are future leaders as they will lead us and our country once they step into this world after completing professional programmes, they must understand that as they expect best from their families and society, in turn family and society also expect best from them, it is the responsibility of every student to perform well in their studies and consider education along with qualification as integral part of their life.

Every student can not top their academic activities or institutions, because every student's capacity & capability is different, what they can do is to give their best, problem happens when a student having the ability to score 70% scores 60% and so on, where as if they apply themselves, students having the ability to score 70% can score 75%, that is simply by changing their attitude, setting their priorities by accepting the challenge of the hour.

Student must try to understand the complexity of life, which is the most precious thing nature has gifted to us, its complexity reflects that what we as a human being don't like to do is very much required to be best in the respective field, be it sports, education, music, literature, art, technology, science or any other profession, beauty of life is that in the beginning it does not come easily but once we start taking interest with clear thinking and removing distractions, it starts moving slowly by applying ourselves steadily towards the goal with positivity there is no doubt that we will achieve our target or be near to it.

One very important thing I would like to mention here that all the participants taking part in any competition or competitive examination will not get medal or selected, as number of seats are limited but with the preparation they have done to compete, all of them will be much better than as they were before competition or examination. There is a say "Go and aim for moon, if you don't reach there, you might land up on stars".

Along with winning, fighting well is also the key of human life which opens the lock for many other possibilities.

Top Gear (Positive); A student when pass out of school and trying to start learning about life and career, h/her life revolves around choosing line of action regarding desired career, what s/he intends to do with his life or in which field s/he wants to excel, every student wants to get admission in the best institute related to their field, if it is technology, student's aim is getting admitted into one of the IITs, if it is management every student wants admission into one of the IIMs, if it's Medicine every student would like to be in AIIMS and so on, but it is not possible for every student to get the institute of h/her choice, A student's **strength** lies in giving its best and come out as a winner even if she does not get the admission in the desired institute, adjusting with culture and atmosphere of their present institute and doing well with the available resources is symbol of strength, strength lies in when s/he is ready to compete in every field whether it's sports, cultural or academics, it is during student life when we develop the attitude for winning and character to accept the defeat with grace.

Scenario; Sonal is one of the best student of her class and has just completed bachelors degree in commerce and preparing for CAT exam to get admission in one of the top ranking IIMs, but after the declaration of counselling result she could not get admission in any of the IIMs even after scoring 98.2 percentile, for few days she could not believe and felt really depressed, after few days she gather courage & **strength** and applied for admission in another reputed professional institute to pursue her dream of becoming expert in data analysis. During her course she was one of the best badminton players in the institute along with her studies and got placement in one of the multinational corporations, after few years while sitting in her cabin Sonal was thinking about her strengthful journey. She is always interested in sharing her journey with juniors to spread strength and motivate them.

Brake (Negative): During student life most of us have more negatives than positive ones or have more **weaknesses** than strength. What is the key to a good career and living meaningful life? During student life we are indulge in everything other than studies, we mark our calendar for going out with friends, do not hesitate to try those banned antisocial things or become experts in making excuses to our teachers and parents or busy in making comparisons to justify our poor performance in studies. A student may get easily distracted by other's capability or wealth.

Second weakness is failure to connect with others because of superiority complex, family or educational background. Answer to the above asked question is identifying those weaknesses which have become hindrance in achieving goal, once we start removing those hindrances truth will surface telling us that at this point of time "Knowledge is more important than branded clothes and faster mode of conveyances. Knowledge acquired during student life will help us in achieving our goal and will have long lasting impression in our life.

Scenario; Sonal coming from a financially average family is one of the brilliant students of her college, she got admission in one of the top ranked management institutes on the basis her CAT score to pursue her Masters degree in statistics, from very first day of joining the institute, Sonal was feeling low because of branded clothes her classmates wear, use costly mode of communication & transportation and visit expensive coffee bars nearby to refresh, it requires lot of efforts from Sonal to overcome this inferiority complex, she counselled self that all individuals are born and brought in different financial, social & educational background, but there is one thing which can remove these differences is acquiring knowledge in the respective field and attaining her goal for the betterment of self & family by removing the **weaknesses** she is surrounded by.

Neutral Gear (Plus): A student may get good **opportunity** after getting admission in one of the best institutes of choice, taught by best teachers and able to match with their speed and enjoying healthy competition, good peers & friends and above all a disciplined life. When a student got the opportunity and platform of her dreams, s/he must set her eyes on international or world standards be it in sports, academics or any other field, there is always one step higher which is not visible at this point of time, but dream of doing some thing more than average or above normal with wings expanded to cover the unchartered horizon, will be a great boon if any one of us can convert this **opportunity** to bring laurels to self and country at world level.

Scenario; Sonal got the opportunity to do doctoral programme in her field of specialisation, coming from financially average background but understanding the importance of education which will take him to next level in life, because of coming from average financial family background she has only one aim that is to complete her doctoral programme and find a decent job thereafter to support her family, one evening she was reading the autobiography of Dr. A.P.J. Abdul Kalam and was very much inspired by the autobiography in which Dr. Kalam was able to spread the message about an average individual coming from very ordinary background become a top scientist and become President of India there after. Sonal also started thinking of doing something extra ordinary at world level, after completing her doctoral programme, she started applying for reputed international universities for post doctoral programme, being one of the best in her field, she got admission and scholarship in a top ranked University, completed her post doctoral from there and dedicated self in research work successfully which makes her one of the top scientist in her domain, Sonal sitting in her cabin thinking about ten years back when he was about to except an offer of appointment just after completing her Ph.D. but her decision of expanding her 'wings of fire' brought laurels to self &

country and moreover her various patented inventions were very useful in the field.

Flat Tyre (Minus): During student life an individual is full of confusion due to lack of guidance in understanding and direction to move, which course to take to earn livelihood, what will be the guarantee of job if we get the course of our choice, how to handle the negativity spread by friends and relatives. Most of the energy is consumed in thinking and nothing seems to be going in right direction, second most intriguing thing happens during this period is production of hormones in one's body which generates natural attraction towards opposite sex, h/her only goal turns out to be, how to be one with the individual whom h/she likes, without calculating pros & cons of it, s/he is mainly interested in impressing each other by false ways and spending time with the individual of his liking. It is real **'Threat',** real threat in the sense that if it is not controlled it can derail life's plan and realising own 'dream' will become a distant 'dream'.

Scenario: Sonal while doing her Ph.D., came very close to one of her classmate who was also one of the brilliant student of institute, they both started doing assignments together, he was the first person whom she approach to solve any academic challenge same condition was with that boy, in the beginning they meet with the purpose of solving academic problems and completing assignments but after some times assignments were kept aside now the meeting has sole purpose of spending time together resulting in academic activities going off the track.

Their guide Dr. Kumar was observing this when situation was about to getting out of control, he called both of them and clearly told them about their activities impacting their academics and make them realise the real purpose of taking admission in Ph.D. programme, he told both of them that few things in the life of every human being is very natural one of them is attraction towards opposite sex, but it becomes big problem if it's not controlled and kept above other priorities of life. Dr. Kumar told them to think about their career and aspirations of your family. They both understood the situation by bringing their academic activities on track and completing their Ph.D. programme with in given time frame and lived happily there after, whenever they think of Dr. Kumar, a natural feeling of gratitude flows from bottom of their heart for acting as guide not only of their Ph.D. programme but for life as well by saving them from a potential **'Threat'**.

Qualities to be developed during student life; As mentioned many times student life is the most important part of an individual who is interested in leading a meaningful life, as qualities developed during this period makes the foundation for future, deciding about its brightness or dimness. Let us discuss few qualities a student must posses to sail successfully for a bright career.

Hard disc; What does a hard disc represents, what is the reason behind keeping a good quality hard disc with ample memory? We save our valuable content in a hard disc, but before that we prepare valuable content which is very important for an individual, we save important content in order to reproduce it when there is a need.

We as a student has to discover a hard disc in self which can store quality content prepared by self and we have to attach ourselves to the 'system' to prepare and study, which is required to clear the vision and achieve our goal, get excited by any new information or knowledge, dive deep from basic information about a topic to specialized one, once you make a habit of exploring new topics by self gives you a new high, your hard disc contains not only academic interest but other aspects as well, which may vary from sports, drama, culture, reading, art or music. You understand that to have a good hard disc, wide variety of content is required from different aspects of life and topics ranging from international relations, climate change to stock market, a student with hard disc quality is attracted towards any new topic and want to understand it.

Scenario; B.Tech. class of 2024 has planned to visit Andaman & Nicobar islands on a recreation tour, everybody was excited to have good time in terms of company, food, leisure time and fun, but a hard disc student is along with these is much more excited to know the importance of place in countries history, incidents or stories attached to it and its place in country's freedom struggle, in other words a hard disc student will go beyond average to make every moment more valuable, s/he is interested in utilizing every occasion to make it more meaning full. A hard disc student will adjust self to remain in the race by learning new things and storing it for use in near or far future.

Owner; What does an owner means? A good owner not only looks after assets well but also takes full responsibility of what he does with these assets, what ever decision an owner takes with respect to assets and make it worthwhile by making any modification or improvements, similarly a student needs to discover owner's quality, a student needs to honour h/her decision of taking admission in a course, because it is this course which will bring colours to life and create a responsible citizen for country. As discussed earlier regarding modification or improvement, if a student think that s/he has taken up wrong course or programme, must take suitable step immediately to change it like an owner who changes his assets, a student owner must change & adjust his direction to move along with the programme, some time the programme you have chosen, does not suit your aptitude, but with a mixture of youth and maturity you have to complete it.

Scenario; Anshul has taken admission in B.Arch. programme in a prestigious institute, by the mid of third year he realised that he is not fit for this field and wanted to try his hands in cinematography, when he discussed the matter with his father, who put up one condition that he will support him for his career in cinematography only if he completes his B.Arch. programme with decent grades. Anshul agreed to this condition and worked reasonably hard to complete the course with good grades, when he entered in the field of cinematography, he couldn't get success initially but when he remembers his hard work and application during last year of B. Arch. course, he assures himself that if he sticks to his commitment, he can be successful in the field of cinematography too. That commitment with self resulted in a successful career in cinematography. Ownership quality gives you the confidence that you can accept and meet new challenges and live life of your choice or fight for some thing more attractive. In a team discovering the quality of owner will help to kickstart something new on his own and delivering quality stuff with in given time frame.

Archer; Why a shooter like qualities need to be discovered in and by the student? What does an archer or shooter do? An archer aims for bull's eye to win or accomplish the goal, no confusion, only bull's eye, but before setting your goal one must know what is required to reach the set goal, with out this knowledge of equipment's and material required no archer will be able to hit the bullseye. Every student must know what it takes to fulfill the desired goal, which road to prepare and which road to avoid.

Scenario; After completing her 12th class with subjects Physics, Chemistry & Mathematics Ankita wants to join IIT, she used to study approximately six hours study in a day, but while taking coaching for IIT-JEE, she came to realize that six hours study per day is not enough, every other student is putting 9-10 hours of study, what she should do? If she wants to be ahead of all other fellow students, she has to work harder than other students to crack IIT-JEE. A master archer while aiming for bull's eye must know the direction of wind, when to hold and release the breath to score perfect 10, An archer has to follow time frame because s/he has accepted a task which needs to be completed in given time, a quality which needs to be developed by archer to see straight towards his path as a horse competing in a race, because a lot of distractions are there to derail the process, as a matter of fact that few distractions need ones attention, one of the most famous distraction is "What people will say"?

Few readers will say that archers do not respect human emotions and relations, where as my thinking is on the other side, archers respect human relationship and feeling as much as anybody else sometimes even more than that, an archer loves give his/her best once the target is finalised, s/he did not settle for less than ten out of ten, archer loves to display strength to every team member and motivates others to follow the suite. Discovery of an archer will lead to an atmosphere of moving towards excellence in a team, an archer will aim at what s/he can do best to stand at number one spot on the podium, for an archer every other thing is immaterial and can be ignored, during the game time s/he has the quality to avoid every distraction and hit the bull's eye to bring laurels to the team.

Organizer; What an organizer is expected to do for team? An organizer is expected to put together all the parts & participants together to put up a fantastic show. Where as all other will look here and there to avoid the chaos, an organizer has his mind started running and loves to see something coming out beautifully by arranging all the pieces of puzzle, as a student discovering the qualities of organizer will help you a lot, because a organizer also panics but keep it to self and continues moving without showing any outer disturbance, organizer is attracted towards difficult situations but has the attitude & confidence for making things easier and ability to absorb last minute changes, resulting in no-turbulence shown on the ground.

Scenario; if an organizer is given the task of arranging an office picnic, s/he will give equal importance and feel responsible like any other official task of organization, in other words, for him/her organizing a picnic is equally important as preparing an annual audit or inspection report, for office picnic s/he will take care everybody's food preferences, will also have in mind to have optional venue if it rains or snow on that day. Organizer will give instructions when in charge, irrespective of people not like to be instructed, while giving instructions s/he also don't like it but suppressed his or her feelings as s/he knew that getting the things done is integral part of task, organizer's initial instruction turns out to be positive reaction once the task is completed, every team member hails h/her efforts for completing the job wonderfully, organizer also practice how to explain the things to a senior team member if they are assigned the responsibilities below their designation, an organizer is like any software, for example if we enter destination, itinerary, money we get a valid travelling ticket, or our organizer may behave like a chef, give h/him required ingredients, without bothering about the heat of the kitchen s/he will pull out very tasty and exotic dishes for everybody. Our organizer love to be recognized for extra efforts made by him/her in the interest of team & organization.

Conclusion; Study of oneself is very important to bring order in life, in relationship with others and gave birth to understanding which in turn improve our relationship with individuals, society and universe. By knowing ourselves we can make a fair assessment about what we want from life, what are our goals, how we react to a particular situation, what is our strength and weakness, in which field we need to improve.

With this self-knowledge we attain wisdom and become independent of ever fluctuating world and learn to be self-reliant. We need to fulfil the purpose of our precious life. In the end we can sum up with the following lines.

When I was intelligent, I tried to change the world.

When I become wiser, I try to change myself.

Mind is My Best Friend

When I was kid, one of my father's friend visited our house and during our introductory conversation he asked me the name of my best friend in the class, I told him that my best friend is Aakash, but after few months Aakash's father was transferred and Karan became my best friend, after one year my father was transferred to another base and I have to leave my best friend behind, during my university days Anamika became my best friend but after completing her graduation she also went abroad for higher studies.

In this process of gaining and loosing friends I discovered that one thing which has not left me irrespective of any condition, it is an invisible small light house which has guided me through all my ups & downs and keep moving between my heart and brain is my **"MIND"**. My mind has never left me after I befriended it and helped me in taking the right decisions, getting me out of every difficult situation, from there on wards whenever somebody asked me the name of my best friend, first answer which I gave them is about my temporary friend which is a human being, second answer I gave to myself silently by hugging my invisible friend, my mind.

I would like to remove one confusion that under normal circumstance or in general terms mind and brain are considered same, but it is not so, this can be understood by an example, all of us must have seen brain of a human being in pictures or in a biology lab, well preserved with formalin in a glass jar, but has any one seen a photograph of mind, I can say very confidently "no". brain can be mapped, scanned, or operated upon, but mind cannot be. Secondly, have you ever heard or read words brainset or brainful, whereas I am very much sure that most of us have heard & read words 'mindful' and 'mindset'. Third, during any conversation or any negotiation have we ever heard. "I have changed my brain" but we must have heard "I have changed my mind". And above all you must have heard that s/he has been brain washed but you have and will never heard about somebody's mind being washed.

Brain is with us since birth whereas mind starts taking shape from the time when we start thinking, reading, socializing or setting our goals and taking decisions about life. It is up to us how we shape it, if you feed it with positive and encouraging thoughts, we will develop positive mind and vice-versa. Mind is an invisible part of us and its strength depends on us. Our mind holds the key to our physical and mental health, its only our brain which is wired to observe only negative things for example we easily point out a mistake in a picture, a bad habit in a friend, we immediately see something wrong or hear something objectionable or disturbing noises. However, with the help of our mind we can negotiate or ignore those negative aspects and move forward towards our goal.

Have you ever thought that why few people are comfortable and accommodating in every condition or situation while some of the individuals are always struggling? We often wonder why we are thinking this way or that way, why our thoughts are so weird. In this regard we have to understand the difference between thinking with the help of brain or using our mind when our thoughts are weird, we are using our brain to think, but when we make an effort to channelize those weird thoughts into constructive ones we take the help of our mind which helps us to rise above average and clear any confusion or conflict arising due to a particular situation and bend that situation towards our side, using our mind leads us to positive and contented life, from immaturity to maturity. Our mind is the gateway to peace or suffering, thoughts originated in mind decides about the outcome, whether this thought will energize us or suck our energy, give us hope or discomfort. With the help of mind, we can change our condition from suffering to peace.

Scenario; You are sitting in your room and thinking about an incident (how badly your senior has treated you because of notes misplaced by one of your room-mates, for which you were not responsible) of past which has given you immense pain when your pain reaches its highest level and you can't bear it anymore what you should do to avoid pain, you start thinking that whatever happens cannot be reversed, considering it as a learning experience by not to repeat this mistake again, you switch your thought from unpleasant one to pleasant one, turning your attention in totally opposite direction, giving yourself a sigh of relief by thinking about the performance in annual cultural festival which was applauded by everybody in the college. Our mind which is our best friend and creation will get us rid of pain by directing us towards comfort, now it is evident that **pain is inevitable and suffering is optional**. How much we allow ourselves to suffer or in other words we will feel how we think, feeling is directly related to thinking, if we want to feel good, we should exercise to turn an unbearable situation to bearable one.

    It is very much clear from the above example that we should design and develop our best friend (Mind) in such a way that it can be rotated by 360 degrees in our favour or it shows us the scenery which help us to find our reason and purpose of life & self, during this rotation of 360 degree our best friend guides us to choose what is beneficial for us.

Our best friend helps us in every circumstance and create necessary conditions for our progress and wellbeing, we should develop our mind as our best friend. We use brain in our daily activity resulting in resentment, anger, guilt and unforgiveness but after developing our mind to cope with day-to-day activity, we start loving our surroundings and attain peace.

Researches have shown that there is mind body connection, which states that "A healthy mind lives in a healthy body", more we take care of our body the better we feel developing our mind, which leads to love, affection & positivity. Brain controls our body whereas mind is responsible for our wellbeing & personality and is the prime source of energy, whatever we want to achieve & perform, we can do it with the help of it, some people fail to develop it whereas others who set a tougher goal make the most of it, we cannot alter the functioning of brain but we can develop our mind, due to this reason we have seen some people with physical limitations attaining greater heights where as some able-bodied individuals living below average life.

Mind recognizes efforts and in turn releases energy directly in proportion to that effort and act as a sensor, if we guide our mind to follow the right path it will attract right path and if we decided to take wrong path our mind will guide us towards wrong path, our mind is shaped by what we feed to it, we should feed positive thoughts to it to be enjoy positive aspects of life.

Scenario; there are numerous examples of sports and games in which player or team bouncing back as victorious, we must have heard x football team was trailing by 3-0 during first half but came back fighting and won the match by 5-3, it's not the victory of one team over another it's the victory of mind, because during half time, team which was trailing behind and all the player's brain had accepted the defeat but the mind of few players were not ready to accept the defeat and they want to win, captain of team called all the players in dressing room and motivate them to give their best performance today and told them that we can and we will win. After motivating all the players and leaving behind the thought of losing and they had only one thing in mind that they have to win this game and they won.

Mind is My Best Friend

Scenario; Maj HPS Ahluwalia's mount Everest expedition was full of ups and downs, their camp was hit by fierce avalanche burying all oxygen cylinders under the snow, observing the gravity of the situation the 'Chief' called off the expedition and ordered for pack-up to return, by this time only few members have scaled the mount Everest and the rest of the members was feeling very sad as their dream of summiting mount Everest was shattered by avalanche.

All the team members have accepted the order of chief and started packing to return, but their was one person who is not going to be defeated by avalanche or has not accepted that his dream of scaling mount Everest has come to an end, it was Maj. Ahluwalia who has befriended his mind during course of life and his mind always helped him taking the right decision, mind does not only helps in taking the right decision but also helps in executing that right decision as well, he asked his mind what to do under this condition? After conversing with his mind and passing of avalanche without any damage to human life, He approached chief of expedition and asked the permission to dig for oxygen cylinders, head of the expedition understanding the emotions of team members, gave the permission for digging to find out the buried oxygen cylinders but only for the stipulated time and that time was when they have to start going downwards to culminate this expedition.

Having received the permission to dig for oxygen cylinders, all team members got on the job of finding cylinders, as we all know that luck favours the brave mind, during the digging a solid noise was heard and buried oxygen cylinders were recovered paving the way for rest of the team members to summit the mighty Mount Everest, If Maj. Ahluwalia had accepted the status quo, it would have shattered the dream of summitting the mighty mountain for may team members.

Let us discuss what changed the situation, Maj. Ahluwalia's brain had already accepted the order given by Chief to pack-up and return, but his mind has not, his friendly mind start thinking that this opportunity will never comeback, and must find a way, it's now or never, take some calculated risk and act differently. It is our mind which helps us in taking courageous step after calculating pros and cons, it is our mind through which we overcome fear of being wrong and move with confidence. Mind is the place where dreams are weaved and realized and it is in our mind where passion and patience are nurtured. With the help of our mind, we can exceed our limitation and go beyond brain, use our mind as 'dost'. **Jo doshon ko ast kar de.**

Personality shaper; It is our mind which observes what we lack in having a good personality and start working towards required changes, It is our mind which not only sees what we lacks but also sees what good qualities others have and what steps we have to take to be like them, in other words our mind introduce us to minus points of ourselves and plus points of others, If we can observe the above sentences carefully, difference between brain and mind is clearly visible while brain sees our plus points and minus points in others, whereas a friendly mind with an intention to improve and have better personality does totally opposite i.e. observing minus points in ourselves and plus points in others so that we can compare and develop ourselves.

Scenario; When my mind sees that a friend is going to gym by rising early in the morning, my mind will first question me and try to find out the reason why I am not able to rise early and goes to gym, upon observing this my mind will tell me that basic pre-requisite of getting up early is going to bed early by removing all the unnecessary activities which are stoping me from doing so, It could be understood by one more example When we are falling ill on regular intervals and wasting precious resources and time in medication and recovering, our mind will compare our condition with other team members and find out that they are consuming home cooked food mostly where as my food is always delivered from outside, friendly mind will slowly mould me to keep balance between health and taste.

Reservoir of energy; Every thing in this world whether humans or machines needs energy, that energy is generated by the engine installed in them, for machines it is customised & developed out side, but in human beings this engine is developed and fuelled by the thoughts and efforts of the individual, Studies have shown that all our performances & actions depends on our mind for energy needs and for a living being mind is the biggest reservoir of energy, when we decide to do simple task mind releases lesser amount of energy, when we decide to do challenging tasks mind releases energy in the same proportion. It all depends on how much we have unfolded our mind and prepare to receive energy in proportion. All our action big or small is directly related to our mind, it is our mind which is master of all activity.

Scenario; It's 7.30 p.m., I have just come back from office and wanted to take half an hour's rest, suddenly I received a call from my friend informing me that he is in town, coming for dinner and will be staying back for night, I forget all my tiredness, requesting wife to prepare dinner for the occasion, rushing to nearby market for purchasing refreshment & groceries to make this get-together memorable, I observe my physical condition before & after the phone call of my friend and understood the power of mind.

Static & Dynamic side of mind; Static mind tries to maintain status quo, avoid taking first step or initiating any positive move, even if its sure that these steps are beneficial in moving forward, people with static mind are contented with their present situation and dread making any change. It is very much clear that static mind is a follower.

Whereas people with dynamic mind tries to find out various other ways to move ahead with the intention to make things better, any improvement gives them satisfaction, with dynamic mindset a professional takes more interest in executing a process or task in an improved manner benefiting self & team, professional with dynamic mindset have the ability to takes first move, taking initiative and courageous step if they think that by moving first will benefit their team & organization, they clear the path for green flag.

Now the question arises does a dynamic mind always think in forward direction? The answer is 'NO', a dynamic mind has the ability to move both ways, like any normal thinking mind it first moves towards negative side of the situation and all its efforts are towards avoiding losses, but after remaining on the negative turf for some duration, a dynamic mind started weighing both options i.e., backward & forward and decides as per the circumstances & available resources. It is not necessary that a dynamic mind always move forward, it can step backward if it is in the interest of self & team, but it will not remain stand still and wait for things to happen, taking proactive measures is the next level a dynamic mind would like to achieve by always having hunger for knowledge by exposing & visualising from various aspects. This could be understood by given scenario.

Scenario; Mohit and Amit are two friends; Mohit is investment advisor and Amit has just left his job after working in the corporate sector for 25 years. Mohit & Amit met to discuss the future course of action to engage Amit in other profession to earn his livelihood, Mohit offered Amit to teach him the basics of stock market to start with, Amit accepted this offer and started learning the skills for trading in Share Market, after six months of time, Mohit called Amit and informed him about the stock of ASD corporation which is being traded at very low price but as per his information & calculation this stock is about to appreciate in a very short period of time, Mohit also added that it is penny share and falls in the category of "high risk high gain", upon hearing this Amit started thinking of dealing with this particular stock, In the beginning Amit was very much in favour of earning profit in short term, but his dynamic mind told him to step back as there is huge difference between the circumstances and resources of the two, Mohit being a seasoned trader and Amit has just learn the art of trading, Mohit can afford the loss but Amit cannot, so Amit's dynamic mind suggested to step back and avoid taking high risk & high gain route in this particular case.

Mindstation; One must be surprised to know about the new word 'mindstation'. Mindstation is like a railway station where train stops and passenger with valid ticket check their train number and coach before boarding the right train, imagine if a passenger does not check its ticket and board the first train which comes to platform resulting in huge loss of time & resources. Similarly, 'mind station' is where our brain stops before converting thoughts into action, by stopping at mindstation we check the action to be taken and moreover the consequences of it.

As in a train, passengers are deboarding and on-boarding, deboard your negative thoughts and on-board your purposeful and knowledgeable thoughts while travelling through Mindstation', I am not talking about only positive thoughts sometimes negative thoughts are also very helpful in choosing the right path. During decision making process one must use our **'Mindstation'** so that we can take decision by a thoughtful process and sincerely pick the best available option in trichual interest. Stopping at 'Mindstation' is very necessary to avoid an accident and prevent losses in the form of material, human and financial. Developing a mindstation will help us taking decision in an evolved state, as we do not jump directly from thoughts to action, we take a break at right point of time for selecting or choosing the correct path for reaching our goal.

During our association with an organization, we have to deal with and exhibit emotions to get the work done by giving or taking orders, receiving feedback or managing work, sometimes we control our mind sometimes we can't. when we are able to control our mind, everything seems to be moving in right direction but when we are unable to control our mind, every thing seems to be moving into unknown direction resulting in precious loss of resources, when we stop at 'mindstation' before taking any action we do the right thing, but if we jump 'mindstation' we tend to derail our activity.

Mindstation for Leader; Developing a mindstation is very important for a Leader, as a Leader one has to take decisions for effective & efficient functioning of team and organization, having proper understanding of mindstation will help a leader to execute responsibilities in a smooth manner. In the absence of Mindstation and in order to take quick decisions a leader might loses credibility resulting in irreparable damage to organization & team. A developed mindstation plays a very important role in the life of a leader which helps to stop & think clearly in favour of organisation and take decisions which have long lasting impact, accepted by most of team members, ably supported by past and making future better for every one in team.

Scenario; Ramesh is serving ABC enterprises since last one and a half year as CEO and managing his team well. Since last month he was facing some problem regarding performance of one of the team members, named Himanshu whose behaviour was little bit frustrating and different from usual, once again Ramesh has to seek an explanation from Himanshu for delay in the job assigned. Ramesh was thinking of replacing Himanshu and want to send him to back-office operations.

Ramesh was about to call Himanshu to inform him about his decision but before taking a final decision he stopped at his Mindstation and called his deputy to discuss the matter. Ramesh's deputy informed him that Himanshu is facing some personal problem related to his wife and in-laws due to which he is unable to execute his responsibilities in proper manner. After hearing this Ramesh called Himanshu in front of his deputy, discuss the matter and want to know about the time frame by which Himanshu will be able to give his 100% contribution to organisation, Himanshu informed Ramesh that things will settle in a week's time, Ramesh suggested Himanshu to take leave for that duration and join back with renewed energy. Stopping at mindstation saves one good employee from being getting demoralized and an organization from losing a good employee.

Moving from static mind to dynamic mind for Leader; A CEO must understand that alien mind is static and friendly mind is dynamic and has the capability to bring change, we can bring positivity by calling our friendly mind which is always very near to us if we have developed and befriended it in a correct way. Leader will attain success by always putting be-friended mind first in taking action & decision and will be doing a huge favour to organisation, because action & decision taken with friendly mind will always be in tune with the time and accompanied by progressive point of view. History is full of examples when worlds top corporate giants (Nokia and Zerox) went bankrupt and faded into history when their CEOs and top management took decisions with static mind. Secondly, if a CEO wants to teach something or pass on to team leader, it should be the ability to think and take action with the help of befriended mind.

Scenario; When Ashok took charge of CEO first time, he was supposed to address his organisation in the company's auditorium, there was only one barrier in this, Ashok suffers from stage fear and don't want to address team from stage, he discussed the matter with his deputy, who in turn advised him that avoiding first address would send wrong signal to team, Ashok must address his team in order to earn their confidence and be with them, Ashok tried everything to refrain himself from addressing, his alien mind told him that ' you are the CEO of the organisation, it does not make any difference' whether you follow the protocol or not, your position will remain the same, but when Ashok approached his friendly mind which told him that being CEO one needs to follow protocol set by organisation's culture, he must approach formal address with positive mind, being executing the responsibility of CEO, not only formal address but has to do so many other things first time, one can always practice new activity even if it's not the best performance first time but it will prepare the foundation for future action and best performance. Having listen to his friendly mind Ashok practiced the content of formal address and delivered it in a decent manner.

Scenario; A CEO is not only responsible for his performance but also for his team members upliftment as well, Akash is facing a problem regarding one of the important team members named Nimit, who has developed a habit of procrastination due to which whole team is facing lot of problems. Akash was thinking about how to move ahead in solving this problem, first thing come to his alien mind that this situation cannot be changed, but after thinking sometimes his friendly mind started getting signal that with right counselling and communication, problem of procrastination can be handled. He called upon team leader and make him aware of the challenges being faced by his team and organisation as well, after this discussion it was decided to take Nimit into confidence and make him believe that this type of problem can be solved by undergoing counselling sessions, he was made to understand that one can overcome the limitation of alien mind by replacing it with friendly mind.

Mindstation for Team leader; A team leader is the backbone of any organization and responsible for developing a winning team, taking decision, and mending ways to be in top bracket. A team leader is responsible for utilizing material and human asset as well to keep things moving in right direction. Developing a mindstation and stopping at it, will bear good results and convert the team into a well-knit unit. When a team leader starts working with the knowledge of mind station s/he can rotate self in 360 degrees for the best solution, by rotating self in 360 degrees s/he not only move forward but can move backward as well if it is in the interest of team and organisation.

Scenario; Tanu is associated with ABC enterprises as team leader, is known for her fair play policy and down to earth behaviour while managing or leading, She was sitting in her cabin suddenly her subordinate entered and started complaining about one supervisor for a blunder due to which department has to face breakdown resulting in re-scheduling the delivery of product, hearing this Tanu immediately decided to take appropriate action by calling human resources executive, suddenly she decided to stop at Mindstation and send back human resource executive by telling him to come tomorrow after lunch with personal file of supervisor. While going through the personal file of supervisor, Tanu observed that there are no red marks in his entire service of twelve years, all team leaders have praised the behaviour and expertise of supervisor. Tanu called supervisor and warned him about his carelessness, telling him to learn from this mistake so that it is not repeated in future. Once again presence of **Mindstation** has prevented loss to the organisation and bring about confidence in decision making mechanism system in lower ring of team.

Moving from static mind to dynamic mind for Team Leader; A team leader is in-charge of newly inducted team members, is responsible for introduction of friendly mind concept to them as well in order to develop team in to a learning one, simultaneously s/he must introduce the concept of static mind so that team members are able to alienate themselves from it, move towards dynamic mind for exceeding their limitations and removing the mental blocks coming in the way of learning. Secondly, a team leader must share their professional journey's experiences, in which incident s/he has overcome static mind and took decision by using friendly mind emphasising that change is not very hard but it is must.

      A team leader can develop one quality which will take entire team to higher level is accepting mistakes, open to correction and ready to learn new things. By being open to receive feedback in open mode, where as there are other team members who consider themselves to be perfect and closes the door for any improvement. If this one quality i.e., accepting mistakes and open to correction is encouraged among team members, will be beneficial not only for team members but to team leader as well, improving overall functioning of department.

Scenario; Vineet is working as maintenance engineer in ABC corporation, during night shift he has to supervise the lubrication schedule of machines involved in manufacturing process, during one maintenance schedule he was supposed to pour 05 litres of oil into machine, but due to miscalculation he is left with only 04 litres of oil which he poured into machine closing down maintenance schedule and mentioning it into logbook that everything went as per plan and lubrication of machines done as per specification. His static mind told him to hide the above incident as nobody will come to know about the less oil being poured into machine. Suddenly he imagined the aftereffects of his wrong information being penned in logbook, it may be complete break down of whole production chain, resulting in financial loses to company and affecting him directly & indirectly as well, last but not the least his boss will be held responsible for this incident and might be asked for explanation by higher authorities.

Vineet has great respect for his head of department as he is the one who had supported him during his tenure and offered a solution for every problem he faced; it will not be in the interest of team if he is in trouble because of his misconduct. Vineet's friendly mind took charge of the situation, prompted Vineet to call his boss and inform him about the whole situation, who in turn told him to access store with the help of security guard and take the required amount of oil, for which formalities will be completed once factory opens in the morning. In this way being friendly with his mind or making his friendly mind stronger has helped Vineet to take decision in the right way saving him, his boss and organisation from big trouble.

Mindstation for Team Member; An individual team member who has just entered the corporate world, is full of energy but lacks experience. Developing a Mindstation will help a team member in achieving their long-term goal. Stopping at Mindstation will make them better & matured professional, mixing action with patience and youthfulness. Understanding and developing their own respective **Mindstation** indicates that a team member wants to choose the best possible option available and needs to be very careful while communicating or taking any decision, it is very important to understand the benefit of Mindstation and developing it, when a team member decided to use Mindstation as a stop, can start taking mock decisions in those matters in which s/he is not directly involved, testing and sharpening decision taking ability and in due course of time comparing both the decisions i.e., formal decision and mock decision taken.

Scenario; Anil and Anirudh are working as team members in a production unit, during one monthly departmental meeting Anil has proposed one change in procurement procedure to cut short the time, but Anirudh was not positive about this idea as it might cut short the time required but excludes the accountability of professional involved, Anirudh's point was considered by seniors and Anil's proposal was side-lined, making him uncomfortable. Now Anil is looking for the time when he can oppose any suggestion made by Anirudh during team meeting, but before taking any concrete step he decided to stop at Mindstation, during his stay at mindstation he observed that Anirudh is not his enemy but one of the team members with whom he has to work for the success of his department, secondly after revisiting his thoughts he realizes that Anirudh was somewhat correct in giving right opinion in the interest of the department. Now Anil decided not to oppose every proposal or suggestion made by Anirudh and decided to take decision on merit only.

Moving from static mind to dynamic mind for Team Member; A team member who has just joined a corporate sector, understanding the difference between static mind & friendly mind is very important, a static mind will tell you that you are doing good by surviving in this job, your dynamic mind will tell you that your job is not to survive but to excel in your domain and move ahead in career by making self professionally rich. Dynamic mind will tell you that if you befriend me, I will help and guide you in overcoming stagnant thoughts, do not surrender to current circumstances something new can be learned, it may be communication skills or decision taking ability. Static mind will tell us that we are struck and friendly mind will find out the way to move forward.

Scenario; Asim is working as trainee engineer in ABC Corporation, during his college days he was unable to understand the concept of hydraulic braking systems thoroughly. Unfortunately, during his duty hours, hydraulic brake system of an important machine broke down, bringing whole manufacturing process to stand still. While the repairing of hydraulic system was undertaken, Asim did not come into forefront as his static mind told him that he does not know much about it so it is better to hide self and remain docile part of team till the hydraulic system is repaired and full functioning of machine restored.

Asim's friendly mind asked him what will happen if this hydraulic system breaks down again, behind whom you will hide again, as an important team member it is your responsibility to keep the things moving. What step you have taken to remove this draw back? This conversation with dynamic mind awakened Asim. He asked the manual of hydraulic system from senior engineer, studied it properly and went through maintenance log to find out the reason behind breakdown.

Static mind tells us to undertake only those tasks in which we are proficient. If we undertake those tasks which we have never done and fails, we will be labelled as failure or inefficient. Whereas dynamic mind will motivate to commit yourself to learning new set of knowledge by trying unexplored arena, accepting new challenges by venturing in to the unknown.

Mindstation for Students; Students while new to many things in this world are told not to fall behind any other fellow students and ready to react to every action, as an in-experienced human being at this stage of life they tend to jump mindstation at most of the time and land themselves in problem, in some cases putting their careers and reputation of family at stake. It is very necessary for a student to understand the concept of 'Mindstation', it will not only help them smoothen their path but also learn to decide in favour of those activities and decisions which are beneficial to them, befriending 'Mindstation' will help every student to make it a habit to carry it throughout their life.

Scenario; Ravi was studying in twelfth standard of a reputed boarding school and his final exams are near, he has to appear in internal examination as part of the preparation for final exams. His performance in chemistry practical exams was not satisfactory for which he blames his subject teacher for not giving them enough time to practice in lab, so he decided to do some mischief in chemistry lab resulting in financial loss to school, the day before he decided to do the mischief, he stopped at his **mindstation** where he remembers how four of his seniors were expelled from the school for damaging computers in electronics lab for the same reason, parents of all those four students were summoned by principal and handed over the expulsion letter resulting in huge career & financial losses to all of them. Being afraid of the results of doing wrong, he decided to meet chemistry teacher to remove his doubts and make improvement in the subject. Visiting his mindstation saves Ravi from humiliation and probable financial loss.

In conversation through brain; In the beginning of student life when a student start thinking or conversing with them selves is not aware of right way to think, after some hit and miss, using trial & error method students slowly start learning right way of thinking by differentiating between brain and mind When we converse with our selves through brain, we see things as they are, For example, if we perform in a test with good grades, what fellow students will think if I don't repeat my performance will they think that was a fluke. Conversation through brain is first step for visualising or imaging any scenario. A student should be able to move from thinking with the help of brain to applying their mind for better results.

In conversation through Mind; Continuing from above paragraph, when we as a student learn to converse through mind, we conclude that nobody can repeat performance every time whether its student, sports person or any other professional, none of them can win gold medal every time, I will not lose my confidence if I don't come first every time but make effort to approach difficult circumstances with learning attitude, I will always give my hundred percent during preparation for every activity which comes in my way, sometimes I will win sometimes others might win, those who have performed better than me must have better abilities and accepts this truth without blaming anybody by getting in touch with my teacher to plug the loop hole for improvement in my performance next time.

Moving from static mind to dynamic mind for students; It is very important for students to understand the functioning of both minds i.e., static and dynamic mind, as students are just entering into a new world, at every step they will find something which they have not experienced it earlier, after understanding the working of both minds, students need to differentiate between them and feed the one which they find beneficial for their career. After understanding the working of both minds a wise student will prefer to feed dynamic mind. During student life it is dynamic mind which tells us that every negative activity can be overcome and limitations overcome, expanding talent & intelligence for a successful life. A student must understand that dynamic mind holds the key to achieve desired results in professional and personal life.

Scenario; Akhilesh was habitual of eating out during his student time, as he does not like food from hostel's mess, while eating out every day he promised self not to eat outside food tomorrow as he was suffering from some stomach related problems, but due to static mind, which always tells him that eating out will cost only Rs. 250-300/= per meal, so he continue eating out as he can afford this amount, but again he was having medical problem related to his stomach, Akhilesh look forward to find out the solution and approached his dynamic mind after feeding it properly, his dynamic mind converted the fact into truth by informing Akhilesh that eating out once in a while as per requirement is absolutely fine, but eating out seven times a week is putting pressure on his stomach and pocket too, as he has to spend substantial amount of his budget on medical treatment. A dynamic mind is always interested in guiding its owner towards best option available.

Scenario; Ashima is watching web series on OTT platform, immediately there starts a conversation between her two minds i.e. static and dynamic, static mind will advocate instant pleasure by communicating that it will take only one hour per episode and bring lot of pleasure, on the other side dynamic mind will signal that this is not the right time to watch web series, as final exams are near and this time period is most suitable for studying sincerely which will help her in getting the desired goal which eventually bring satisfaction for whole family and friends. She listens to her dynamic mind which took her back to previous night and ask, what she got after watching two episodes of web series? The answer was that she was knowing everything about web series and can participate in the conversation when it is discussed among friends. Friendly mind told her that it was temporary pleasure and last for few minutes, one should look for permanent happiness which is attained by answering the questions asked by teacher and doing well in the course which Ashima has enrolled for. Understanding the signal given by friendly mind Ashima gradually started reducing the time spending on OTT platforms, simultaneously increasing time on studies, securing better grades.

Scenario; When as a student we take admission in any course, we have to clear the exams by understanding the content of the syllabus earmarked for particular subject, in every semester or year. When our static mind sees the syllabus, it communicates to us that we will study & understand the syllabus & topics during our preparatory leaves. Whereas when we look up to our friendly mind it communicates and guides us that it is advisable to break whole syllabus into small segments as it is not possible to understand whole syllabus assigned for one semester during preparatory leaves, preparatory leaves are for the purpose of revision and clearing doubts if there is any. By dividing the syllabus into small parts and working on it regularly along with the lectures taken for that subject will remove the undue stress and pressure during exams ultimately helping us in achieving the desired result.

Scenario; Kanwal is getting ready to leave for appearing in his semester exam, he had his bathroom geyser switched on to take bath suddenly there is power failure, on experiencing this Kanwal lost cool and his static mind goes haywire, whereas situation was not that much serious, there was other alternative available for water heating i.e., gas stove, but static mind could not make it out. Static mind disturbed Kanwal and he appeared in examination without taking bath, during whole exam he was feeling itchy and sleepy. Dynamic mind always takes the correct approach, it does not lose sight of goal if small speed breaker comes in the way, for optimum results it continues the journey keeping in view the larger picture, does not depend on 'mood' it keeps operating on the 'mode' it is set.

Scenario; Ashwin's exam centre was at the far end of city, due to some unruly behaviour of traffic police, public transporters has declared strike for next two days, instead of getting disturbed Ashwin's friendly mind tells him to shift at one of his relative's place which is near examination centre. Without loosing any time Ashwin followed the suggestion of dynamic mind and able to write his exams properly.

Subconscious mind; There is one more side of our mind which is known as '**subconscious mind'**, subconscious mind is that invisible part of an individual which has the power to make a dream come true, it attracts what you think with positivity, it creates circumstances and conditions unknowingly for an individual so that s/he is able to achieve that goal which seems very difficult and distant during conceptual stage but it's there in the corner of our heart, waiting for the right time to become visible, it is the result of moving in the right direction with confidence and faith even when a clear picture is not visible, All the success stories are the result having positive subconscious mind, be it a mediocre student dreaming of becoming a civil servant by cracking UPSC, an intelligent individual coming from poor family background getting admission in to IIT, through crowd funding or an entrepreneur started his journey in a small room with a dream turning start-up into Unicorn, a extra artist becoming successful actor/actress in film line or a young boy started his production unit in a garage with the dream of becoming a successful industrialist.

All the stories mentioned above have one thing in common that they are combination of a dream realised through subconscious mind. Subconscious mind moves an individual from slave of circumstances to the creator of circumstances. When we dream about a goal first thing which comes to our mind are the obstacles lying on the path, subconscious mind helps us to remove those obstacles step by step and clears our path if we continue moving in right direction.

Winning or achieving our goal; Life of a human being revolves around winning or achieving it's pre-set goals & targets, be it in studies, sports or in any other field, it is only when we be-friend our mind we can achieve the set goal and can be a successful academician, soldier, sportsperson, writer, musician, singer, artist, industrialist, businessmen, political leader or any other professional we would like to be, every individual wants to be somebody and achieve something during his span of life spend at this planet. There is one invisible friend which helps us to achieve our goals and that is our befriended mind, because whatever we want to do or achieve in life, first step is to visualise it with the help of it which will tell us that life is very precious, if we take care of life, it will care us back.

We have to understand how one life revolves around so many lives and those lives revolve around one life. Life is full of surprises, not always fair and no one knows what is going to happen next moment, so start moving towards your goal from this very moment, when we understand the fragility of life thoroughly, we decide to enjoy and utilise it fully by moving sincerely to achieve our goal.

Biggest benefit of a be-friended mind is that it constantly keeps you saying that when others can achieve this milestone **why can't you.** You are equal to everybody, may be there are certain circumstances which at present are in favour of winner, but sooner or later you can also with the help of your attitude can turn the tide and become one. Life is not about defining ourselves; life is about creating ourselves from the stuff which is given to us.

Making Happiness a Habit; Before learning how to be happy we must know the real meaning and what the happiness is all about, most of the people confuse happiness with pleasure, in their terminology happiness is going out with family & friends, having tasty food of our choice, watching comedy film or cracking jokes in the group but in my opinion all this activity comes under category of pleasure which is short lived and temporary.

Happiness is permanent identity of one's personality which can be defined in one line **"ability to replace negative thoughts with positive one',** once our friendly mind is able to do it for us, we will be happy in real terms, happiness is not absence of negative thoughts, happiness is clarity of thoughts &

action and living by choice or able to do what we want to do, or happiness is controlling our life, not life controlling us, whatever we think or do personally & professionally our ultimate aim is to have an element of happiness in that, moving one step further we can define happiness as a journey which can be discovered along the road and not at the end of road.

Most of us think that I will be happy if I get promotion, get married or achieve any milestone, but we have experienced these things before as well, we should question ourselves does those things have made us happy, a simple introspection will tell us that this type of pleasure is temporary and will last only for small duration.

One should aspire for permanent happiness which comes from within by bringing contentment, stillness and refined intelligence, when we think that we will be happy and healthy after becoming successful or achieving our goal, we are not thinking in right way because it's the other way around as our befriended mind will tell us that we can be successful in real terms only when we are happy, or in other words we wait for a reason to be happy, if that reason does not happen we are not happy, our befriended mind will make us learn how to be happy without any reason, there is no way to be happy, happiness is the way, we need to extend our diameter of happiness and find it in small things and activities, when we extend our diameter of happiness, things which were earlier not in our list of reason to be happy we include those thoughts and actions also. When we look at hundreds of things we enjoy, then the few things we don't have will cease to bother us, when we chose happiness over unhappiness, then we really understand the meaning of life because to be happy or not **is our choice, not chance.**

When we are not happy, our befriended mind will tell us that the happiest people don't necessarily have the best of everything; Happiest people just make the best of everything they have. Be happy, not because everything is good, but because you can see the good in everything. Friendly mind will guide us to see something good or positive in everything & under every circumstances. Being happy does not mean that everything is perfect. It means that our friendly mind has decided to look beyond imperfection.

We have to make happiness a habit to live a life full of harmony, by making our friendly mind guide & convince ourselves that whatever happens we should not lose our goal to be happy, it's a commitment with self. As soon as you identify that you are bending towards negative side or getting moody, strongly affirm your decision to be happy, we may not be able to change the circumstances but we can control the reaction. This simple ability will change our lives and make us happier.

How to Handle Failure. Since childhood we have been reading and knowing about great personalities, successful scientists, sports personalities, wealthy industrialists, Nobel prize winners, Oscar winning artists & musicians and many other success stories in and around our family & society, we also want to be successful and earning fortune like them, but when we think about these successful personalities, we have only one thing in mind that how lucky they are and how easy their life is, if we can be like them we don't have to do any thing for living and our life will be basking in glory. But things are not like this, if we closely watch their lives and read about them, we will find one thing in common that all of them have over come failures & adversity by be-friending their mind.

Failure, adversity, setbacks, accidents or unfortunate mishap is one thing which is Integral part of everybody's life and all of us have to face it or deal with it at one or other point of life, some face it early or some during the later course of life, when things don't happen as we have planned. What should we do? Answer is that we have to befriend our mind which will guide us to get ourselves to see the way out. No great personality has shined with the smooth path, sailors become skilled captain when they are introduced to rough sea and learn to manoeuvre the ship. Difficulty has greater role to play in building personality rather than facility, personality build through adversity have permanent impressions, because it is one's own efforts, not a borrowed one.

Success over failure; As we all know that one should have decent academic record to do well in life and become independent, but many of us don't understand the importance of good academic record and knowledge during our course of study. We can achieve good academic grades with the help of our friendly mind only, which always tells us that we are not less than anybody, we can also score good marks, this our mind has to say to us because of a wrong notion, which states that all those who are good in studies and score high grades are more intelligent than those who are scoring less marks or are weak in studies, students who are scoring high grades are having better intelligent quotient, but they are more hard and smart working than those students who scores low grades or in other words low scoring students can also improve their score tremendously if they start smart and hard work, low scoring students lose their interest in studies and just carry on averagely imagining that they can't compete with high graders because they are less intelligent, whereas success and failure has little to do with IQ, all achievements are result of resilience and hard work. Same approach can be applied to be successful in other field of profession whether in sports, science, medicine, writing etc.

Brain will always calculate 2+2 = 4, whereas be-friended mind has the capacity to dive deep and think beyond normal. Same approach is applicable to handle failure in other aspect of life, a befriended mind will not accept the failure as permanent and find out different ways to win in next encounter by working on weaknesses or reason of loss, it is the trust that this too shall pass if we hold on our fort, our hopes are kept alive with the help of faith and confidence. To err is human and forgive is divine, forgive yourself and move forward by engaging in introspection and self-reassessment.

Only human beings have the characteristic to turn a difficult condition into achievement. If a person receives setbacks or failure chooses to fight back instead of regretting is a victor not a victim. Regretting is negative and motivation to correct self is positive and transcend failure & rejection. Befriended mind will help us to overcome pain arising out of failure & defeat, best thing a befriended mind does is to stop pain turning into suffering, because after a defeat or failure pain is inevitable, but suffering is a choice, if we can minimise suffering arising out of pain, we have won half of the battle, suffering consumes lot of positive energy by drawing a vicious circle and we keeps on revolving around it without moving an inch towards our recovery path, befriended mind wake us to get up and target our goal with lot of courage & enthusiasm.

Changing habits; We all comes from different social, financial and educational backgrounds but we have only one goal, that is we want to be successful and financially independent to lead a good life, fulfil the dreams of self and our near & dear ones or we want to do be recognised and known for our achievements it has been observed that there are few individuals who are able to achieve their goals and rest keeps on revolving around the circle of confusion and not inching forward. What is the difference between the two? The difference is ability to changing habits as per the need and requirement of the situation or goal which helps an individual to change its habits.

In the beginning of our life our brain shaped habits as per our resources, surroundings and upbringing, but we will reach nowhere if we continue with our old habits, we have to change our habits in accordance with our aim & goal, if we want to be a world class sportsperson or athlete we have to change ourselves as per the parameter of that sports, if we want to be scientist we have to make habits accordingly, if we want to be a soldier we have to start preparation by keeping in view the mental and physical standard of defence forces and so on, every goal, every target has different specifications and parameters to fulfil.

    Who will help us to change accordingly? Off course, it will be our be-friended mind which will take over from brain and guide us towards change. If one of the basic requirements to achieve any goal is getting up early and sleep less, our mind will tell us that there is equal amount of discomfort if we get up at five o' clock or nine o'clock in the morning, but by getting up at 5.00. a.m. in the morning we will be closer to our goal or one step nearer to our target. If having less weight on our body is one of the basic requirements to achieve our target, our mind will tell us that being healthy or having correct weight in proportion to body's mass and height will not only help us to achieve our target but it will have long-lasting impact on our life as well, in this condition our mind will stop us at mindstation and make sure we develop healthy eating habits. If one of the primary requirements is to have adequate finance, our mind will interrupt us when we are making extravagant spending, by telling us that we can save money by eating home cooked food or clothes we are planning to buy are not required at this moment because same type of clothes is lying idle in our cupboard and not used since last six months. In all three scenarios we will tell our mind, please one more day to sleep by 9.00. a.m., one more extra cheese pizza for dinner last time or one more new jeans & T-shirt to be kept in my ward robe, after listening your request mind will tell you that it is not denying the pleasure you want or deserve, but the goal is more important than sleeping late, eating extra cheese pizza or buying new jeans & T-shirt. Mind is simply telling us to be more disciplined and postponed those unnecessary activities which comes in the way of achieving our target.

Compounding; Compounding, as we all know that is a mathematical process, in the process of compounding small numbers keeps on adding on regular interval resulting in huge sum beyond our imagination. This theory of compounding can be very aptly used in our daily life by those who wants to bring change. One very interesting thing which our be-friended mind will tell us that if we have decided to go for bigger goal, we have to bring small changes regularly and those small changes when added up turn out to be a big change in the form of result.

In this regard I can share you a real example of self, When I decided to write this book, I was scared and was not sure whether I will be able to fulfil my dream (writing a book), how I will accomplish this mammoth task, especially for a professional who has not published a single article or paper till date, Then my be-friended mind comes into picture by motivating me to do the most important part of any project or dream and that is taking the first step and started moving in the right direction, my be-friended mind told me to pickup my notes & laptop, start writing & typing what ever comes to my mind which is related to the topic of my book, I told my befriended mind that it is very difficult for me to write a book of three hundred fifty pages, My be-friended mind told me that "Yes, it is not very easy to write a book of three hundred fifty pages, who is telling you to write 350 pages in one sitting, but it is very easy to write one page daily for next 350 days". I very well agreed with my be-friended mind and started writing a page daily, which bore fruit and result is on my table in the form of book which I had dreamed of writing.

Compounding not only helps in adding good habits to one's personality, reverse compounding helps us to get rid of any bad habit as well, any individual or professional in any field can introduce self to the concept of reverse compounding and realise the dream with it's help, it could be a chain smoker who can reduce smoking by one cigarette per day or it be any one who want to lose fat by burning small amount of calories slowly on regular basis, or a student wanted to add hours to h/her study schedule or an athlete want to break the record in 100 meter sprint at international level improving by fraction of seconds regularly.

Conclusion; An average human life through out his span of life revolves around survival, maintaining status quo, changing habits for betterment, winning or achieving goal, handling failure or sorrow. All these parts of life are governed by only one thing that is '**mind**' if we are able to develop our mind to a dynamic mind, we will sail through our life smoothly, all the above-mentioned part of human life is bound to happen to every human being irrespective of rich or poor, intelligent or average, healthy or unhealthy.

Brains capacity is limited whereas mind has infinite capacity, it can be expanded by making brains muscle stronger, for example we bought a computer having a ram of 256 GB but after using for sometimes we want more speed for work, then we decided to increase its RAM, similarly when we are struck in some problem or mental block, we expand our level of thinking with the help of that beautiful part of ourselves i.e., mind.

Same could be understood by a simple example, I have a pre-conceived notion that watching movies is totally a waste of time, but when I am feeling bored my mind will tell me that there is no harm in spending half an hour in front of television to distract my brain from negative & energy sucking thoughts which occurs during moments of boredom. In other words, 'Pakao' jokes are better than no jokes.

A static mind may be considered as an individual who is known to you which lives far away and unable to listen that you need some solution or need to change a habit or to start a new activity, whereas a friendly mind is always near you because you have developed it and consider it as your friend, it will tell us that whatever the condition is, it can be improved upon. static mind is very often against the change, it will tell you that it is difficult to change any habit, friendly mind also backs this opinion of static mind of making any change is difficult but moves one step further by saying to itself "change is possible", which means we can replace any undesired habit with good one with the help of will power and create a winning edge.

Good habits are core of the success, as we all come from different backgrounds but we have to hit one target i.e., success, for being successful in professional & personal life there are certain qualities and habits which needs to be inculcated in our personality and to revolve into correct orbit so that we complete our journey successfully. Friendly mind will guide us to those small things in a beautiful manner giving small tasks its due importance. If we are more towards our static mind, we lose our focus on drop of a hat and looking for goal which we already knew but could not find it near our eyes because static mind is so fragile that even a small unwanted thought or activity will blur its vision and unable to decide the need of the hour.

Attitude

Suresh has received an e-mail from human resources department informing him lapsing of sick leaves for this calendar year, Suresh is associated with ABC corporation as CEO since last two years during these two years of service he had barely taken any sick leave, although he has taken leave for going outstations with family to spend vacation, to attend family function or to attend professional courses related to his specialisation.

What is the reason behind his good health? He does not do anything extra, follows same daily routine like other team members. Secret of his good health lies in his positive attitude towards his organisation, everything he do is with full commitment and enthusiasm. There were some incidents which disturbed him but he never allows those incidents to shake his attitude towards organisation, he feels very much contented when he is respected in the family & society due to the position he enjoys and able to meet his family and social responsibilities.

Ashok is working as team leader in ABC corporation, he is the bridge between top management and team members, he very well understands the importance of positive attitude in maintaining high level of productivity, under every circumstance he tries to maintain favourable attitude of his team members. He heads marketing department with a team of 27 people.

Today he seems to be a bit puzzled after few days of declaration of result of performance appraisal, none of his team members is promoted and rightly so his whole team seems to lost its motivation to work hard, leave apart work hard his team is unable to maintain bare minimum standard since last few days. Ashok was sitting in his office thinking how to solve this problem and bring a change in the attitude of his team members, suddenly one idea came to his mind.

He called all the team members over a cup of coffee and reminded them about last year's annual appraisal result in which highest number of promotions was given to their department. Humans are wired to forget good things happened to them and tendency to remember negative things happened to them, our reaction to good things are very sublime where as we react to negative things in a very disproportionate manner. Keeping this thing in mind he counselled his team members to change their attitude and lift their motivation level to bring back their performance at previous level and counselled team members by telling them that organisation also have some limitations we should respect the decision taken by higher authorities, should not lose focus and always have bigger picture in the mind.

Ashwini is working as Executive (accounts) in ABC enterprises, he was selected through campus placement drive three years back, in the beginning he was very happy as his goal of getting decent job through placement has been realised which allows him to meet the need of his family and self. But after working for three odd years, he is not enjoying his job, day by day his interest keeps on declining, reason being that all his family are doing business and few family members of his age are earning more than him at this point of time despite being less qualified and without any professional qualification, he was really confused what to do, how to keep working with same enthusiasm.

He discussed the matter with his team leader, luckily his senior also went through the same confusion during early years of his career. His team leader counselled him by saying that. In any case we have to work whether we became entrepreneur, trader or corporate professionals, to attain a respectable status in society and for our existence as well, there is no comparison between different nature of professions as every profession or mode of earning is totally different from each other, team leader told him that being a professionally qualified individual he has an unmatched advantage in the form of dual setting, which allows a professional to turn self into entrepreneur, trader or businessman at any point of time or as per the need arises but an unqualified individual cannot switch mode of earning according to will, Second advice he gave to Ashok that aim of life should not be to earn more money than others, it should be to live a life by choice and enjoy the profession you have chosen, after listening this piece of advice, the attitude of Ashwini takes a U-Turn, he left the office of his team leader with thankful note as his confusion has been removed, clearing the path for better personal & professional life.

Ritika is studying B.Tech. (Electrical) programme in a prestigious institute, today she came back home in a bad mood because she had not scored good marks in third semester exams. His father being a seasoned professional saw all this happening, he called Ritika in his room to discuss the matter. Ritika told him about her bad performance in third semester exams and not securing good grades despite of studying hard. Ritika's father told her that he observed her studying and concluded that she was studying to pass the exams, where as if one has to score good grades, they must try to understand the subject and gain knowledge about it, nobody gets good grades merely by studying important topics only. After seeking guidance from her father, Ritika started studying as per her father's advice because she knew that as a qualified professional and her best well-wisher, his suggestions are the safest to be followed. Keeping his advice in mind she started studying the way as told by her father resulted in securing good grades in next semester exams.

All the four scenarios discussed above about leader, team leader, team member and student have one thing in common i.e., ability to listen, understand and change their course of action in positive direction thus bringing improvement. It is there openminded and positive attitude which was instrumental in securing good grades, saving career, improving performance, and achieving organisational excellence. Imagine what would have happened if all the four characters mentioned above does not take action in positive way.

It is very much clear that positive attitude is the most important ingredient for personal and professional life, correction in attitude can bring you back when life does summersault and helps to fly when you are sprinting. With the right attitude one can make their dreams come true and attract success. When we develop right attitude, it opens the doors to happen miracles.

Attitude is a state of mind of an individual towards something. It may be defined as a tendency to feel and behave in a particular way towards objects, people or events. Attitude can be termed as person's preferred reaction towards a situation, opinion or condition. In long term an individual's attitude is influenced by things he admires, respects or fear and align its attitude with the behaviour of the people whom he looks up to. Attitude can be changed by providing new information, by resolving differences, by involving people & giving or receiving right type of feedback.

In this topic we will discuss about the attitude required during our student and professional life. As we all know that attitude towards anything could be positive or negative, we can express or show our attitude in favour of something or against it, it could be a change, activity or habit. As described earlier, the best thing about attitude is that it can be changed for better personal, professional or student life, as we enter our real life where we are in the process of proving ourselves and learning to lead it towards a meaningful destination. One thing which will take us to high altitude is not our attitude but our right attitude. In other words, we need right attitude to fly high and it could be negative or positive, all of you reading this might be little confused because till date we have read or heard the word "positive attitude" only. Let us discuss about need of both type of attitude, a professional is fine if he had negative attitude towards backstabbing, lying or any unethical practice and positive attitude towards fair-play, respect for knowledge and sincerity etc. to be a good student one has to develop negative (unfavourable) attitude towards using unfair-means during exams, procrastination or unhealthy eating habits and positive (favourable) attitude towards punctuality, hard work and discipline.

All of us should understand that we can have blissful life only if we take responsibilities of our action, as nobody else can breathe for us or nobody can think for us, blissful life can be attained with the help of right attitude only.

Functions; Main function of attitude is to adjust or adapt to environment to form the basis of future behaviours. Attitude helps in expressing values and a standard of reference which allows people to understand and explain their environment. What ever we do as human being good or bad, positive or negative, we express our attitude towards these activities. Function of attitude in any individual is to motivate self to take path as per understanding of attitude.

Attitude for CEO. Subhash is working as Chief Executive Officer of ABC enterprises, at present he is travelling to Bangalore from Delhi and thinking about his professional journey, if he has to give credit to only one thing which had helped him to reach at this height of corporate life, that is his positive attitude towards organisation, due to which he always gives his best and firmly believes that product of its factories can globally compete with any product of same specification, he reinforced his values by never compromising on the quality of the material to be used and is of the opinion that happy team members makes a successful organisation, he never missed any opportunity to make his team & team member feel important. In other words, he has full faith in capability & capacity of every team member.

Attitude about self. Subhash as CEO has always positive attitude towards self and holds self in high esteem by understanding the importance of correct attitude for a leader, a leader can exhibit best qualities and produce extraordinary results only if s/he is able to affect the entire team with correct attitude. He remembers that during his entire career he had turn every difficult situation in his favour with correct attitude and having firm belief in his capabilities. One of the prerequisites to be a successful professional is the presence of correct attitude towards whatever s/he is engaged in doing.

Scenario; Change in attitude. Once Subhash was heading a project in which he has to handle team members from different specialities, few of the team members were technically more knowledgeable and experienced than him, few team members were not in good terms with each other, In the beginning it was looking little difficult to deliver the project on scheduled time, in order to find a solution he noted down the steps he has to take for successful execution of project, he zeroed on two steps, first step was identification of team members with negative & non-co-operative attitude and second step was to bring change in attitude of those who were identified with negative attitude, when he called the meeting of team members identified with non co-operative attitude, he informs all of them the importance of project for the organisation, its impact on their annual appraisal thereafter and told them firmly that if they don't mend their ways he is left with no other option but to take strict action. Question arises how Subhash was able to take corrective measures with respect to the attitude of team members for this particular project. Subhash had gone through the same situation ten years back during middle of his career but he was also able to bring positive result just by changing his attitude from negative to correct.

Attitude towards organisation or organisational commitment; Subhash saw his success due to his positive attitude towards his organizations where ever he had served, he always developed a sense of loyalty & right attitude towards all the organizations, during his career span of twenty seven years he was associated with five organisations, but he gives them equal importance in terms of loyalty and attitude, one may be surprised by above definition of loyalty, it is very much clear that one may remain loyal to a particular organisation during his stay only, if a professional changes organisation his loyalty will also shift to the current organisation.

Subhash could show organisational commitment because of his right attitude as he understands that whatever position he is holding is due to this present organisation, which has given him chance to fulfil his professional ambition, social & family responsibility. It is the responsibility of a professional to rate h/her organisation above everything as a soldier is attached to his 'Paltan'.

Attitude towards meaningful life; One more attitude which Subhash has nurtured at the bottom of his heart is towards life, he understands that all of those who have come on this mother earth has to spend some time here depending upon their destiny, so why not spend it with full fanfare, live every moment with full of energy and execute all the assigned task with best of the ability by excelling in what ever they do or told to do.

Benefit of having positive attitude towards meaningful life has been the core of thoughts for him during his entire career, leading a meaningful life for him means not spending any moment or thoughts on wasteful activity and understand the preciousness of time. He had developed this positive attitude since college time when he was introduced to good literature and self-help books by one of his teachers, whom he always thanked from bottom of his heart whenever he receives appreciation or move forward in life. Second benefit of having a positive attitude towards a meaningful life is that his action and behaviour has become inspiration for many team members, family members & friends, by establishing a reputation of a positive human being, colleague and senior, he takes decisions after considering both side of the coin i.e., negative & positive, and clearly explain the benefit of going with the correct one, in this way he is able to mentor young minds and pass it to the next generation.

Benefits of Negative (Unfavourable) Attitude; Subhash as CEO has unfavourable attitude towards corruption and illegal practices, his un-liking for corrupt practices was deep-rooted in his mind due to one incident in his family, one of his maternal uncle who was in government job was suspended on graft charges, due to which family of maternal uncle faced lot of humiliation, keeping that incident in mind, Subhash has decided to always follow the law and abide by all the rules and regulations of organisation.

Negative attitude towards wrong practices has helped him maintaining the dignity of human nature, as he was able to fend off many temptations which could have put him and his family in difficult condition by bringing bad name to entire organisation as well. Subhash always remains grateful to family upbringing for his inclination towards being a rule following and law-abiding citizen.

Attitude

Knowing about other's Attitude; As a CEO Aman was very well aware of his attitude and how to use it to lead the organisation and bringing change for smooth functioning, but still things were not up-to the mark. After giving it a thought for quite a while and spending lot of time to understand how to manage team members and keep them motivated to execute their responsibilities properly, He suddenly realises that developing right attitude to be a CEO is different matter, but to remain CEO one has to know about the other's attitude as well because that is the key to know your team members, once you know your team member's attitude it becomes very easy to allocate the right kind of responsibility and get the best out of them.

Scenario; Aman was looking at his team members to lead this prestigious project they have won, after having elaborate discussion with senior team members he narrowed his choice to Ankit and Alok, board members were in favour of Ankit who was senior and more qualified whereas Aman's choice was Alok who was just one grade junior to Ankit but a very good team player along with friendly & adjusting attitude.

Aman as CEO informed board members that he is in favour of Alok because of his positive attitude, Board also gave its approval to Aman's choice, as they were also interested in projecting themselves as progressive organization and interested in practicing modern ways of managing things. Result of this appointment was immediately visible, while addressing his first team meeting, Alok addressed all his senior team members and especially mentioned the name of Ankit with great deal of respect and seek his guidance to accomplish this prestigious project in the interest of organisation. Simply finding his name mentioned with great deal of respect, Ankit forgets all the grudges and devoted himself fully towards execution of project.

Desirable Attitude for CEO. There are some attitudes which are must for successful execution of a particular role in professional life or in other words one can say that if a particular role holder is aware of the need of these attitudes will make their journey effective and reflect a professional approach towards their job responsibilities, in my views a CEO should be familiar with these five attitudes discussed below, although there is no end to have good qualities and attitudes to perform professionally.

Loyal; Loyalty towards present organisation is one of the prerequisites to attract good results, loyalty here does not means that one must stick to an organisation throughout whole life, as it is not possible for a professional to serve in one organisation throughout h/her entire career, but being loyal here means what ever s/he does in current role and to its present organisation or whatever one plans to do is always keeping the interest of organisation in mind till s/he is associated with it.

Being loyal to its present role will attract positivity and help the professional to chart new paths. we can understand loyalty by an individual's thoughts or what one speaks about it's organisation, it could be few decisions made by keeping the attitude of loyalty in mind, those decisions may not be looking very fruitful at that point of time but will have long lasting impact in future, loyalty here means standing in front of that individual who has any intention to harm the interest of the organisation, Loyalty can be seen in a CEO's conduct on the last day of notice period when s/he is giving her 110% by applying h/her knowledge and experience in executing last task for the present organisation. In an appropriate definition "Loyalty is that invisible undercurrent which brings lot of pearls to the shore".

Committed. Being committed towards present organisation means doing everything one can do to move it forward and make it successful not only in terms of earning profit, but in keeping in tune with time, bringing modern techniques & management practices, sometimes commitment requires personal sacrifice also, these can be sum up by a situation where his/her organisation is in need of some liquid money as due to poor cash flow this situation has surfaced.

A committed CEO will lend helping hand to the organisation to avoid any misinformation being spread. Being committed will establish reputation of a leader on top. Commitment is clearly visible in a professional's efforts while running the show which is also an indication that under every circumstance a given task has to be executed, no obstacle can stop a committed professional, this obstacle could be in the form of medical problems, resource constraints or sudden exit of a team member, a committed professional will undertake every task by keeping in mind the contingency plan, once a task is accepted s/he will not leave any stone unturned to complete it, a committed professional is very much aware of h/her reputation and in no case would like to have a dent on it.

Impartial. Leader is a father figure for every team member and the best way to lead an organisation is by taking impartial, unbiased and transparent decisions, once all team members have confidence that their efforts are being judged by a Leader who is impartial and unbiased, will take efficiency & productivity of team members to next level, which is the ultimate goal of every organisation. A Leader's top most priority should be to encourage impartial and unbiased action, behaviour and decisions not only from self but s/he should express the desire that all team members must follow this practice as well.

Impartial and unbiased not only with each other, but with organisation as well, when we learn to be impartial & unbiased with our organisation, we do not hide any mistake which in due course of time might become the reason of loss in any form. Leader having impartial attitude is the best asset to an organisation and becomes main reason for its success.

Positive. A CEO being head of the organisation must have positive attitude towards what is happening in the organisation, don't get confused about 'whatever happening' in the organisation, positivity here means if any thing negative or wrong activity comes to the notice of CEO s/he should approach it with positive attitude and must have the confidence that s/he will deal with this negativity with full force and find a amicable solution in the interest of the organisation, be it conflict management, malafide publicity or loss making, with the positive approach a CEO must have the will to get out of these situations winningly.

Every team member would like to work with a CEO who is having positive frame of mind which fills the team member with confidence and motivate them to give their best, team members are confident that in every difficult or trying circumstances their CEO is available to guide them towards right direction. Positive attitude of CEO is infectious by making other team members more positive which is reflected in team's approach while handling high level of stressful jobs. Positivity attracts positivity and make an unbreakable chain.

Flexible. Flexible attitude of a CEO is that one quality which can be said to be lubricant of every team and the key for managing team and organisation efficiently. Every organisation is run by rules & policies for proper functioning, but sometimes these rules and policies needs to be changed with the moving times to suit present condition & generation of team members. Flexible attitude will help making changes in these rules and policies in the interest of the organisation. If one is not able to make frequent changes, then taking decisions by using authority also indicates sign of flexibility. Secondly, Flexibility also indicates promoting those actions which a leader is not in its favour personally, but it is in the interest of organisation & team, moulding self to benefit others for getting best out of them and developing efficient human resources.

In other words, flexibility can be termed as that style of leading which states that rules and regulations are for the smooth functioning of organisation, not to create barriers in the path. Flexible attitude of a CEO is very helpful in keeping the team members remain dedicated towards organisation. This could be understood by this real incident, in my previous organisation there was LTA (Leave Travelling Allowance) which any employee can avail as per their grade, while filling the claim form, I have to attach tickets and boarding pass as proof of travelling but by mistake I have misplaced our boarding passes and could not attached the same. Accounts department rejected my claim due to non-production of boarding passes, When I requested my CEO to approve the bill by describing the whole case, he immediately called accounts head on intercom and conveyed his approval for the same. This flexible approach of my CEO has made me more dedicated team member of organisation.

Attitude for Team Leader; Neetu is associated with ABC enterprises as team leader (Marketing) since last four years and has very positive attitude towards her department (marketing), because of organisation's employee friendly and transparent policies which motivates her to give best performance. She receives adequate support from organisation and was able to use this attitude for the betterment of team.

Attitude towards team and team members; Neetu is associated with her present organisation since last four years, her job has been made easy by none other than but her positive attitude towards team members and their professional commitments, we can give a score of 8/10 to her attitude towards team, despite of various ups and downs she never loses faith in her team. Let us inquire from where Neetu got this attitude to lead her team.

She learned the art of positive attitude from her previous boss, it is not that her previous boss was having positive attitude towards his team, in fact his previous boss has absolutely negative attitude towards his team and always views himself as the solo actor, but Neetu being a thoughtful and progressive professional saw the impact of negative attitude on a failed team which could not deliver any project on time because of boss not showing any faith and confidence in the ability of team members, not giving them freedom to take risk, no space for improved communication. After having seen her previous boss failing, Neetu decided to do just opposite when she got a chance to lead. For being a successful leader, one should have the ability to learn from other's mistake as well.

Scenario; Attitude of Neetu towards her team members has always been positive, she very well understands that in a team 70% of task is done by 30% of team members, rest 70% are in supporting mode, but it does not mean that those supporting team members comprising 70% of total strength should be ignored and no step for their professional development should be taken. Every team member if given proper guidance and opportunity has the potential to reach next level, as we never know which team members can contribute more than expected, she is always looking to polish the hidden gem by making team better and more valuable.

Attitude towards top Management; One more attitude which kept her motivation at higher level is her attitude towards top management, top management of her organisation is very professional in true sense, they not only mean business but consider themselves as custodians of employees and treat them as their extended family members. Whenever there is a need of support from top management for any personal or professional problem, proper support is always there.

Scenario; In corporate sector it is common notion that top management is always interested in revenue and profit only, this false notion makes team members developing negative attitude towards top management. Neetu very well understands this, from time to time she keeps on telling team members that it is due to the money invested by top management, we are earning our livelihood and able to execute our social & professional responsibility. If we keep negative attitude towards top management, it will be reflected in our action and thoughts pulling us further away from top management. It is very much necessary to be positive towards top management and understand their limitations as well.

Neetu always keeps on reminding the good deed done by Top Management, whether it is helping financially to needy team members, setting up a kitty with major contribution from their side as welfare measure for education of children of team members, When a machine operator lost one of his upper limb in the accident he was aptly helped during medical treatment and given safer job after recovery, not only this but top management took decision to replace the older machine and provided funds to procure latest & safer machines. Neetu's effort in spreading positive attitude towards top management bore fruit and every team member is executing the given task responsibly.

Attitude towards her job; Neetu always considers her job responsibility as number one in life and her attitude towards the job has given her immense amount of satisfaction, being satisfied in the job is one of the best assets of a professional, which results in good physical & mental health by taking them to higher level. If a professional team leader is not satisfied with job s/he will not be able to perform well and set higher standard for team, it is the responsibility of team leader to keep her attitude positive and intact.

Scenario; Neetu as a professional and serving team leader of marketing department has very positive attitude towards her job and shared same attitude with team members by promoting positive attitude towards job responsibilities which has made her team perform exceptionally well. Neetu during informal communication with team members highlights the importance of a job in the life of a professional, it is God's gift to showcase one's ability and differentiate humans from other creatures. No other species earn its livelihood like humans do, every team member should feel lucky to have a job and build a career out of it by rising higher on the corporate ladder.

Change in attitude; One of the most important job of a team leader is to keep the attitude of their team members positive and correct to take team in forward direction, but as we all know that sometimes all team members do not exhibit same attitude, when any one or two team members start thinking or acting in different direction, pulling the team in opposite direction resulting in wastage of resources and time. What steps a team leader should take? A leader is left with no other alternative but communicate and counsel team members to come back on the platform on which whole team is standing, it could be by taking tough corrective measures in the interest of team and themselves.

Scenario; Neetu's team was smoothly moving in right direction, but since last two weeks she was experiencing some downward in the performance of the team, after observing & using her experience, she zeroed on two team members who were not able to contribute there hundred percent, one of them was Nishith who was trying to move abroad with his parents and his legal formalities were still three to four months away from being completed and second one was Shruti who was having some personal problems and taking advantage of that she was asking for excuses every time.

Neetu called them one by one in his cabin and have detailed conversation, she conveyed to Nishith that It is good that you are moving abroad with your family but that should not be the reason for lowering your performance level intentionally, you might need our help once you return back after completing your tenure of three years, Nishith understood the point and started working with usual level of efficiency. While counselling Shruti, Neetu advised her to take long leave till she finds the solution of her personal problem, because working half heartedly with distracted mind will not be in the interest team and organisation. Shruti took Neetu's advice sincerely by immediately applying for long leave.

Benefits of unfavourable attitude. Neetu as deputy of Subhash has unfavourable attitude towards backstabbing and gossiping in the department, as a team leader she never backstabs or indulge in gossiping about any other team member for the purpose of time pass or making other team member feeling low, she want her team members to understand and know about the fine lines demarcating jokes, laughter, humour and gossip, neither she uses his authority to show others about his superior position instead she uses knowledge and experience to impress upon her team members. This unfavourable attitude of Neetu has kept her team in the best form, she encourages them to use organisation's library and gym in free time instead of finding faults in other team members and making them feel low.

Attitude

Knowing about other's Attitude; As a team leader one has to deal with different level of professionals to keep the show running, these professionals may be vertically placed at same level in different departments, junior or entry level executives of same department, knowing about the attitude of subordinates and same grade professional is not enough, one has to understands the attitude of seniors as well to meet their aspirations. As a team leader they not only have to assign task to entry level or junior executives but have to seek co-operation from same grade department heads or they have to seek approval from CEO for any action to be taken, knowing about others attitude is very positive step towards getting the things done efficiently and take pro-action to resolve any issue which is obstructing the way.

Scenario; Avdhesh is working as team leader in IT department of ABY corporation, apart from one of the best hardware specialist in organisation, he tries to understand the attitude of his team members including CEO, which makes his task much easier, since last few days he was finding it little bit difficult to work on current project as two of his team members taking advantage of their seniority and specialisation have started coming late to office and leaving early, Avdhesh was of the opinion that they are involved in "moonlighting," but without any concrete proof he could not do much. But when things started going out of control, he wanted to discuss the matter with CEO, considering the attitude of CEO very positive towards discipline and punctuality, after listening Avdhesh's problem, CEO called head of the H.R. department and instructed her to re-frame the current policy as in current policy senior team members were given relaxation for leaving or coming to office without taking any formal permission, but due to continuous misuse of this policy by seniors resulted in loss to the organisation, this problem was curtailed due to CEO's positive approach and attitude towards indiscipline and unauthorised use of power, Avdhesh's problem was solved due to his knowledge about CEO's attitude.

Desirable attitude for Team Leader; A team leader being a bridge between Top Management & team, is the first contact point of junior team members as they look for motivation and follow the examples set by team leader, it is very desirable for a team leader to have or develop following attitudes in the **trichual** interest of self, team and organisation. Let us discuss these attitudes one by one.

Confident; A confident attitude for a team leader is very desirable for self and team , a team leader full of confidence spread positive vibes among team members helps in two ways, first while dealing with higher authorities a confident team leader is able to put forward h/her point of view in much more effective manner as most of the requests and suggestions to higher authorities are regarding providing better facilities to team members, asking for more resources or making policies for better culture & working atmosphere.

If a team leader is unable to put forward h/her point of view in a confident manner, suggestions and recommendations put forward by them won't be considered seriously. Secondly, being a role model for young team members, attitude of confidence counts a lot, as every team leader has to accomplish the task with the contribution from team members, lack of confidence will bring their position dwindling in front of team members, as they have to produce results, teach & train young minds to get their work done for which confidence is one of the main ingredients to make sure that transfer of knowledge is done efficiently.

Optimistic. Optimism is also one of the attitudes which a team leader must display while handling day to day functioning & road blocks, optimism shown by a team leader increases credibility, being optimistic depicts that we will overcome any mishap or negative activity. Secondly, to keep the working atmosphere in vibrating mode while facing any problem, a team leader approaches CEO to find the solution to any problem, similarly team members who are at entry or junior level, approaches team leader to seek solution for any problem or query.

If team leader is optimist, then his approach towards every problem will be solution-oriented filling his team with confidence and spreading positive vibes in entire department, one more effect of optimistic team leader is that s/he gives new team members opportunity to learn, relearn and unlearn, one mistake by a team member is not taken as permanent impression but given the chance to correct that mistake because an optimist always believe that everybody has the ability to improve self.

Realistic. Being a realistic in attitude, a team leader makes things easier for team, a realistic professional sees the situation as it is, in other words s/he sees the glass of water as it is, not half nor full instead s/he thinks how to utilise this glass of water to quench thirst or in other words, meet the desired goal. While being realistic, a team leader does not choose options which are superficial or imaginary. A realistic team leader is able to use past incidences to take decision and opportunity to set targets as per the capability of team which in turn takes performance of team members to next level, because realistic targets are met by team members with success which further encourages them to accept next target with enthusiasm.

Friendly. Friendly attitude towards team members will be a magical ward for a team leader for two very important reasons, first, mostly a team leader has to deal with team members who are relatively quite younger and most of them are first timers and trying to find their way for establishing themselves in a new professional world, it is of immense help if they find their team leader being friendly towards them, it is win-win situation for both of them.

On one hand a friendly team leader is able to clear every doubt of their team members and in turn team members don't hesitate to approach their leader as they know they will be treated in fair manner which in turn paves the way for smooth functioning of department, Secondly, A friendly attitude of team leader will help whole team to convert into a well knit group and able to ward off small misunderstandings & confusions without much problem, lot of time and resources are saved when internal problems are solved by taking informal solution.

Courageous. A team leader needs a pinch of courage to keep team & department running in electrifying manner which includes taking decisions quickly and sometimes approaching a situation in unconventional way to bring positive result. Courage is required when a team leader has to take approval from CEO for a decision to travel on the path which was not taken earlier or where little bit of risk is involved but if succeeded will bring extraordinary results and open new avenues for organisation. Second benefit of a team leader having courageous attitude is that s/he stands firm with the team in case of any injustice is done to a team member, team is not treated well or not getting enough support or co-operation from any other department, a team leader with attitude of courage chose to put forward the case in strong manner rather than to be in good books of others, courageous attitude of a team leader shows that for h/her team's interest is above everything.

Attitude for team member; It is very necessary for a team member to have favourable attitude towards their job and in turn it is the responsibility of organisation as well to continuously educate their team members about the importance and benefit of maintaining the favourable attitude while executing the assigned task.

Due to negative attitude towards his job Akshaya could not get promotion since last five years, he performs only those tasks which are sufficient to keep his job intact, leave apart participating in any training course. This negative attitude has made it very difficult for Akshaya to perform efficiently. It is of utmost importance that attitude of team members should be kept positive with the policies of organisation and good human resources policies & practices which includes understanding the attitude of team members, moving towards positivity and training for re-adjustment of attitude if required. If a team member during first or second job is finding it difficult to adjust or unable to give its best performance, is indication for a need of adjustment in attitude. H/her disinterest might be due to unfavourable attitude towards job because of one reason or the other. It becomes the responsibility of that individual and team leader to help h/her to re-adjust for the benefit of self and team.

Attitude towards nature of job; As a team member best thing you can do for yourself is to have positive attitude towards your nature of job, in the beginning of the career when you are in the process of building base of your life and becoming financial independence by clinching your first job which will fulfil your dreams and something which you have to do for your next twenty five years of life, to sail through it smoothly one has to love it as second girlfriend, because when you love something you are not tired by making efforts and commitments promised to it. There are some instances when a professional does not get job of choice but as a human being, we have the capability to turn this unfavourable condition into a favourable one, just by replacing thoughts and change in attitudes. History is filled with numerous examples where humans who have touched the highest point of their career and life have never thought of entering into particular field doing it but when they entered in that field accidently, they gave their best and become the 'best'.

Attitude towards performance appraisal; One of the most important positive attitude building should be in the direction of organisation's performance appraisal mechanism, because it has been observed that generation 'Z' when joined a job, is in search of fast movement of career which lead to some impractical notions about upward movement on corporate ladder, whereas they must understand that every organisation has some policies regarding promotion and increment which are followed for the purpose of developing & retaining their human assets, it cannot be changed at the will of any individual. While executing their job, generation 'Z' developed some unreasonable expectations, if not fulfilled leads to dejection and wrong decisions like quitting or below average performance.

Benefits of Unfavourable Attitude; An individual team member must develop unfavourable attitude towards gossiping, wasting time by excessively using social media during office hours, unfavourable attitude towards these practices will ultimately help him/her in giving hundred percent while executing a task by realising that gossiping and using social media during office hours is making loss to the organisation, if organisation suffers, it is loss to all those who are associated with it, it is very important to understand this simple mechanism.

Knowing about other's Attitude; A team member being a fresher has to work with same level of executives and senior level professionals. It is very helpful if one understands the attitude of others in order to adjust self and be a part of the team. In the beginning of one's professional career understanding other's attitude helps an entry level team member to learn, move ahead in his role and helps to gel with other team members by taking proactive actions and move smoothly with the team.

Attitude

Scenario; Komal has just joined a multinational organisation as management trainee, she was trying to get herself fit into the organisational culture with little bit of efforts, after keenly observing her team leader while he allocates job responsibilities to each of his team members, as if he knows the qualities and attitude of each of them, keeping in view this Komal also started paying attention to attitude of each of her team members.

During such one incident her knowledge about other team member's attitude bore good fruit, her team leader has given her to prepare a report regarding financial matter, which makes her little bit uneasy, as during MBA program her major subject was marketing, but knowing the co-operating attitude of one of team members who has specialisation in finance help Komal to approach him not only for getting the report prepared but also learn the key point of finance.

Desirable attitude in a team member. There are certain attitudes which are very beneficial to a team member during early stages of their career, or in other words we can say that they are must to reach next level of career and complete this phase in a successful manner. In my views they are not only desirable but these attitudes are expected from young generation, there is some change in the definition we can define a professional to be young only if s/he is executing their job responsibility happily and with great deal of enthusiasm. Let us discuss those attitudes one by one.

Energetic. In the beginning of the career a team member needs to display good amount of energy as s/he is expected to learn and execute the knowledge in so many different spheres. Being energetic is sign of good mental & physical health as well, when a professional is medically fit and do not take leave for health reasons, thus present during most of the important occasions, paying proper attention, on some occasions one can stay back after office hours and not get disoriented due to fatigue.

It is expected from a young professional to come forward to take extra load and additional responsibility when ever a situation arises and must accept this opportunity happily with an intention to learn something new. A team member full of energy is considered an asset by seniors as they know that they can depend on h/her when need arises.

Enterprising. An enterprising attitude is very good for an entry level team member, which makes a team member curious about various activities happening around, an enterprising & curious individual looks for better ways to execute the task and does not want to follow the conventional ways of doing it, s/he wants to observe and learn interesting way to do a task which takes less time & less resources consuming, bringing better results in the form of innovations and new process.

An enterprising team member sees any process from many different angles with an intention to add something better, this enterprising attitude of a team member breaks the monotony and encourages other team members to follow suite. I would like to add one more thing in this perspective that this enterprising attitude is not limited to physically visible activities but it is visible in thoughts and behaviour as well, which means that an enterprising individual team member is always interested in better and improved manner of communication, better negotiation skills or any new trend which makes h/her soft skills better and spreading it by way of exhibiting the same.

Reliable. Reliable attitude helps an entry level team member to be confident of seniors and colleagues, it's a boon if senior has confidence that whatever job is assigned to h/her will be executed to the best of ability of that individual, Reliability can be defined in other words also, which clearly says that one relies on other for every option whether it is 'yes' or 'no' because an individual should be able to tell the correct picture will he be able to execute the task or not, if not why? If yes what are the requirements to complete it, a reliable professional is one who is not ashamed of asking for help, h/her whole activity surrounds around task completion.

A reliable team member is a gem for any team because s/he can take load of those tasks which others are not interested in, reliability is not limited to those tasks in which s/he is proficient, but seniors are interested in assigning those tasks as well in which s/he is not expert but keeping h/her reliable attitude they now that s/he will make every effort to execute it even if it requires learning new skills or gaining knowledge in new field. A team member with reliable attitude is one on which we do not have to keep a watch for completing any task assigned and will give its best **when nobody is watching**.

Humble. A humble attitude is the safest way towards being part of a new team, humbleness is that one quality which gives enough space to remove any drawback if there is any, for an entry level team member every action is new in this corporate world s/he is bound to be confused or make mistakes, for which he may be scolded by his seniors or mocked at.

A humble individual develops the ability to absorb tough times in the interest of learning and moving ahead in career, being humble makes an individual to avoid any knee-jerk reaction to an unpleasant situation. A humble attitude is icing on the cake for a team member as most of human being developed inflated ego after completing a task, shouting like 'Tarzan', I have done this, I have done that which creates lot of disturbance in the team, whereas a humble team member gives credit to team after completing the task and moves towards next task with out much 'ho-halla'.

Attitude

Attitude for Students; A student's far most responsibility is to maintain favourable attitude towards formal education, under any circumstances a student should not lose connection with formal education and try to complete it with the best of his ability. During student life one will face many trying times due to one reason or the other, every student must understand that situation is not favourable for any one of them, but you have to make them favourable by adjustment or correction of attitude.

With the advent of social media and information explosion, students spend time reading about celebrities and successful page three artists, who does not hold any professional degree but their pictures are published with lot of fanfare, this fills the youth with doubt and they started pointing out the very existence of formal education. As a young and budding citizen of country, they must understand the importance of formal education which will bring permanent laurels to them and happiness to their families, biggest benefit of formal education is that nobody can steal knowledge and degree from you. If they keenly observe the life of a successful celebrity who could not attain formal education, their success span is of very short duration and inconsistent, whereas success achieved with the help of knowledge and qualification is consistent in nature and fulfilling. A student having positive attitude towards formal education leads a successful life personally & professionally.

Scenario; Sachin joined a prestigious B-school by way of competition, he holds favourable attitude towards formal education and study seriously to pass this programme, on the other hand When Ajay joined the same school along with Sachin, he holds unfavourable attitude towards formal education because he had read few articles published on page three of newspapers & magazines about so many celebrities and successful businessmen who does not have formal education or hold any professional degree. Student life is that ground on which every individual prepares the foundation of future, s/he has to work in every sphere of his life, gaining knowledge, working on his interests to lead a successful life. all this can be made possible only if a student has learned or developed a positive attitude towards life and its various aspects.

Attitude towards life and self; A student when gets out of protected shell of family has already attitudes fixed for different things, relations, and circumstances. But every student is expected to view life through lens of positive attitude, life given by nature to every individual is special and unique in its own form, we can have positive attitude towards it only if we realise that how precious our life is and we have to make it meaningful with the help of our attitude.

Whether we are weak or strong, average or exceptional, poor or rich, we have to stop comparing it with others and live life as it comes, keeping in view that life has given something to everybody to rejoice about. Secondly, as a student one should have positive attitude towards self with the notion that I will face every challenge in life to realise my dreams irrespective of any circumstances.

Attitude towards teachers and reputation of institute; A positive attitude towards their teachers, guides and educational institute gives a student very good backing and protection. It has been observed that students keep on criticising their teachers & facilities of the institute. It is very unethical to criticise the individual and place which is responsible for our life and career, who guides us to sail through exams and programmes. Who is the catalyst to our next transition to society?

Do you remember when you helped your friend by giving extra pen during an important lecture, how good you have felt when your friend mentioned your help (giving pen) in front of everybody. Whereas in the case of teachers and guides they share their knowledge and experiences of life time to complete your education which fulfils your and your parents dream, on a realistic note what you will think about your teacher and institute, same will reflect on your academic performance.

In other words, we can say that we get what we think, as far as my knowledge is concern no teacher or professional wants to perform below his standard or work against the interest of the students, secondly, instead of finding fault in others we must look at ourselves and improve wherever it is required, we also get what we deserve, if we want to get better from any field, we have to raise our level too, it is sin if we spread negative words for those who brings positivity in our life.

Scenario; When Akshaya joined L.L.M. programme, after few days of attending lectures, he was told by one of his seniors that Prof. Sharma is not a good teacher. But when he gave a serious thought about it, could not find anything wrong in the teaching style of Prof. Sharma, later he came to know that senior who was complaining about Prof. Sharma, could not perform well in that very subject and that is why he is spreading false information about Prof. Sharma. Imagine what would have happened if Akshay had blindly accepted the feedback given by his senior without thinking independently of the opinion formed by his senior.

Attitude towards companionship & friendship; As a student when we move into higher institutions we meet new classmates, teachers, seniors & other official staff about whom we have already framed our attitude by the opinions received from our siblings, neighbours or our friends, but we have to keep our attitude positive towards all of the professionals and individuals mentioned above, otherwise all our efforts to sail through with flying colours in our professional programme will go in drain.

In this case we should think with clarity & positive state of mind by developing independent opinion, we should look out for friendship with like minded individuals and believe in the policy of give and take i.e., only by giving first we become eligible for taking. Positive attitude towards friendship keeps us fresh and safe because we can take shelter under it during difficult times but before that we have to act as umbrella for someone who is facing storm.

Correction of attitude; After having gone through above important points students are advised to take utmost care about choosing their attitudes for a successful personal & professional life, but due to one reason or the other students may not have positive attitude towards any one of the above-mentioned points, as a human being we have the power to correct attitude in our own interest.

A student must have adequate knowledge of attitude, if h/her attitude is different from what it should be for a particular condition, s/he should make sincere effort to correct it, it is must to sail smoothly in turbulent waters. When we learn to identify and change our attitude accordingly as per requirement, we have won half of the battle or in other words if we handle current challenges with our old attitude, will drag ourselves us deeper into problem.

Benefits of unfavourable attitude; As we all know that attitudes are of two types favourable or unfavourable, we should have favourable attitude towards positive conditions and should have unfavourable attitude towards negative conditions, having unfavourable attitude has its benefit as well.

During student life one must develop unfavourable attitude towards using unfair means for passing the exams, indiscipline, procrastination or any wrong thing prohibited by society & law of the land, developing unfavourable attitude towards wrong practices during student life build the right foundation for ethical behaviour which becomes very helpful in taking right decisions during course of career. Behaving ethically is one of the prime requirements to be successful in personal &

professional life, behaving ethically is the best decision any one can take irrespective of its resultant.

Knowing about other's Attitude; Continuing the discussion about having the knowledge of other team members with respect to students, its during student life one comes to understand the meaning of self and other's attitude as student life is the beginning of corporate dream and the first step towards understanding & developing attitude to lead a successful life. Student's team consists of their parents, teachers, seniors and classmates, a student is expected to deal with team members successfully, by being a keen observer a student comes to know about the attitudinal action or reaction of their team members and act or do not act accordingly.

Scenario; Smita was doing graduation from one of the colleges of Delhi University, along with good in studies she was excellent in playing badminton, represented her school in inter-state championship and won silver medal. She wanted to continue the winning streak during her graduations as well.

She was practising very hard to take part in national championship as dates of the championship was announced and scheduled to be held from 15th to 23rd of next month, Smita was planning to participate with great enthusiasm by practising day and night. Suddenly her whole enthusiasm comes to halt as she has just received her exam date sheet, as per date sheet she is going to miss her last exam if she decided to participate in national championship, she discuss the matter with her sports in-charge, who in turn advised her to submit an application for re-exam of the last paper, sports in-charge knowing the attitude of Principal towards games and sports, was confident of getting permission for re-examination of last paper, as assumed by sports in-charge Smita was given special permission by Principal to appear in the last exam after competing in national championship, By getting permitted to participate in national championship Smita got a boost to her thinking that sports and study can be handled side by side if we approach it with correct attitude, she intended to pass on the same attitude in future if she happens to be in deciding position.

Desirable attitude for Students; Student who has just stepped in to a new world to fulfil goal of being a good citizen and a successful professional. All of us have come into this world to play different roles at different stages of our life and must understand that in order to play every role competently one has to rise to the occasion by learning different qualities or in other words we cannot play different roles by remaining stagnant, we have to grow to meet the demands of every new role. I have zeroed in five attitudes which will be helpful during student life and have positive impact on a student.

Respectful. Possessing a respectful attitude is a must for student to sail through successfully during student life. A student will be seeking guidance from every individual around be it their parents, teachers, seniors or peers. It has been observed that students have a pre conceived notion while joining new educational institute that they have to win over everybody in order to survive in the institute/college. But a student does not join any institute to survive they need to excel in what ever they do. A respectful attitude towards their team will take them from survival to excellence.

Motivated. A student needs to find motivation & purpose of life towards their goal, without positive motivation students cannot survive modern day system of education, motivation is the key to overcome distractions or any mishappening occurred during student life and remove any unexpected obstacle blocking the way, absence of favourable attitude towards motivation will make a student stand still after going through difficult circumstances, motivation is the energy which helps us to get up when we are down, motivation are those eyes which helps us to see through obstruction and visualise it as a transparent or in other words motivation is very much required for taking next step when nothing is visible clearly, but moving ahead is matter of life and death.

Cheerful. Being cheerful indicates a student is taking everything into its stride and happily continuing this journey to achieve the set target. A cheerful attitude attracts good company and despite of burdensome activities, makes the atmosphere charged and light, possessing cheerful attitude means one is in control of its mood and no negativity can derail its motive and continues infecting others who came in contact with, making its surroundings a playground and producing desired results.

Willing. A willing attitude means ready to explore new things, willing to help others, willing to participate in new activities etc. a willing attitude is considered one of the prime attitudes for students to move with team. When one shows willing attitude all its team members become friendly and share those things which they have not shared with the one with unwilling attitude.

Learning. A learner's attitude is the most desirable attitudes for a student to bring its goal from imagination to realisation, you must be wondering if it is the most desirable attitude then why it has been notified last, it's done because learner attitude is combination of first four desirable attitudes. During student life a learner's attitude make sure we acquire information & knowledge successfully to get good grades and can be sum up in this way, as we all possess different mental capacity few student can grasp their subjects quickly, where as some take little more time to gain knowledge of their subjects, a student with learner's attitude understands that s/he has to learn the subject even if it takes some more time than others, but in any case I have to learn, deliver or reproduce it during exams. Learner attitude does not remain confined to studies only it is spread to other activities which are new to students and supplement a good personality as well.

Adjustment of attitude through Self-Communication; Best way to develop a positive and productive attitude is to indulge in self-communication technique, before taking the right decision with correct attitude there is small difference between correct attitude and positive attitude, one cannot be positive about everything, for some activities we have to develop unfavourable attitude as well, Self-communication can be explained in below scenario.

Scenario; Student of a prestigious management college were packing their bags to go home after finishing days lectures and practical, suddenly they receive an information that in order to cover the syllabus one extra lecture has been scheduled, students don't like this announcement as they were mentally prepared to go home, Students with negative or positive attitude don't like it, they all responded in same manner but took different action. Student with negative attitude decided to bunk this extra lecture, citing lack of energy to continue. Whereas students with positive attitude communicated to self that even if we are tired, we will grasp at least some part of what will be taught and there is a chance that questions from this chapter might be asked in exams, they went to washroom wash their faces & eyes, sip adequate quantity of water and set in alert mode for lecture with correct attitude.

When the attitude is tested? For example, if we are travelling on smooth road everything seems to be fine but when road is rough, we have to take certain unwanted turns and avoid pot holes to reach our destination safely with minimum loss. Similar is the case of attitude in our life. We need correct attitude to come out of difficult times. This can be understood by following scenario.

Scenario; Nimesh was working in ZOC Corporation as an entry level executive since last six months, he was assigned a task to develop new program, at first instance he could not develop the program due to lack of experience & knowledge and felt very bad. As he was in his bed one night and thinking of changing his job, after few days of confusion he decided to meet his senior who had assigned him the job and informed him about his decision to quit, his boss being a seasoned professional told him that he had given him the task deliberately to check his attitude, He was well aware that as an in-experienced professional in that particular field he won't be able to execute the given task,

Coming back to the point of quitting he told Nimesh that his decision to run away from problem is not correct attitude as a young professional he must develop an attitude of learning new things related to his profession, in case he is successful in switching the job but the problem will not switch it will remain with him till the correction of attitude, he told Nimesh that same situation might be present in your new assignment, so where will you run. To be a successful not only in the profession but in life also focus yourself in learning new things.

Nurture Positivity; Positivity can be nurtured with the help of right attitude, because right attitude first sees negative side of every situation and after sometimes it moves over negative aspect to positive one, when we are moving on road, we can easily point out a small hole or a small fault of our friend despite of so many good qualities, our brain is wired to finding fault, we are always complaining about weather, traffic, subordinates.

When in negative mode we develop a disease called "blamelogy", in this disease everybody is doing wrong things except patient itself, resulting in constant complaints about rude peoples & friends, in this mode an individual who is suffering from **'blamelogy'** don't take responsibility for its action, not meeting his targets but in making excuses. Patient of blamelogy is covered with dust of negativity s/he think, act and perceive negatively everywhere, if s/he has to get well, has to clear the dust as we clear our home with the help of broom and wiper called continuous effort and consciousness which help us to come out with positive attitude and develop self knowledge, this changes the state of our mind and way of thinking, positivity helps us to lead a balanced life, we smile when everything is moving as per our desires but real test lies in smiling in adversity.

We become what we think, our thoughts are responsible for our wellbeing or vice-versa. Our thoughts are like seeds; some seeds give fruits with in weeks some seeds take years. When we feel responsible and take initiative to fulfil our dreams we act positively and overcome negativity. Instead of complaining, making excuses and finding faults in others we should channelize our energy in finding all that's positive. If we want to lead, we have to take load. Our brain and eyes are wired to see objectionable things, unpleasant sight, awful smells and disturbing noises.

To nurture positivity, we can start focusing on right and stop focusing on wrong when our mind starts focusing on right will spread positive vibes resulting in increased capability of our intellect and energy which in turn help us in achieving our goal, we have to understand that blaming others takes us nowhere and saps our energy. So, question arises how we can nurture positivity, first we have to identify do we suffer from disease called blamelogy and then slowly start focusing on white is right rather than what is wrong, start embracing what we have rather than what we don't have. When we nurture positivity, we are able to realize our full potential, widen our horizon and seeing positivity in every aspect, we become grateful to nature and started counting our blessings and as law of attraction has it, receives back them multiple times.

Conclusion; We can choose our attitude and turnaround our personality which decides our future and life, attitude is not a default setting nor it happens automatically, we have to tune it with our life's frequency and adjust accordingly to get the best response for leading a wonderful life. Attitude is more than a choice; we create it and conduct accordingly by developing any skill in a disciplined way and shape our mind, attitude is that intangible thing which makes all other things tangible and can be defined as an internal mechanism developed by overcoming negativity, not the absence of negativity.

Communication

Communication is that tool through which a professional can open the lock of emotions, stress and decision-making mechanism, every activity in this corporate world or in the life of a professional need this tool to get things done and accomplish assigned task or targets. Communication is perhaps one tool which is available in both versions i.e., tangible as well as intangible, if this tool is not handled properly, it can bring opposite results in place of the desired ones, a very good decision if not communicated properly turns into meagre one. Communication is that catalyst when put at right place make a chain reaction possible which can attain desired trajectory for any organisation to fly high.

Scenario; I called my subordinate and told him to prepare a report, simply ordering him in a one-way communication, The whole conversation is given below.

Me; Rajesh, come here.

Rajesh; Yes Sir.

Me; Prepare a report on financial module for Project 'A', submit it within three days,

Rajesh submitted the report in five days citing some reasons.

When I called Rajesh next time to prepare the financial module for project 'B', type of conversation we had, is given below.

Me; Rajesh, please meet me in my cabin.

Rajesh; coming.

Communication

(Rajesh entered my cabin)

Me; Please take a seat.

Rajesh; Thanks Sir.

Me; How is everybody at your home? has your mother recovered from medical treatment she has undergone.

Rajesh; Yes Sir, my mother has recovered well and everybody at my home is fine.

Me; Rajesh, we have to prepare a report on financial module for project 'B' with in three days. If you need any help, please let me know.

Rajesh; Sir, I will try to prepare it with in given time and let you know if any requirement arises.

Rajesh completed the report with in given timeframe. I was thinking and trying to find out the reason behind delay in first assignment and timely submission of second assignment, I zeroed in that it was my style of communication which makes the difference, while ordering first assignment I communicated as manager, who is simply interested in getting the task done, whereas while assigning second assignment I was interested in knowing about his family as well and did not order blankly involve my self also in the task, which prompted Rajesh to complete it with in given time frame, by spending extra two minutes while assigning the task for project 'B' in comparison to the orders given for first task related to project 'A', makes the difference of two days, this is the power of appropriate communication and clearly shows the difference between order and conversation.

Characteristics; Communication should be friendly and information disseminated which is expected to be fair & frank with element of firmness and room for flexibility. Individuals or groups when attempts to exchange ideas, feelings and emotions for sharing information or co-ordinating action, make aware them what to do, what are their goals, receiving and issuing instructions, to develop plans & take decisions. Good communication helps in achieving managerial & organizational effectiveness, it links the members of organization and enhances co-operative action. Leader, team leader, individual and student must communicate to his team in the same way in which they want to be communicated back.

Process; When Subhash was thinking of overcoming a challenge, he developed a source and decided to send a message to all the HODs, comprising of appropriate words, charts or Symbols and transmit it through formal means of communication, when this e-mail was received, understood and well accepted by every HOD. Objective of that message was information Sharing about the new idea and taking feedback from HODs to control the outcome by Influencing through his authority when came across a challenge, he meets it by taking appropriate decision and facilitate change with the help of team.

Purpose of sending that e-mail was planning of a new project with the aim of establishing leadership and practicing managerial efficiency by giving clear instruction about taking right decisions which can keep their team members motivated for the smooth functioning. When Subhash e-mailed the instruction with absolute clarity to his colleagues and peers, he was successful in seeking attention as his communication is very consistence with great deal of adequacy and integrated approach with perfect timing with request of giving feedback.

Forms of Communication;

Written; Writing as a form of communication is used in corporate sector for formal communication, it can be an announcement of opening of new branch office in other city, in praise of a team achieving targets, a decision regarding any new policy to be implemented, annual report to be circulated by top management, approval or non-approval of leaves, any suggestion or modification.

Written words are the backbone of formal communication and has to be followed by receiver as they are and can not make any change as per h/her convenience. While sending any instruction, information or appreciation through written form of communication a leader, team leader, team member or student should be very careful with respect to sender, figures, date & time, appropriate use of words, purpose of the communication and what action needs to be taken by the recipient. All the written communications are a sort of record and must be kept safely in a folder (soft copy) or file (print outs). In modern corporate set-up almost all the written and formal communication takes place through electronic medium. Various software is in use for different purpose, for submitting leave application, indenting any material, circulation of new brochure etc., use of hard copy is generally discouraged.

Speaking (Verbal); Verbal communication forms the core of trust among team members because once it is delivered it can not be produced in exactly the same manner nor it can be recorded and produced again or can be stored, verbal information & instructions are that mode of communication through which 70% of all conversation is done, all though it is the most common and easiest form of communication through which we converse, one has to be very careful while speaking or passing on information or giving instructions verbally.

When we are speaking to someone, we are in dual mode, in the sense we are telling some one exactly what we want to tell or we have to tell something and we are telling something else, while we are communicating verbally everything which is inside us is reflected, knowingly or unknowingly our pitch & tone of voice tells a lot. If we want to have positive impact of our words on others, one must learn to take interest in others resulting in smooth conversation. Graceful speaking is one of the positive signs of a good personality which clearly reflects who you are & who you will be.

Reading; Reading as form of communication is a basic requirement for every individual whether in corporate sector or in student life, it is through reading we are able to learn what is new (Knowledge) to us or any information which needs to be remembered. Every team member, whether CEO, team leader, team member or future star of corporate sector i.e., a student has to be proficient in reading to execute the given task and very careful & focussed while reading written formal communication. After reading we prepare ourselves to act as instructed, one wrongly read or interpreted written communication might create trouble for entire team or organisation.

Careful reading will help us to write better in the form of information, instruction or a report. It is very important to read twice every instruction or information we are about to pass on to our colleagues or seniors. When we read material prepared by self, it serves two purposes, one it exhibits the intention that we want to execute every task in proper manner and second purpose is to avoid any time wastage or damage occurring due to a mistake or lack of clarity in the message. Reading a self-composed message before pressing the 'send' button is sign of every good professional.

Listening; Listening is that part of the communication skill through which we receive information and decide what to do with this message, listening almost constitutes 50-60% of the total communication in every arena of professional or personal life, it has been observed that people listen with less attention and that too not to understand but to reply. Listening carefully should be on top priority for a professional, because we can re-read written communication but verbal communication cannot be heard or repeated.

Good listener makes list of points in mind during formal communication and maintains eye contact while receiving any information or instruction, good listener do not react or involve themselves emotionally before the conversation is complete. Our focus should be on content not on delivery, while listening we must take mental notes and should be able to provide feedback once the communication is over. We can improve listening by doing a good job of comprehending and understanding others. Takes own time, avoid hurriedness ability to put self in other's shoes to see things from their perspective as well. Do not confuse the person with problem: What the person did, who the person is. Say what you feel: Thoughts, words, feelings & actions should send the same message.

Hearing & Listening: Hearing is involuntary and act of perceiving sound while listening is selective in which we take part voluntarily whether its active or passive, active listening is with a purpose and motivation to solve any existing problem, share interest, whereas in passive listening receiver has little interest or motivation in the subject. Major difference between listening & hearing is we are accountable for listening however we are not accountable for hearing.

Asking; Asking is that form of communication which is practiced by every sincere professional, A leader might ask self 'what he is doing'? is he doing the right thing or making things right, not only to self but can ask his team members what he can do to make them execute their duties in a better way.

A team leader in a similar manner can ask self, is his contribution helping the organisation and fellow team members to grow, a team member might ask himself about being on the right track for a successful career, a team member can ask team leader about h/her performance, similarly a student might ask self is s/he moving towards achieving the target s/he has aspired for. Asking self and others is a sign of strength, which takes a professional to next level of thinking and raises the bar for self and others as well. Strength here refers to the pure intention of correcting self if any feedback is received by setting the example for juniors and peers.

Silence; One may be wondering that how silence can be an important form of communication, but it is a truth that silence is such a wonderful tool which can save a leader from getting into trouble, a team leader from making a poor statement, a team member by choosing to remain silent in some circumstances might create positive atmosphere for self in near future. A student who chooses to remain silent during trying circumstances conserve energy and clarity to take next step. Silence is such an underrated communication tool which has the power to create a storm or a 'VIBGYOR'.

If corporate professional can understand the power of silence and use it wisely, they can move forward in career smoothly by removing roadblocks by remaining silent as and when required. A gesture of silence when senior is not in good temper forces the senior to rethink about his action of loosing control, silence when peers are talking shows respect, senior communicating via silence gives the message of acknowledging the knowledge of a junior. Silence is a wonderful form of communication which can express so much without saying a word.

Communication by leader. Communication from leader should be very carefully crafted keeping in view the past, present & future of the organisation and to whom it is addressed, a leader's words should be able to remove the stress, fill the listener with confidence and self-respect avoiding any personal remarks. Now days leaders try to move away from managerial style of communication to leadership style of communication which is open end communication, this type of communication leaves space for correction and modification by keeping in mind the receiver's opinion and attitude as well. Leaders must give space while assigning new task or enquiring about the status of task their team members are currently engaged in.

Communicate to Motivate.; Leader's prime responsibility is not to execute tasks, but to keep entire team members motivated who are engaged in executing the given task, communication plays a very decisive role in this, team members interpret every communication as per their understanding and need, in order to get the best results.

    A leader must learn to communicate to keep his team motivated, for this they need to develop a mechanism which sends clear message to team members that I am always available for conversation and in case of any challenge or mistake firmly stands with and behind every team member, other form of communication which keeps the right doer motivated is that wrong doer will be dealt firmly and shown their place.

    A leader is expected to acquire a style of communication which is very comforting and have soothing effect on team members, after conversing with Leader a team member should feel important and motivated. Best thing a Leader can do is to call team members by their names, listening their names gives confidence to team members and feels that they are recognised and s/he is not an unnoticed fish in a big pond.

Communication

Scenario: Team Leader; May I come in Sir?

CEO; Please come in.

Team Leader; I want to discuss one modification in the process of project which is currently going on, this modification will increase the cost of product by 1.25%, but improves the quality, putting us ahead of our competitors, but if it does not materialise than coming back to original plan will increase the time frame by another 15 days. We want your approval for the same.

CEO; (After studying the modification) I think we can move ahead with this positively, I know that our organisation can depend on you and your team, if anything goes wrong or any correction is required, I am here with all of you. Best of luck.

Formal & Written Communication; A Leader has to do most of the formal communication done in an organisation due to title of formal authority, through proper channel establishes authority and fixes responsibility, it's an order issued to execute certain task with clearly telling who is responsible for what.

in this modern time of paperless communication leader has to be very careful because his one typing or dictation mistake can create lot of confusion. They become little bit careless assuming that since the communication is from leader it will be understood in any case, but it is not so. A leader has to use adequate number of words and giving every detail, writing an e-mail is not same as writing for twitter. Because saving a minute in giving in-appropriate written instructions will waste many hours of their team members.

Example; Avdhesh as CEO of organisation XYZ has written an e-mail after a training class, which states that all employees who have attended training class will have to appear in a tent tomorrow by 11.30 a.m., everybody was confused to see this mail, when they approached CEO's office then it was clarified it was 'test' not 'tent'. A typing mistake has not only created lot of confusion but had made mockery of the CEO's office, it would have been better if the sender had read the e-mail for probable correction before pressing the 'send' button.

Informal; Informal communications plays very important role in every organisation, especially by CEO, CEO very well understands the value of informal communication and will encourage it almost on every occasion, informal communication if handles properly can save lot of time and create wonderful working atmosphere, as subordinates hesitate to approach CEO for small things It is the responsibility of CEO to approach them and ask informally.

Informal communication between CEO & subordinate can take place during office parties, occasional get-togethers. personal celebrations or lunch breaks. There is very fine line between informal or casual communication, A CEO should avoid raising religious and personal matters, keep the environment light and healthy. A CEO can use informal communication to motivate someone who is having some bad time or can take advise for betterment of organization and team. Quality of informal communication reflects the culture of a company.

Reading; 'Reading' for leader is the core of its communication, A leader has to read requests or proposals from team leaders and team members and has to read the reply of his e-mails and written instructions, in this s/he has to be very careful and must develop the habit of reading without any prejudice. While reading, leader should give importance to the content and not to sender.

A sender who is not in good books of leader can also send a good proposal or a team leader whose past record is not up-to the mark can prepare a good report which can be game changer for team. Secondly, every communication which s/he is doing must be read very carefully before sending or passing on to team members, because every communication is not meant for all team members, some communications are confidential and meant for few seniors or designated team members when reaching at wrong desk can create lot of misunderstanding.

Scenario; A CEO wants to invite all team members for high tea to celebrate winning of a prestigious project, told her secretary to send an e-mail to all the concerns 'immediately', all concerns received an e-mail for the gathering in conference hall by 10.30. a.m. followed by tea and snacks, when everybody has assembled, CEO rose from his chair and congratulate business development team for winning this prestigious project which organisation was eyeing since last six months, he asked for everybody's support and contribution to execute this project on time. But while addressing the gathering he could not find few familiar faces from procurement department, reason for their absence lies with the leader herself because while instructing her secretary she had used word 'immediately' putting her secretary in panic mode and her secretary forgetting to add the e-mail address of procurement head while sending common e-mail, although it was not that much urgent matter in which action has to be taken in panic mode which resulted in misunderstanding between CEO and procurement head.

Verbal Communication; A leader has to communicate formally and informally to team members, verbal communication is the core and shows the trust generated by the behaviour of leader, a team member can start working on an important matter before receiving official communication in order to save time subject to the reputation of leader.

A leader has to speak on few occasions, while addressing a small departmental gathering for appreciation, for planning a new project, to discuss confidential matters or has to address full staff gathering on annual day or during a crisis. Leader's words have long lasting impact on team, it is advisable for leaders to practice before speaking, be specific and avoid casual words. While informal verbal communication can also play key role, its effective use can avoid many problems before they turn into fireball.

Scenario; CEO called Deepak in his cabin and inform him that he is receiving continuous complaint from his team leader about his late coming and absenteeism, which is hampering the smooth functioning of department, other team members are also raising objections about his irresponsible behaviour, he warned Deepak to mend his behaviour or ready to face the consequences and told Deepak that at this moment he is not giving him written warning. Judicial use of spoken words was enough to put Deepak on right track, Deepak also felt very thankful to CEO, because a written warning would have become permanent part of his personal file. In this case spoken words were more effective than written words.

Listening; Listening should be one of the top priorities of CEO while communicating with team members, it has been observed due to position of authority most of the CEOs have not been giving due importance listening, they are only interested in giving orders or instructions verbally, it is very much in the interest of team and CEO to give listening its due importance. Listening covers approximately 50-60%% of the total communication in a professional's life, a CEO has to listen to his department head and team members about suggestions, information & complaints, attentive listening gives lot of confidence to the team members and solve many problems before taking ugly shape. Biggest barrier in listening is 'boss syndrome' which states that "I am here to dictate and others are here to listen".

Scenario; CEO Avadhesh was continuously receiving request from Ashok for a face to face meeting, but due to lack of time Avadhesh was not able to give appointment and thinking why Ashok is insisting on meeting personally, when Ashok met CEO he complained about misbehaviour of his senior during weekly staff meeting, CEO listened very patiently and assured Ashok that he will take appropriate step at the suitable time, and communicated to Ashok that "In my opinion there was no personal agenda of your senior to humiliate you, he simply lost control during one conversation only, I will look in to the matter as soon as possible". After having met personally and received very patient listening from CEO, Ashok was feeling very light and positive.

Asking; Asking is a tool of communication which is very strength full and allows a professional to introspect self before or after executing a task or taking a decision. Asking has two dimensions in communication one is asking from self or self-communication and second dimension is asking from other team members about self. When a professional practices 'Asking' in both dimensions indicates positive mindset for learning and improving.

Asking self: While practising asking, a leader can ask self about h/her performance, asking oneself is a very sincere but less difficult option from the two dimensions of asking, s/he can ask others how s/he is doing, any correction or improvement is required in leadership style. When a leader has the courage to ask about his performance shows that s/he is interested in giving best to team and organisation, resulting in efficient functioning of system.

Scenario; Reema is CEO of ABC corporation, her organisation is about to launch a new product which is a toy for the children's below the age of seven, after the formal launch of product (toy), feedback from distributor's was not very encouraging as there was one pointed part in the toy which is hurting kids, ABC organisation has to recall all the pieces of toys, there was little damage in terms of money as small numbers of toys were released in the first lot, which can be absorbed by 20 years old organisation but reputation of the company nose dived.

Reema felt very bad, as CEO she is responsible for every activity whether it is good or bad. She asked herself where did she went wrong, why she could not check the defect in the product before launch, as it was the most important thing to do, after lot of introspection she came to understand the reason behind this mistake, she was not delegating few tasks to keep herself available for the important one to avoid any goof up. In this way asking herself few questions gave Reema the required solution of a problem.

Asking team members; A true leader indulge in one of the toughest activity if s/he has the courage to ask colleagues and juniors about h/her performance, about his approach towards handling any conflict, about h/her behaviour, any change which can bring to have better understanding of team, as there is a gap of approximately 05-15 years between them, it is always wise to ask other team members. Asking is also seen as a welcome step by team members, resulting in reduced friction if there is any and opens all the channels of communication for fruitful conversation and result thereafter.

Scenario; Sonal is working as General Manager of a production unit, since last few weeks she is not performing at his best and few of his decision went wrong, she was perplexed by this situation but unable to decide what is not on track. She wanted to ask from his subordinates and called an informal meeting to discuss the same. During casual conversation she asked about the problem she is facing, she received few suggestions, but the best suggestion she felt was one in which one of her subordinates suggested that she has not taken leave since last three months which is taking toll on her efficiency. Sonal decided to take one week break from office and joined back with a fresh and rejuvenated mode.

Silence; How silence can be a mode of communication, but it is a fact that silence is always used by wise professionals to communicate their preferences and decisions, Some times a leader has to choose silence as mode of communication to handle difficult situation, Silence has to be chosen when leader does not have immediate answer to a difficult situation or conflict, silence is to be exhibited when final decision has to be taken in due course of time and currently things have to be cooled off for the time being.

Scenario; Sonal is sitting in her cabin when she receives a call from her PA regarding two of his subordinates wants to meet her, she thought they might want to discuss some official matter but after taking first sip of tea, they started complaining about a trainee who has joined six months back, while listening about the trainee's complaint Sonal did not utter a word which was indication to team leaders to leave and first try to handle it by themselves.

Barriers in communication for a Leader; A leader has to face the barrier of confidentiality as s/he has to contain some information to self or sometimes different statement is given about same matter to different level to team members, when truth comes out, team member who was given not so correct information felt bad and the leader lost some credibility. So, what is the solution for this? Solution for this has to be apply by leader only, s/he has to be very careful to remove a barrier if there is any, leader's communication informal or formal, is taken seriously. Same can be understood by following scenario.

Scenario; CEO; (Sitting in the office with Team Leaders) I have good news for all of us, we have won the project which we have been trying for last two months, only formal contract is yet to be received. (Here CEO forget to tell his team leaders not to disclosed it until we receive formal contract). As CEO was moving in the corridor and stop by to accept greetings from one of the team members.

Team Member; Congratulations Sir, we have won the project.

CEO: Who told you, still lot is to be done in this matter.

Team Member; (in a confused manner), Yes Sir.

It is very much clear from the above scenario that nobody is at fault, but due to confidentiality barrier faced by CEO, he has to convey same message to two different grade team members in two different ways.

Second most potent barrier encountered by a leader is lack of time, a leader is accountable and responsible for everything happening in organisation, s/he is always in hurry and short of time, which sends the delivering of proper communication to back seat, resulting in improper disbursal of information leading to misunderstanding and confusion.

Communication by Team Leader

Formal, Written & One way; While receiving or giving directions to its team. A team leader has to indulge in one way communication, it is one way because this is a kind of order which one has to follow in the interest of the organisation and team, it again becomes one way when recipient of the order has to pass it on to team to get the things done. A team leader has to be very careful while passing on one way order and should not look like rude or strict and must chose the tone & pitch very carefully.

Team leader is leader of h/her department and has to perform all those tasks which leader of the organisation is performing for organisation. For a team leader writing includes replying to the e-mails received from CEO, it may be answering about the progress report or any other ongoing work, process or product. Team leader has to write to team members regarding motivation, continuous evaluation of progress made in the project, problems faced or guidance needed.

Scenario; Anuj is working as a production head (Team Leader) in a manufacturing unit producing foam mattress and has just come back after meeting his senior, who informed Anuj that our organisation has just received a big export order details of which is already shared with him, please take extra care to get this order delivered on time.

While sharing this information with his team Anuj has to add one more clause, which was the most difficult part, that all the leaves sanctioned earlier have been cancelled, with this information he added that timely delivery of the consignment will get his team due share during annual appraisal review pacifying those team members whose leaves are cancelled. A simple act of forethinking and diligent one-way communication resulted in timely execution of project.

Two way & Downward; Most of the times a department head has to be involved in two-way communication, it may be taking feedback or during a discussion to solve an internal problem, it requires great deal of maturity to conduct two-way communication, especially with those team members one has to deal and meet daily.

A team member looks at team leader as the one who can solve h/her problem and remove obstacles if there is any, it may be any grievances or funding of training programme for career upliftment. Two-way communication can be between team leader and a team member, between two team members of same position or between worker and supervisor.

Scenario; Raman who is team leader (Exports division) of FGD corporation, is engaged in producing steering wheels and other spare parts for a reputed automobile company, any wrong or negative communication will have its impact on daily working. Raman wanted to convey a message of the top management to team members that during board meeting and declaration of quarterly results it was found that due to ongoing international conflicts around the world our exports have decreased which in turn has reduced our profits by 3%, if this trend continues, management has to think of cost cutting which might include human resources as well. Team members taking view of this serious situation responded in one voice that they will try to find out new avenues for exports and maintain the profitable status of the organisation.

Formal & upward; Raman conveyed the message of team members to CEO regarding ongoing conversation with his team and assured that they will leave no stone unturned to meet our targets, cost cutting should be considered as last resort, CEO was more than satisfied, appreciated the fair and frank way of communication adopted by Raman to avoid any confusion and kept the motivation level of the team members at higher side.

Informal; Informal communication plays very important role in binding the team, a team leader can communicate informally through verbal mode, by body language or through WhatsApp groups, it is the quality of informal communication which shows a lot about the personality of a professional. Most of the informal communication is done during official get togethers, meeting any team member in the corridor or parking, during lunch hours, over a cup of coffee.

Informal communication may be conveyed with gesture, glance, nod, smile or silence and has the capacity to overcome many challenges without raising a voice or creating a scene to attract attention or coming into limelight. A team leader must involve self in informal communication with team members when ever s/he finds time or create this opportunity intentionally to know team member well and their attitude towards other team members.

Lateral; Team leaders and department heads have to communicate outside their chain of command, this type of communication comes under lateral category and is cross boundary, cross functional and Inter-disciplinary. Lateral communication is equally important part of an organisation because it requires good inter-personal skill and team spirit.

When production head share the schedule with engineering department head for servicing of machines or it may be a request to canteen manager to arrange food on weekly off as some of his team-members may be staying back overtime to complete the assigned task. Remember that these colleagues and peers are also important part of your work life, all communication should be positive and full of respect towards each other, To have healthy relations with other team leaders one has to be proactive by keeping personal likes and dislikes aside in the interest of organisation. Use every meeting and request to strengthen inter-personal relations, listen others with open mind and try to understand other's preferences as well. Do not assume that your point of view will be accepted blindly by others.

Scenario; Akanksha is working as Team leader of IT department, today her personal assistant is on leave and she needs to type a lengthy report to be submitted to his senior, she had requested another team leader to provide her personal assistant for typing job, who accepted her request, because Akanksha keeps on communicating with him and other same level officers informally as well it may be greeting them on new year, on their birthdays, asking well being of their family members and helping them if any thing is requested through informal channel,

Communicate to inspire: A team leader must communicate to inspire team members as s/he is approximately 8-10 years more experienced than other team members and indulge in inspiring them by telling stories, sharing experiences and real-life incidents. Inspired team members are real assets of every team as they take every responsibility positively.

Inspiring team members to exceed their limits, continuously motivating by telling them that they can do better and achieve more, develop a rapport that whenever a team member converse with you, expects to take away something new and inspiring, whether it is in the form of humour, teaching or learning, if a team member comes to you bruised, a team leader's responsibility after conversing with him is to send him healed. A team leader must converse with team sending signals of giving, his words should be channelised towards openness and a kind of invitation for team members, take whatever you can take from me, it is up to you how deep you can dive and find the pearl by enriching themselves in the 'trichual' interest of self, team and organisation.

Scenario: Team leader: Akshay, please come to my cabin.

Akshay; Yes Sir.

Team Leader; I have been observing since last two weeks that you are not giving your best in the team. Can you please open please.

Akshay; I also want to discuss the same with you, Since Anil has joined our department all data related work has been given to him and he has become very important for all senior staff members.

Team Leader; There is no such thing it is only your perception, as you know that Data Analysis is a new concept which every organisation is getting into and using it for professional excellence. Keeping in view the above requirement a new vacancy was created and filled by Anil as he is a qualified Data Analyst who knows his job well. I was looking at your personal file, you have not done any professional course since last three years to upgrade yourself, you should take up continuous learning programmes, time is changing very fast if one has to keep pace with it and for a secured future, every professional must keep on advancing in h/her field

Akshay; Thanks Sir, for removing my doubts and showing me the way, I will find out a course which is professionally suitable for my career upgradation. Once again thanks not only for your valuable advice but also for taking personal interest in me.

Team leader; It is my duty to keep the morale of my team members high, all the best dear.

Scenario; Shailesh is heading technical department of ZAS corporation, since last few weeks he was been observing that his team is not performing well and not achieving the given targets, he thought of communicating with his team through a common e-mail to address this issue, he sent a common e-mail to all his team members.

Dear team members.

Greetings of the day

As we all know that our department is going through rough times in terms of performance due to reason well known to us and within our control, sometimes its absenteeism, other times its non-availability of spare parts or wrong diagnosis of problem, our average standard of performance is reducing the profitability of our organisation, we all depends on this organisation to fulfil our professional and social responsibility.

I have been working with all of you since last two years and know all of you personally and professionally, it is our responsibility to give hundred percent in the interest of the organisation and self, we all are capable of a turnaround and must be aware about the consequences of average performance in a professional setup. All of you are advised to take steps in the right direction before our performance dips from average to poor.

Communication

I am extremely hopeful of positive support from your side in the mutual interest of both.

Sincerely yours.

Shailesh

Technical Head.

In the above message Shailesh was able to motivate and encourage his team members to improve upon and side by side he was able to inform and warn them about consequences of not being able to meeting their assigned targets.

Verbal Communication; A team leader's best bet is on verbal communication, gaining mastery in verbal communication will solve lot of problems and save time but before that s/he has to understand the meaning of phrase **'respect for words'** and develop the strength to listen back what s/he has said during any verbal conversation with one of his colleagues or to his team at any point of time, a team leader's credibility lies on their spoken words and converting them into action as s/he has to use verbal communication upwardly, downwardly, informally or formally to give orders, instructions, suggestions or explanation regarding any delay or irresponsible act to his seniors. Team leader must use words very strengthfully for two reasons, for leaving long lasting impressions and setting up example for team members to follow.

Scenario; Team Leader; I have assigned you one task, have you completed it.

Team Member; Sorry Sir, I could not complete due to pre occupation of my current assignment.

Team Leader; You should have told me earlier. I would have assigned it to another team member.

Communication

Team member; Silently, in his own thoughts, you have not asked Sir.

Team Leader; Silently, in his own thoughts, from next time I will ask before assigning additional task. I should have given some space to you.

Listening; A team leader must adopt listening as one of the most important forms of communication for team and self, as sandwiched between CEO and team members, sometimes has to listen few rough words from CEO due to his team's mistake and to listen about challenges in department or performance of his team, as team leader has to play the role of **conflict resolver and problem solver** both these roles require very patient listening from various fronts. The art of listening will help a team leader to understand those words which are not spoken by team members and prompt him to take pro-action.

Asking. Asking is that tool of communication which helps a team member to take right decisions and corrective actions if a wrong decision has been implemented, with the help of asking self or other team members one can find fault and mend it. Asking helps a team leader to set good example of developing and executing a plan by checking and including every nut & bolt of system.

Asking self; Manoj has joined a multinational organization as team leader few days back, he is sitting in cabin and asking self, will he be able to fit in new culture of MNC, then he self-assured that he is experienced & knowledgeable professional and will learn anything new required to excel in this culture, he remember two other organizations where he worked earlier and does remarkably well on the basis of two qualities i.e., simplicity & integrity, which he nurtured over a period of time.

Scenario: Manoj was in conversation with self during morning hours and thinking about what he can do to improve his team's performance. He wanted to introduce new concept of productivity which he had learn during a training program in previous organisation, He called upon the meeting of his team members over a cup of tea and discuss the matter by inviting them through a common e-mail.

Manoj don't want to invite them for teaching something, however he is interested in sharing the knowledge which he had acquired over a period of time, main content of his e-mail read as "all of us are already doing the assigned tasks in a professional manner, but we can always find a better way to do our job. If all of you are comfortable, we can have one session of discussion benefiting all of us".

Asking team members ; Asking from team members should be a regular practice for a team leader as he is holding the position of bridge connecting top management and team members, to remain in top form one must know where s/he stands, remember team member here means superiors as well, because as a general practice we don't ask from our superiors " How I am doing"? nor we ask our juniors the same question because we think what we are doing is best and no improvement is possible further. But asking opens a frank conversation, in its absence we might miss a few negative things which can be corrected in 'trichual' interest.

Scenario; Manoj is enjoying his tenure as team leader in current organization and discussing project execution with team, after having discussed every aspect and allocating responsibility to every team member as per their domain, he did not forget to ask for open discussion and frank feedback from team members, one of the team members suggested that it will be better if you keep us guiding during project and be regularly in touch with project team for status. on hearing this Manoj said "I was also considering the same but some of you might take it as micro managing and lack of trust in the team". Team member immediately responded by saying that "Sir, we very well understand the difference between micro managing and guidance".

Silence; Silence as a mode of communication helps a team leader to avoid many difficult and controversial situations, a team leader who is sandwiched between top management and team members has to juggle a lot. Keeping silence during invoking or controversial conversations helps a team leader to keep calm and be less stressful. Silence as a tool of communication can be used mostly on two occasions, first if top management or CEO is trying to correct a mistake made by team or self, in this way team leader is sending a message that s/he is accepting and agreeing by their constructive feedback and thus making sure that precautionary measures are in place so that this mistake is not repeated. Secondly, when a team leader keep silence and gave a cold look to an unjust demand put forward by any team member, communicating that your demand has not been considered for further action.

Barriers in communication for Team Leader;

Silent Expectations; There are few barriers in communication which a team leader must know and take corrective action, if not corrected will make communication losses its purpose and meaning, one of the barriers is silent expectation from team members, which means that team leader is assuming about a team member to perform in a certain manner without communicating the same due to one reason or the other. It is the responsibility of team leader to clearly tell a team member how to do an assigned task, in the absence of proper communication an individual team member finds it difficult to execute that job properly. It is better for a team leader to avoid silent expectations, s/he must understand that an in-experienced team member has to be guided at every step to complete a given task.

Selective Perception: Selective perception is also one of the barriers created by a team leader and has some pre-conceived notions based on family, cultural background, past experiences, values or needs, this could be understood by an example given below.

Due to team leader's past experience with a female team member who could not perform satisfactorily on the field job, now while conducting an interview for field executives he perceives that women are not suitable for field job, and is reflected in most of the decisions thus creating a barrier.

Defensiveness; Defensiveness is one of the reasons which can block communication between two parties, barrier of defensiveness is created when few assumptions take place before the beginning of communication process. In the absence of proper communication there is surety of confusion and wrong interpretation of message.

While communicating with juniors a team leader must keep in mind that a junior team member may not engage in open and fair communication because of defensive mode and similarly while engaging in communication with the leader, a team leader will be in defensive mode, it is responsibility of team leader to remove the barrier of defensiveness while communicating both ways i.e., upward or downward.

Scenario; Production head of ABC Corporation was informed by marketing head to provide stipulated number of units within given time frame, production head did not give any heed to his demand because as per his last experience marketing head was very unjustly demanding and last lot of products are still lying in warehouse to be distributed to dealers for sale.

Another barrier we mostly encounter during communication between team leader and team members is when they both communicate with each other while keeping previous words, performance and action in mind which derails the conversation by creating confusion. But we must understand that human being is susceptible to change for better and we should avoid judging their current status by keeping their past in mind.

Scenario; Rahul (Team Leader); please provide me data of our product sales for last six months. (While giving instructions team leader was keeping past performance in the mind as this team member has done lot of mistakes while preparing data last time.

Ideal conversation would have been team leader telling the team member precisely which mistakes to be avoided and what corrections to be made, by simply ordering the preparation of data is not going to work until previous doubts are cleared and new expectations are conveyed. A team leader and team member must make an effort to remove probable barriers for smooth functioning of their department.

Communication by Team Member;

A team member has to communicate with customers & clients which requires adequate level of training as one has to speak and write only those words which are specific in nature, communication with customers & clients is totally formal and how one conveys the massage exemplifies the quality of sender and level of organisation, Internally a team member has to communicate with colleagues and reporting team leader, internal communication could be formal or informal, verbal or non-verbal depending on the requirement of the situation, mostly s/he communicates or share its general views, suggestions, proposals and grievances within the parameters allowed as per the protocol of the organisation.

It may be about non-cleaning of toilet, serving of cold food in canteen, non-approval of leave, non-availability of office conveyance or stationery etc., on higher side it may be for task co-ordination, problem solving or conflict resolving, information sharing. Communication is that part of one's personality which differentiate between an amateur and a professional. At this point of career, a team member must start learning the art of communication.

Communicate to impress ; An entry level team member who is new to corporate world must learn to communicate to impress colleagues and seniors, impression is just not about looks or physical appearance, an individual team member communicating through an improved version of self which shows the amount of interest in learning & creating better version of self.

While communicating with colleagues an individual team member must try to impress them with element of humbleness, knowledge and other qualities such as being co-operative leaving permanent impact. When an individual team member shows his inclination to do better it reinforces the action of team leader who in turn gives more efforts to inspire and creating an unbreakable circle. This type of action and conversation has infectious effect on other team members as well who started thinking and acting in the same direction.

Scenario; Team Leader; Romesh, please prepare the Data for the upcoming product to be launched by our company.

Romesh; Yes Sir.

Team leader; When can you provide me Data?

Romesh; In three days Sir.

Team leader; But last time you took approximately four days.

Romesh; Yes Sir, I took approximately four days last time, but I thought there must be some better way to prepare this data, so I approached my senior who was earlier doing this job and requested her to teach me the process to reduce the time taken for data report preparation, she agreed and taught me few shortcuts to operate 'excel' which helps me to reduce the time taken.

Team Leader; Very good, that is really positive approach.

Listening; Listening is that mode of communication which all team members have to go through daily, being the junior most in corporate ladder, they have to listen to their seniors, team leader and CEO. team member must listen very carefully to what is told to them, what is told to other team members and above all what is not told to them. For an entry level team member practicing how to listen carefully should be one of the important exercises, at this stage of career s/he has to mostly listen to the suggestions, corrections and take orders from superiors.

No senior would like to repeat any instruction, every senior expects you to listen & understand conversation in one sitting. Although there may be some instances when a team member is unable to understand because of not paying proper attention but that can be sorted out by requesting them to repeat the same. Individual team member must make it a habit of listening to gain new experiences, to create mutual understanding and learning,

Example 1; when Rohit reached his work place, he saw his boss warning his colleague for spending too much time in cafeteria and warn him about his non-serious approach towards assigned job, Rohit listens carefully and started spending required time only away from his cubical.

Example 2; Boss; See me at four.

Rohit; Yes Sir.

Around 5.00 pm Boss called up Rohit, asking about his where about as he was waiting for Rohit since 4.00 p.m. Rohit replied that he is waiting for him at 'Shore' (office cafeteria).

Verbal; A team member has to speak to his superiors and colleagues, they must learn the art of speaking formally and informally both, during formal verbal communication one has to explain or gave clarification about an action or one has to convince seniors for any improvement in the already existing procedure or an informal chat which might take place in parking lot, asking wellbeing of family and kids.

Thumb rule while communicating informally with your senior is that your senior can be casual in conversation but don't expect junior staff to be casual. Even during informal communication greet and address with full respect. When informal communication is taking place with same level team members show affection, motivate them, share your experiences,

Scenario; Shraya has been offered letter of appointment and absorbed in the public sector undertaking after completing her internship, along with other reasons such as academics and personality she enjoys one added advantage over others and that is her very good verbal communication skills, every body in the organization likes to converse with her, whenever she speaks formally or informally is a treat to watch, she gives due respect to all team members and seniors, her colleagues & seniors are highly impressed by her ability to speak in a very balanced way, as she take utmost care by drawing a line between formal & informal communication.

It is very much clear from this scenario that good verbal communication is of utmost importance to move upwards in corporate ladder as every team member whether junior or senior like to be respected not only for their authority but by the words spoken to them.

Written; A team member has to use writing as mode of communication mostly when they have to submit regular reports on standard formats for which they have to get themselves acquainted with the vocabulary related to their profession, always backing their finding with best possible evidences or support. An individual team member has to write an application for leave, for release of perks or for shift adjustment due to personal reasons. While writing one must choose words carefully and in a professional manner.

Scenario; Tina is working as senior team member in Human Resource department of DFG corporation, main business of her organization is making advertisements for various reputed corporate groups, she has other interest in person and that is reading short stories, due to this hobby her content development and letter drafting capability has increased many folds, Tina was able to make written communication very interesting and positive, her every letter or anything related to words were written in golden ink which every team member likes to read. When this news reached top management, with the consent of Tina and her team leader they transferred Tina to content development department, she proved herself by becoming a valuable team member in this department as well. Writing is a wonderful art it can bring laurels to any one who takes it seriously.

Reading; One has to be very careful while reading every correspondence because one has to reply back to it, a small mistake will send wrong signal of carelessness and above all might result in loss of resources to the organization. It is highly recommended that as a young team member one must make it a habit of reading good books related to their profession and keep abreast themselves updated about the latest developments, develop positivity in views, learn to think with open mind so that one can handle the complexity of a professional life beautifully.

Scenario; Ananya is working as office in-charge of CEO, she has done her Master's degree in commerce and doing her job efficiently, resulting in receiving praise from every corner of organisation, she has one very good quality on the basis of which she is able to execute all the tasks effectively & efficiently and that quality is 'curiosity' she read every document, every pamphlet & every purchase order not as per her duty but in order to know and learn any thing new which can add to her knowledge. When a job is less stressful when it becomes combination of duty and interest.

Today CEO has asked Ananya to send a common mail to all concern that prices of one of the products has been revised, from now onwards we have to quote new prices and this price will be Rs. 4700/= per kg. Ananya was about to write the e-mail to all concerns, suddenly she re-call that Rs. 4700/= was the production cost, she immediately rushed to CEOs office and clarified the matter, on clarification CEO accepted his mistake as he had quoted production cost in place of selling price and thanked Ananya for being extra careful in these important matters, and in turn Ananya thanked her reading habits for doing her job sincerely.

Asking; For a team member asking is that mode of communication with self, which can guard from many problems, when a team member makes a habit of asking (self communication), s/he is moving in the right direction for a better self and bright future. Asking self may be about goal of the future, about professional excellence in the organisation, parameters required to reach there and the steps & resources required to achieve it. Asking self opens various internal thought processes which is the gateway to next level.

Scenario; James is working as team member in ABC Corporation, since last few weeks he was little disturbed for the reason being that one more team member has joined the team at the same grade and doing equally well, after reaching home James sit down in a quite corner and ask self the reason behind this disturbance, finds out that team member has done MBA from a college which is ranked ten points below to the college from where James has done MBA but he is placed in same pay grade, having a matured view James find out that it could happen to him as well if he joins any other corporation, corporation in its own interest to keep the things moving might hire him @ 15-20% more than his current salary and will make him better paid than other team members presently working in that organisation, after having thinking in right direction he corrected himself for inner peace.

Now let us move to the next level of 'asking' which is little difficult and requires fair amount of courage, because in this part we will be asking our seniors and colleagues about ourselves, in the beginning it is little difficult but when it becomes normal practice helps a professional to know where it stands, to know about self from others shows professional maturity and prevents mistakes from turning into blunder.

Scenario; Team Member: Sir, can you spare ten minutes, I want to ask you something about myself.

Team leader; Yes, why not, please come to my cabin.

Team member; Can you please tell me about my performance, what improvement I can make to be a better professional and team member.

Team leader; I am observing you since last two weeks and trying to find out the reason for your inconsistent performance, you are always in a hurry, you need to improve your listening skills for betterment.

Team member; Thank you very much Sir, for your constructive feedback, this will be of great help for me to cast my future in right direction.

Silence; A team member is junior most in hierarchy should learn the art of keeping silence as and when situation arises, but a team member who is relatively young in terms of age is eager to show knowledge, experiences and exposure to his colleagues & seniors, speaking at every possible opportunity available, not keeping silence when it matters is inviting problem, a team member should exhibit mix of youth & maturity by using **stop, think and proceed** formula to participate in any conversation, specially when s/he reached any place where conversation is already going on, silence is the best mode of communication when an individual is unaware of the situation, Silence during a conversation shows that an individual has the power of self control

Barriers in communication for a team member;

Static Communication; Biggest barrier created by a team member is static communication, which means an in-experienced team member assumes that whatever s/he is going to communicate is right and no modification is required, whereas as communication should be open and can be improved upon.

A team member is advised to remain open and should be mentally prepared to receive any improvement, should follow three Ps, i.e., **Prepare, Practice and Proceed.** It is very necessary for a team member to indulge in professional and healthy communication for proper execution of task, healthy communication will remove doubts if there is any.

Filtering: Manipulation by the sender to obtain favourable response, e.g., informing about positive or negative things only. It means sender gives information which is cooked in his favour. For example, when Kamal informs about late coming of Ramesh, he adds his previous mistakes also, to the point communication is the need of the hour or talk only about those subjects which is asked for, no addition of personal information is welcomed.

Communication for students;

Student life is the beginning of all learning activities, communication is also one of the most important of it, a student who want to lead a meaningful life has to be proficient in all the forms & types of communication be it, Listening, Reading, Writing, Speaking, Asking, Silence, Informal and Formal etc. All paths leading towards goals of any student pass through one of the **'mindstation'** called communication, however intelligent or smart working one may be, if a student is not able to express views or knowledge in right way will not be able to reach higher in life and achieve desired goals. Since foundation of all the good qualities required to lead a meaningful life is laid in the beginning and during student life, every student must put learning good communication skills on top priority.

Communicate to learn; What is the most important goal in a student's life? It is learning, gaining knowledge, exposing themselves to different conditions with a little pint of courage. All communication by students must be directed towards only one goal, that is to gain as much knowledge as possible whether it is through self study or by asking teachers for more, a student must pursue this goal and show that s/he gives prime importance to learning. Learning during student life is not limited to qualification, it is to develop self into a whole personality and a student must be interested in being educated along with qualified, having good communication skill is must for moving from merely qualified to well educated.

Communication between Teacher & Student; A student must understand that most important communication during this period takes place with the teacher, if a student is able to understand the words communicated by his teacher, half of the job is done, other half of job needs to be completed by making teacher understands the improved and adjusted way of communication as per need of the hour.

Communication

Communication between teacher & student should be filled with compassion and understanding, sometimes a student may not like teacher's way of communication, but s/he should understand that whatever a teacher does is for their betterment and to prepare students for a meaningful life, a student should show respect and include element of gratitude while communicating with teachers. Generally formal communication between student and teacher takes place regarding syllabus completion, teaching method, scheduling of exam and completion of assignments. Communication should be showing mutual respect which may include some humour also.

Communication between student and student; During student life a student's best companion is another student with whom they spend major part of their time and share physical space, secrets of youths and moments of happiness or sorrow. Communication between a student and another student should be filled with the intention of helping and bringing out best in each other instead of finding faults in each other generally students discuss information to be shared in group, about personal life of each other, about assignment completion or any help is required for examinations.

During student life relationship of lifetime are made and that could be possible only when we have good communication skills, learning appropriate communication skills helps a student to understands the words communicated by other student which ultimately helps them to make choice between good and bad company, ultimate aim of a student is in the company of like-minded individuals.

Reading; Reading as form of communication plays the most important role in the life of a student, student has to master the reading skills to be good in their studies because reading is the first step to reach next steps i.e., writing & speaking, in order to write and speak well a student should be proficient in reading.

Students have to read their course material, journals, newspaper and above all question papers, answering these question papers efficiently will sail them through a semester successfully, students must make it a habit of reading with interest and care. If they learn to read with interest, it will be easier for them to understand any chapter or topic. Students must make it habit of reading other than their course work such as national & international magazines, newspapers and self-help books for overall improvement in personality and understanding the finer aspect of life.

Scenario; Rahul; Question paper was very lengthy; I have attempted all six questions.

Rohit; But we have to attempt only five questions. It means you have not read instructions carefully before start writing answers.

(Rahul had wasted approximately 35 minutes by attempting one extra question, those thirty-five minutes could have been utilized in writing better answers to the attempted Questions, if he had read instructions on question paper carefully.)

Verbal; Learning the art of verbal communication helps a student in great deal, Verbal communication has two parts, one is formal and another is informal, formal verbal communication is practiced by students when they have to converse with their teachers, seniors, class mates, their evaluators and examiners during viva-voce or practical exams. Student life is the best time to learn and make base for future verbal communication which is almost 65% of total communication in a human being's life. Thumb rule of verbal communication is that one should speak only in a way s/he wanted to be replied back i.e., with dignity and respect.

Informal communication takes place during lunch hour, while travelling to college or when group of students had gone to participate in cultural or sports event, informal verbal communication tells us about the family background, individuals own personality and become reason for making friendship with those we want, students are noted for their informal communication by their teachers and seniors as well.

Example; Student; With all due respect Madam I could not understand last point of this theory if time permits, please repeat it.

Teacher; I am sorry dear, time does not permit this, you may come to my room between 3.30 to 4.00 p.m.

Students; Thankyou Madam, I will be present in your room during that time.

Second Example; Student to senior; Sir, I request you to give me question papers and notes of previous years, I will get them photocopied and return.

Senior; Sure, you can collect them from my room in the evening, and don't forget to return them in a week's time.

Written Communication; Writing is that means of communication through which a student communicates to teacher about the knowledge s/he possess, students have to write their assignments, answers, dissertation and thesis etc. If written properly it can fetch best returns on their time and money. A student has to learn to write formal applications for leave, any scholarship scheme, asking for relaxation in timing due to some unavoidable reason, explanation about any indiscipline activity etc.

Writing skills have to be practiced with lot of sincerity as it is the only skill during student life which reaches to teacher for evaluation, it exhibits not only one's knowledge but the preparation and efforts behind it to secure good grades, however intelligent and knowledgeable a student may be, if s/he is not able to produce that knowledge on paper for evaluation in the form of answer sheets or assignments s/he won't be able to secure desired grades.

A student should write an answer under these heading, a) Meaning & Definition, b) History c) Main Content d) application/implication e) example f) critical evaluation. g) my own point of view. h) Conclusion.

Example; Question; Define theory X in detail.

Answer should be under these headings.

a) Meaning & Definition; Theory X states that.......

b) History; This theory was developed/founded by Mr. Z. in the year y. and first time it was published in the book or journal ....

c) Main Content; What this theory is all about.......

d) Application. This theory can be applied for understanding.......

e) Example; Same can be explained by suitable given example..........

f) Critical Evaluation; This theory is backed evidences/ empirical research or not......

g) Own point of view. I am of the view this theory holds good or does not hold good.

h) Conclusion;

Listening; listening is one of the equally important activities which every student has to master during student life, they have to listen to their parents, teachers, seniors and classmates. While in college they have to listen to their teachers while attending lectures and during practical training. Quality of being a good listener will help them to understand the course-curriculum and produce same on answer sheets to get good grades. Giving adequate importance to listening will help them to avoid any confusion and bring clarity, not listening properly may lead to loses in the form of poor grades.

Asking; Asking as a form of communication should be very important part of student life which can be divided into two. Asking from self is the first part, where student learns to communicate with self, it is the beginning when a student is introduced to communicate with self and understand the need & importance of the same, introspection is an important activity which should be done on regular basis by every student.

A student may ask self, am I doing enough to achieve my goal for which I am here for, am I on the right path if not, what is the reason for deviation, reason is internal or external what step I have to take to get back on the right track? There may be so many questions depending on the situation it may be relations with peers and seniors, medical reason, financial indiscipline or any other reason, asking will help a student to find the way out.

Second part of asking is from teachers, peers and seniors, it is a courageous step, because nobody wants to listen negative words for self, but only a frank and fair conversation will bring out positive results, when you ask somebody, who is your teacher or senior, in first instance they will look at you from head to toe and move, but one has to gather courage and ask again, as it is something which is new to them, they might be taken for surprise, but once you start asking on regular mode, teachers and seniors will start taking interest in this new activity and make some preparation for this and reply aptly.

Silence. Silence for students is golden way of communication, along with verbal communication they should make silence also their friend, when they consider silence their friend silence in turn will act accordingly and keep them away from many possible disturbances and turbulences.

Most important part of silence is to remain silent from inside, learning to remain silent from within will help a student to handle turbulent time with ease, silence does not mean absence of activity, silence inside a student will help to keep unwanted noises away from self and continue working on its priority as per scheduled plan. This ability to maintain silence under trying circumstances should be an important part of every student's life, student will encounter many conditions & circumstances which she or he has not expected or imagined before, silence within will help a student to develop self into a keen observer and ability to negotiate those difficult turns successfully, rather than getting disturbed and deviating from desired path.

Barriers in communication for Students; Students have a perception that real student life is shown in movies and social media, in the beginning and during early stages of student life they suffer from superiority or inferiority complex as they belong to different walks of life such as wealthy family, middle or lower income group, from business class or government job some are from private sector background, it is their family and economic background which makes the basis for their style of communication, some become extrovert and some become introvert, treat and got treated by others accordingly. Some students are full of negativity and arrogance which is reflected in their communication, they give importance to themselves only and hardly takes others point of view in consideration, apart from family background there are some other communication barriers are language and culture etc.

Language: Words convey different meanings to different people; same word may be interpreted for different meanings. Different language has to be used while dealing with different set of team members.

Culture: This barrier is caused by combination of ignorance and disregard on the part of issue, for example American work culture is totally different from Japanese work culture. One has to be very careful while dealing with team members coming from different cultural background.

Scenario; It is the beginning of new session in a professional institute, Aseem and Kalyan, two friends have taken admission into this institute, as they were talking in the corridor, Raman also a fresher wants to join them but they ignore and finish the conversation with minimal words, reason is that while coming to college they saw Raman using public transport, whereas they both use bikes to commute, here economic status becomes barrier for proper communication.

We must try to remove communication barriers, if cannot remove try to minimize it as it will help in developing good personality during student life and getting maximum exposure, when a communication barrier is minimized, students from different walks of life come close and make the most of student life, main aim of student life is not only to earn good grades but becoming a responsible citizen and understand the meaning of life.

Conclusion; Communication is that invisible tool which has the ability to cause damage or create magic, communicating clearly and effectively is very much required for every professional in a corporate setup, whether s/he wants to be a good leader, team leader, team member or a student. We choose different set of outfits for different occasions similarly we have to use different words and style of communication while dealing with different rank professionals. The two most important words in professional conversation are 'sorry' (accepting mistake) and 'thank you' (showing gratitude), secondly, we have to follow one unwritten rule which states that 'a senior can crack a joke with junior or talk casually but junior cannot do the same under any circumstances.

Emotional Understanding, Stability & Sensibility

When I joined my first corporate job through campus placement, I was eager to give my best while learning and executing the assigned tasks, but after spending four years in corporate set-up. I was surprised to know that in every team, performance of team members varies from average to best and the most surprising fact was that they posses almost same qualifications and comes from same social & financial backgrounds, after gaining few more years of experience and attending two workshops on emotional intelligence, I realise the importance of emotions in our day-to-day corporate life.

As we all know that equal opportunities and facilities are given to same grade professionals, but reason for variation in performance is due to perceived emotions for and towards organisation, peers, seniors and job, When I watch my team leader cruising along smoothly and executing his job happily by allocating & delegating tasks to his team members near to perfection. His secret recipe for job allocation is understanding the emotions of team members, he takes keen interest in understanding the mood and emotions of team members, he knows when a team member is happy or going through rough patch. Same can be understood by scenario given below.

Scenario; I was sitting in my team leader's office suddenly his intercom rang up it seems to be his deputy who wanted to assign an outstation task to Rakesh, my team leader immediately refused the suggestion of his deputy by telling him to assign this task to Neeraj, as Rakesh has lost his ailing mother two week back, he might be required at home for any ritual as per his religious practices. On hearing these words from the mouth of my senior, I felt very lucky to be working with such a understanding professional who takes care of his team members not only professionally but personally as well. To be a successful leader one has to know your team members personally and what is their current mental, physical or emotional status at this point of life.

But situation in other department was totally different as team leader of this department act as taskmaster and never gave any importance to emotional aspect at professional level, his motto was "we are professionals, we have to execute the task assigned." He simply gave orders and close the door.

In short term both departments led by team leaders with different approach and temperament seems to be equal in performance as they were able to achieve their targets, but in long term difference was clearly visible in the form of less absenteeism, medical leaves and low attrition rate from the department which is led by team leader with higher emotional understanding, where as department headed by team leader with low level of emotional understanding reported higher absenteeism, cases of burnout, data from HR department shows that team members of this department has consumed almost all their medical leaves and above all high performing executive have left the team to join other organisations. It is clearly predictable from the above observation that we should always follow the approach supported with emotional understanding.

Emotional understanding does not only understand the team members for proper functioning of department, team members also reciprocate by understanding the emotions of team leader as well which helps a lot in finding the right path towards success of team, team members working with emotionally understanding team leader are always ready to give their best whether s/he is present or not. They also understand the emotions of their leader, when s/he is in playful mood or struggling with problem or trying to solve a conflict between two team members, what is the right time to approach?

Meaning; I was thinking about the meaning of emotions and its application in corporate world, after having read word 'Emotion' again and again in corporate magazines and management articles, twenty years back emotions were sole property of poets, story writers, film actors or dramatist, nobody had thought emotions are going to play major role in the corporate world as well.

Whether it is motivating a team member, putting a dead wood to work or taking important decisions regarding work force and above all taking appropriate decision about self and getting out of a difficult situation, under all these conditions one takes help of emotions whether it is of others or self. It is not so that we have started taking help of emotions just 25 years back, every worker has used emotions to execute the given task since the beginning of industrial revolution but with more research and expansion of knowledge, corporates have understood the importance of emotions and its application for the benefit of team and organisation as whole.

Word 'emotion' contain itself word 'motion' which we all know is the synonym for **keep moving**, emotions keep us moving and make us dynamic, this dynamic moment could be backward or forward depending upon the type of emotion we are filled with or going through and create conditions for generating emotions for our team members, if we want our team to be on right track.

We must know what moves our team members in individual capacity or team as whole by being a keen observer we can find out what moves them in forward direction, some of us might moved by getting praised for their work, some of them might be interested in getting the right feedback, few of our team members might be triggered by constructive criticism, and what about me I will be happy to move ahead if my team members are following rules & regulations and meeting deadline for the job assigned.

As a leader when we try to understand the nature and emotions of our team members for the purpose of job allocation to get the things right, have we ever understood what will happen if we don't understand our emotions while understanding the emotions of others, all our exercise will go waste. To keep every thing at it's best one must know the state of our mind during decision taking. As we all know that while giving orders our mind moves to **'dictator mode',** means we have already decided what is wrong or what is correct mode of process.

Where our mind should be on 'understanding mode' means a mind in **understanding mode** is open to receiving constructive feedback even while giving orders so that a mutual consensus is created for the outcome of results or in other words order is taken in to create best outcome with order 'giver' and 'taker' are on same platform connecting the right dots for optimum utilisation of resources and creating an atmosphere of trust. An emotionally stable decision taker or decision communicator is rightly in a position to measure stress and take counter measures to deal with it or reduces it to the minimum so as to provide best working atmosphere to its team and organisation in turn.

Definition; When first time I learn the definition of emotional quotient or emotional intelligence, I was little confused about it because 'quotient' is that word which I came across while solving mathematical or numerical problems, wherever intelligence word is directly related to inborn capacity of an individual which can be measured, but emotions cannot be measured by any scale, emotions are combined result of brain, mind and heart. In some emotions brain has its upper hand, in some emotions mind has more say and in some emotions, heart is to be followed. Emotions are largely related to understanding whether it is of self or others.

To keep our team in top form we must understand the example of driving skill, we keep moving our car in forward direction only if we use appropriate gear for hills, city or highways, apply right kind of pressure on brakes while stoping at red light or correct use of accelerator while negotiating a round-about. What will happen if we apply a skill at wrong moment i.e., if we apply brakes when there is no traffic on road, or drive in fourth gear when there is huge traffic on road, using wrong skills at wrong time will either bring car to stand still or we met with fatal accident. Same is with a team, to make sure they reach desired destination we have to apply skill of emotional understanding continuously as and when need arises.

Scenario; Sandeep is CEO of CDB corporation, he was studying the balance sheet of last financial year, which is not reflecting good result as compared to last financial year (YOY). During board meeting it was discussed and an obvious decision was taken to cut cost and reduce over heads. Sandeep after returning to office called upon the meeting of team leaders and asked for their suggestions. HR head while submitting his suggestions & recommendations for cost cutting suggested that our organisation should stop monthly celebration of team member's birthdays, a combined birthday celebration is organised on the last working day of every month for the team members whose birthday falls in this month, by cutting cake and presenting voucher of Rs. Five Hundred to all the invitees. Sandeep rejected this cost cutting measure as he was of the view that it will have adverse effect on the moral of team members and send wrong signal in terms of reputation of the organisation.

Emotions play very important role in everyone's life whether s/he is a student, team member, team leader or CEO. Whatever we do in our professional or personal life emotions are at the helm of affairs, it may be taking tough decisions by a CEO in favour of organization, keeping up the motivation level of his team members by a team leader, receiving instructions or orders from seniors by an entry level team member, trying to understand a difficult topic by a student. It could be anything like relieving of stress, recovering from setback, maintaining present situation or gathering the courage to fly higher, all these actions need emotional stability or emotional sensibility in one form or the other.

What is the need of emphasizing so much on emotional understanding, it is not that emotions were not used in professional set up before the coining of term emotional quotient, but researcher and thinkers moved one step ahead from using emotions to managing emotions & utilizing it for 'trichual' benefit. Secondly, employee and employer has come a long way since the beginning of industrial revolution. We can easily determine this by changes in the title we used to call our team members, from slave to labour to worker to team member to blue collared staff, and look how we changes our team's name over a period of time from staff to personnel to human resource to human assets and designation of leader have also changed from General Manager (Personnel) to GM- HR to Chief People Officer to Chief Happiness Officer.

Scenario; Emotions have very important place in our life we want to be liked, encouraged, greet, enjoy, compliment and share with our colleagues, juniors and seniors. During pandemic (Covid-19) one survey was done in which it was asked about a choice of working place after pandemic, despite of comfort of working from home 70% of subjects were in favour of coming to office because they want to meet their colleagues & friends, discuss personal & professional matters and indulge in gossips, meeting friends & colleagues after long time will help an emotionally drained person to recover and get back his life

Introduction: We as a student, team member, team leader and leader want to excel in life & career, but when we are unable to reach the desired level for the reason not known to us. A feeling of helplessness takes over. What can we do to get out of this? just observe your emotions whether negative or positive, evaluate your actions and make firm commitment with yourself that now onwards you will take or make every action by using emotions sensibly. This commitment will take you from a stressful state to a blissful one, you will emerge as victor by using emotions sensibly for the purpose of bringing harmony in personal and professional life.

An individual's life is a rational combination of Emotional Understanding and Intelligent Quotient (IQ). Intelligent quotient is by birth which is govern by our biological friend 'Brain,' i.e., logic, whereas Emotional Understanding is combination of mind and heart, i.e., reason one must understand for anything we do is either by logic or reason in other words logic is always 2 plus 2 = 4, But when we take road by avoiding logic, and because of a reason by keeping so many things in mind we can create magic by the result which could be 1+1= 11.

In a study it was found that configuration of 80-20 is responsible for success in an individual's life or during his career, 80% of emotional Understanding and 20% of intelligent quotient is needed for a successful career and contented life, whereas it is 60-40 in case highly technical or research-based organization. It is to be noted that IQ is very much required to use emotions effectively.

Scenario; When an individual lost one of near or dear one due to a mishap and is under sever grief, during this period of grief his intelligent quotient (logic) comes to the fore and he starts thinking rationally. Whatever is lost is lost, I have to overcome these emotions and move on for better utilization of whatever is left. In the same manner if a student could not perform well in studies due to some reason or the other, then his intelligent quotient (logic) comes into picture helping to take emotionally sound decisions to perform well and overcome his weakness.

Application of Emotional Understanding; Emotional Understanding is applicable in almost all activities from leadership to decision making and from stress management to time awareness, sometimes it requires action from leader sometimes from team members or sometimes from team. Emotional Understanding got its due importance after discovery of research-oriented approach. There are various emotions like anger, patience, guts, grit, courage, fear, initiative, respect, cheerfulness and personal likes & dislikes in a professional set up but real challenge is to display or control these emotions in a very understanding manner for the benefit of self and team.

One more reason for using the word understanding is because an understanding is always between two entities, it could be between a CEO and Team leader, between a team member and team leader, or it could be between a difficult circumstances and CEO, forcing CEO to sit down and understanding emotions to overcome this difficult situation or it could be between a team leader and a new challenge arising suddenly, by making team leader to slow down and using emotions how to meet this challenge successfully, it could be between a team member and a problem, robing a team member of all his energy by stagnating and using emotional understanding how to defeat this problem.

Interpersonal Emotional Understanding: It is the understanding & awareness about team members ability, how they work, how to get co-operation from them, what motivates them, recognizing emotions in others, how to get the best out of team under all circumstances, Interpersonal emotional understanding is the key to keep the team on track not only first time but every time. When understands the emotions of our team members, we have done half the job required, because by understanding the emotions of our team members we can mould them as per the demand of the hour.

Intrapersonal Emotional Understanding: It is about making an accurate assessment about one's own emotions & ability and using it successfully for the benefit of the team and utilizing it to reach the goal of leadership successfully, i.e., knowing & noticing one's emotions or self-awareness how to get rid of anxiety or any distress feeling and when to soothe self. Biggest benefit of knowing about one's own emotions is to stop at the **'Mindstation'** and decide, am I doing that activity which is the need of the hour.

Awareness about self and others helps us a lot in maintaining harmony in the team. By keeping in mind below points. Team's performance may go up or down. To bring it back to stability extreme emotions should be kept in check. Overwhelming negative emotions disturbs working capacity whereas positive emotions increase efficiency.

Emotional Understanding for Leaders:

Researchers who embarked upon the journey of decoding the DNA of emotional understanding had come to the conclusion that emotional sensibility & stability is involved in all the activities and decisions taken by a leader, whether it's selecting or promoting a team member, leader should keep the team's interest on top, similarly while sacking or demoting a team member a leader should be emotionally strong enough to keep his personal likes and dislikes aside.

Scenario: Kapil is working as CEO of HRT corporation, his company has received a project abroad, Top Management has asked Kapil to name a project manager from present team members to be sent abroad for executing the projects, in the eyes of Kapil there are two probable candidates, Sunil & Sumit who fulfils all the requisite to be one of the team leaders for new project, both are equally capable. Sunil is little more close to Kapil as they are from same home town, but Kapil recommended the name of Sumit, one of the prime reason for his selection was that Sumit is a married man and can better understand the needs & emotions of other team members at new location, under new atmosphere & working condition away from family members, which an unmarried man can not understand, an emotionally strong and understanding professional, Kapil has kept a side his personal preference and decided in the interest of team and organisation.

Continuously motivating his team: A leader should always say 'hurrah' to his team and create an atmosphere of positivity by setting targets as per the capability & capacity of team, nor too boring neither un-achievable. While reviewing progress of the team, leader should always give constructive feedback and avoid any discouraging or negative feedback which might hamper the overall performance of team, leader should display courage in taking responsibility of any failure. If we can read about great leadership examples almost all of them have displayed leadership skills and bring back their team from the jaws of defeat, be it in sports, war or corporate sector. It is an emotionally understanding leader who can raise the level of emotions in their team and make them believe that they can turn an impossible situation into possible one.

Scenario; If you think there is a mistake in the process, before pointing out you must know the correct process or solution, if you do not know the solution accept the same and motivate your members to collectively find the solution. By doing this a leader's credibility increases many fold and team members also understands that a mistake is pointed out to be corrected and not to show authority.

Communicating verbally or non-verbally; Free flow of communication is an integral part of any successful team. Leader must be emotionally stable to accept negative side and must understand that nobody is complete nor indispensable. Since 65% of communication in a team is non-verbal, leaders are advised to be open to self-evaluation & criticism by exercising utmost restraint while showing any undue emotion through any gesture or medium.

    Team performs best when they come to know that their leader is emotionally understanding and ready to consider every suggestion made by them and making this process two-way, when a leader is ready to take suggestions and constructive feedback, s/he can also give suggestions and constructive feed back to it's team member which they will accept without hesitation, you may find nothing new in this, but the twist is that an emotionally understanding leader listens everything with interest what a team member has to say, even if it is of importance or not, because a leader understands that team member will also listen to him sincerely only if they are being given a patient hearing.

Leader's suggestions & feedbacks are important for executing the assigned task as s/he has injected those suggestions with knowledge and experience of lifetime, in order to make those suggestions and feedback work, emotionally understanding leader follow the principle of give and take while managing the team.

Scenario: If a team leader is too reactive and loses his patience at the drop of a hat, team members will start avoiding him and stop discussing out of the box ideas which in turn stops informal communication. Anger receives attention but losses respect. Example: If any team member comes to you with a complaint of another member, you must think twice before giving any verdict or taking any decision immediately. if it is feasible, you can discuss the problem by bringing both face to face. A leader must restrain self in taking impulsive action and should be interested in taking sound decision backed by thoughtful action. There is a say in corporate sector, if you want say to one of your team members.

'You are fired.'

Say it tomorrow, because one needs a cooling period. Even then if you think its right to stick to your decision, then go ahead and implement it.

Developing a safety net with interpersonal and networking skills: Emotionally understanding leaders keep team under there protection by casting a safety net around them by applying best interpersonal & networking skills. Emotionally understanding leader knows that their authority will help team members to execute their duties in a smoother way.

They take proactive steps to prepare ground for smooth movement, it could be having very good relationship with government officials & officials from regulatory bodies, spending time and resources on concern persons outside the organisation is of really great help to junior staff, persons outside of the organisation may include officials issuing various 'NOCs' for Fire Safety, lift operations or continuing the operations etc. By having good relationship with government officials will have wonderful side effect in the form of saving time & manhours, especially for liaison department and field staff. Secondly, it really pays very good returns on time and spend on building relationship with internal team members outside of our departments, as we all need each other help at one point or the other.

Scenario; Emotionally understanding leader always encourages an atmosphere of giving and helping each other at the time of need, if we receive a request from other department e.g., to borrow vehicle, printing paper or any hardware, we must help them keeping in mind that someday we might also need something from any other department in case of vehicle breakdown or malfunctioning of any hardware. It is matter of giving and taking back and creating a win-win situation for every team member.

Educating team members about Emotional Understanding; We can spread the knowledge of Emotional Understanding to make our surroundings positive and working atmosphere flourishing and should be done by leader itself, because only a leader knows that having knowledge of emotional understanding will not be enough for team to give its best.

Every professional while executing the responsibilities and duties of a leader must take interest in transferring knowledge of emotional understanding to other team members as well by introducing them to problem solving & decision making by understanding emotions. With this gesture an emotionally understanding leader can motivate every team member. By learning emotional understanding team members will always remain grateful to their leaders. We can easily imagine the direction in which a team will go in the absence of emotional understanding.

Test for leader; Every leader has to pass certain tests to show the superiority in a humble manner, Biggest test of leader's emotional understanding is when he accepts that one of the team is more knowledgeable in a field due to domain expertise and leader is comfortable in being led by that team member, because in this era of knowledge and technical break throughs no team member can complete a process by itself as every process is executed by joining all the components contributed by team members.

Sometimes a leader has to approach his junior to understand or to clear doubts about a particular component of the field beyond his expertise. In this case a relationship of teacher & student is established by setting example for other team members to follow and not hesitating to clear doubts if there is any, from their juniors, triggering a healthy atmosphere and culture in the making. One more advantage of this emotional understanding is that from now onwards no team member will make mockery of another team member of not knowing something in h/her domain, sending the message that no team member is complete with respect to knowledge in this ever growing and advancing world.

Scenario; Atanu is CEO of XYZ corporation, he is known for his open-minded approach and healthy mentality. While discussing a report with his Chief Finance Officer, he catches a particular entry called 'overheads' in accountancy language, which is showing much higher amount than it was in previous report. Atanu wants to understand the full process of calculating overheads and what are entries taken into. He went to CFO' s chamber and learn all about overhead entries and came back satisfied. `

Hearing 'NO' from a Junior; Another test an emotionally understanding leader has to pass when s/he has to act or react on hearing 'NO' from a team member who is junior, when a team leader or team member who had always replied in 'yes' to a new assignment, but today s/he said 'NO' when an additional task is assigned. What will be the reaction of leader, whether he become furious or took it as a part of professional life.

Earlier in corporate sector there has been tendency and general perception that a junior can not say 'NO' to a senior, but with changing time and more emotionally understanding leaders taking over and switching from conventional method of leading as manager to act as leader by providing space for open communication and clarify the matter for smooth functioning.

Scenario; Atanu called Amish to his cabin and told him to look into one more project, on hearing this Amish replied back to Atanu "Sorry sir I cannot take any more additional responsibilities as I have two more undergoing projects are there to manage". Atanu was little surprised to hear 'NO' from Amish and wanted to shout at Amish for not following his order, but he kept his cool leaving behind managerial mode of leading, telling Amish to meet him tomorrow with fresh approach to find out a solution.

When Amish met Atanu next day and explained the reason behind saying 'NO' to Atanu, Atanu the emotionally understanding leader, was satisfied and decided that Amish has taken right decision in the interest of team, if he had accepted the assignment, it would have led to problem in completing other two projects which he is already handling. Atanu also learn one lesson that before assigning any task to a team member he will first ask about his quantitative engagements in order to avoid this situation surfacing again.

Emotional Sensibility; Emotional Sensibility for a leader can be defined in a way where he is capable enough to solve difficult problem with an intention to do it 'now' attitude to minimize loss. Emotional sensibility makes a leader to act as sniffer dog who smells an IED before blast and diffuses it with in time by taking sensible decisions, emotional sensibility helps a leader to sense where team needs intervention or where it can be left to operate on its own, but in no case any kind of blunder is acceptable.

Scenario; Amit is heading the project team and Deepak joined one month back, both were unable to get along to move the project forward reason being that Amit is more experienced than Deepak whereas Deepak is more qualified than Amit, when CEO learns about slow progress of the project and reason behind it, he called both of them to his office immediately and asked for explanation, after listening their side, he immediately tell both of them to mend their way in their personal as well as organization's interest and instructed Deepak to co-operate with formal authority and suggested Amit to utilized the knowledge of Deepak where ever it is required, as a true leader his (Amit) interest should be to bring quality in the project rather than fighting for individual glory.

    As an emotionally sensible professional Amit should not hesitate to take help from a more qualified professional, whereas Deepak must understand that experience has his own merit and cannot be replaced if one has to excel in project, experience and knowledge must walk together to give wonderful result. Imagine if CEO has not taken the step of solving this immediately or had not kept it on his priority list the damage would have been many folds and project could not have been completed on time, an emotionally sensible leader must understand that tough conversation is very much part of one's professional life.

Emotional Stability; Emotionally stability in a leader can be defined as that quality on the basis of which s/he can be differentiated from a manager; with the help of emotional stability a leader can take tough decision in the interest of team when a she or he has to decide between a team member and the interest of the organization.

Scenario; CEO has come to know that a team leader Karan has been very toxic to his team members, trouble creator in the project is not only bringing loss of time but creating a kind of toxic culture in which other team members started feeling unsecured. CEO decided to take immediate action and want to remove him not only from the project but from organization as well. To terminate a team member needs great deal of emotional stability as it sends the message to other team members that a leader can take extreme step to safeguard the interest of organization and team.

Emotional Understanding for Team Leader;

Team Leader is the back bone of an organization and acts as catalyst between senior management and individual team members, A team leader balances h/her emotions between senior management and team members. Main job responsibility of a team leader is to remove the obstacles & difficulties coming in the way of smooth functioning of department. On the other hand, s/he has to be emotionally understanding while receiving instructions from top brass and passing it on to team.

Biggest achievement of a team leader is when she or he can pass on the message with an intention to get the job done and keep the team motivated, some times there is one negative message to be delivered, an emotionally understanding team leader will use all h/her skills to minimize the damage. An emotionally understanding team leader not only practices emotional understanding by self but also motivates every member of team to acquire knowledge about it.

Saying 'NO' to a Junior; When a team leader has to say 'NO', a team leader is approached by team members for their just or unjust demands, if demand is just then its ok, but if a demand is unjust, then team leader must explain or tell the reason why this request or demand is unacceptable, the way team leader handle these unjust demands paves the way for future functioning of team. During this conversation department head has to say 'NO'. 'NO' should be said in such a way that applicant should leave the table satisfied or it's a win-win situation for both parties.

Scenario; Sumesh who is heading marketing department of a multinational organization was approached by a team member in the middle of the calendar year to forward his request to management for a raise as he has just completed an additional qualification in his domain related field, this team member is one of the most efficient and completes every assignment on or before the deadline. Sumesh told team member that as per organization's policy increment to any team member is given only after annual appraisal which is applicable for previous calendar year. After listening this team member felt satisfied and left the table with happy handshake.

Taking corrective measures; A team leader has to observe and grade quality of work done by his team members, Simultaneously while evaluating the quality of work a team leader has to make corrections also if required, an emotionally understanding team leader while suggesting a modification or improvement has to be very careful, Because a human being does not like to be corrected or being told about their mistakes, any body doing so is a villain, whether it is in personal or professional life, its perhaps the most delicate matter for an emotionally understanding team leader to handle, any mistake or knowledge gap in a team member should be guided to learn and fill the gap with positivity. It has been observed that one mistake done by fresher is quoted in every conversation. A team member along with correcting or modifying a process must be communicated that what ever a team leader is doing is for the benefit of team member.

Scenario; Sumesh who is associated with MKL corporation as team leader, for some times he has been observing one of his team members namely Suresh, while talking to one of female clients is getting too personal & casual, spending lot of office hours during this conversation. Sumesh was thinking of how to solve this problem and was waiting for right moment to handle this situation, one of the reports prepared by Suresh was in-correct and team leader Sumesh has to digest few rough words from top management. Sumesh got the opportunity to correct the long pending mistake of Suresh, Sumesh called him into his cabin and strictly told him to mend his ways or ready to face the consequences, by adding that whatever he is saying is in the interest of Suresh, because as a bright professional he has a long way to go and should not spoil his career by involving self in any irresponsible act, every individual is free to whatever s/he wants to do after office hours. Suresh understands this and corrected his behaviour.

Apologizing without hesitation; A team leader while leading his team is looking for correction and modification in the job done by his team members, when he does a mistake or over look any standard operating procedure resulting in difficult time for team, an emotionally understanding team leader should not pass on the blame to any other team member, but as a show of strength an emotionally understanding team leader should accept the mistake and apologise in the presence of team members with the right version of incident to restore the confidence of team members.

While accepting mistake and apologising afterwards, a team leader can clear self of guilt, secondly, s/he sets the example for team members to follow, that they should never hide any mistake in the interest of team and develop the courage to accept it in front of whole team.

Scenario; Sumesh was not very happy on receiving a phone call from his senior who informs him that a consignment was supposed to reach today has not been delivered. Sumesh remembered that he had assigned the task to one of the team

Emotional Understanding, Stability & Sensibility

members, he immediately rushed to the cubical of this team member and start shouting at him and tell him to apologize to CEO for his irresponsible behaviour, after shouting at team member and without listening anything Sumesh rushed back to his cabin. After half an hour that team member called up Sumesh and informed him that consignment was collected from customs and handed over to the personal assistant of CEO who in turn forget to hand over the consignment to CEO, on hearing this Sumesh felt very bad as he has scolded team member without any fault of him, rushed to team member's cubicle and apologizes in front of all other team members present for shouting without confirming all the facts.

Emotional Stability for a Team leader; Can we guess about one quality which helps a team and its members to execute their tasks in a successful manner, In my views it is 'confidence', confidence is that gel which keeps the rail of tasks on track, One of the most important roles of team leader is to keep their team members filled with confidence by continuously telling them about the importance & purpose of individual team member's role & job, and giving feedback how they are doing and if any guidance and correction is required, or in other words team members feel confident when they find that they are important part of a chain which is accomplishing the task, an emotionally stable team leader in this case is keeping the interest of team members in fore front, Emotionally stable team leader understands that in some cases a team member needs selfless guidance and when we take steps to increase the confidence of team member our objective is completed.

Scenario; During routine round of the department when Sumesh came across a team member who was working on a software monotonously without much enthusiasm, when Sumesh told him the importance of the ERP software, he is working on keeps the track of supply chain of raw material and keep the show running. Secondly, when Sumesh gave him feedback about his work which was rated as above average by his immediate senior, after hearing this feedback team member was filled with confidence & enthusiasm and his performance also rises, reducing margin of error. In this way Sumesh, the team leader was able to install the sense of purpose in team member.

Emotional Sensibility for a Team leader. Emotional Sensibility for team leader is very much required to perform his task in the interest of the organization. Being emotionally sensible results in taking appropriate decisions which in turn brings strength and laurels. When a final decision is taken after adequately choosing an option from many options in the larger interest of organisation.

Scenario 1: A team leader was assigned a task to name one of his subordinates to be sent for training abroad, after thinking for some time the team leader decided in favour of Ratan as he fulfils all the eligibility criteria who can complete the training programme successfully and simultaneously implement & train others for the same to maximize the return on investment. But due to professional reason team leader don't like Ratan personally because on two occasions opinion given by Ratan was accepted by higher authorities instead of team leaders, but keeping in view the long-term interest of the organization, Ratan was sent for training abroad and after returning back he trained all other eligible team members to multiply the effect of knowledge acquired, resulting in the huge improvement in departments performance and bringing laurels to team leader. When team leader saw the result of taking decision in an emotionally stable condition and recommending the name of most eligible team member.

It is very important to take decision related to professional or personal field in an emotionally sensible condition. One can easily imagine what would have happened if team leader had taken the decision in an emotionally insensible condition. He could have falter on two fronts, first, if he had not recommended the right candidate for training, apart from training other team members, s/he could not understand the training module resulting in the huge loss of time and other resources of organization. Secondly, if wrong candidate is sent for training who could not understand the training module and clear the exams thereafter would have brought organization a bad name and question marks the quality of human assets associated with it.

Emotional Understanding, Stability & Sensibility

Emotional Understanding for a Team Member:

A team member has to use emotions very sensibly and stably to excel in team for realizing his dream and move ahead in career. First and far most requirement is gelling with other team members and accepting them as they are, irrespective of which background they come from, once they are named your team member, you have to complete the given task with their co-operation and adjust with them by keeping aside your social and psychological differences or preferences.

Secondly, one has to think like a leader, whose thoughts and activities are channelized for successful completion of task in hand, put your foot in the shoes of leader, sometimes your leader may be negative, non-communicative and might lose temper but there is no personal interest in this, try to understand his position. Sharing is the key for success of a team player one may share his knowledge, experience, professional resources, sometimes food, vehicle, jokes and lighter moments of life and avoid negative emotions like jealousy, hatred, anger etc., and move towards co-operation, initiative and courage.

One thing a team member must understand that this team is your second family and organization is your second home, as no family is complete in all aspects same thing is applicable to your professional team, show and raise your maturity level by gelling with other team members. Your respect and helping nature protect you and your group for any mistake which can be corrected by in-house effort. If a team member wants to excel in personal and professional life, s/he has to learn how to use emotions sensibly and stably.

Emotional stability for a team member; A team member while learning about emotions during early stage of his career, moving forward or backward and adjusting self in the career slot, some times understanding things in a wrong way and some times in a right way, first and far most objective of a team member should be to remain stable during difficult times or in other words not to lose ability to think rationally and take decisions by keeping emotional stability in forefront, showing sign of maturity. A team member who has learn the art of being emotionally stable can remain calm during every personal and professional turbulence.

Scenario; When Rajesh's boss yelled at him Infront of his junior team member for not ordering requisite raw material in time due to which company suffered financial losses, left Rajesh feeling very bad and thinking of immediately leaving this organization, but next day he went back to memory lane, remembering how much his team leader has taught and helped him during initial stages of his career.

Secondly, after stabilizing emotionally he put self in the shoes of his team leader, what would have been his reaction if any one of his subordinates has done same type of lapse, after doing fair assessment of the circumstances he decided to learn from the incident by keeping all the negative sentiments aside.

Developing external & internal relations; A team member has to give lot of importance to networking with the same level team members from other departments like finance, marketing, administration, purchase, commercial and logistics. Due to good networking skills an emotionally understanding team member will be able to remove many hurdles which might comes in the way of smooth functioning of department and team. Understanding and maintaining the relationships with team members from other departments requires time, resources and emotions as well.

Scenario; Sumesh very well knows the importance of internal and external networking and is always ready to accept any invitation, did not forget any occasion to greet every one whom he saw in corridor or meet in parking breaking all the boundaries of cast, creed and religion in a modern organization, which is full of diversity. In one instance when company needed cash, he mobilizes all his resources and told distributors to make advance payment and simultaneously he requested vendors to be ready for delay in payment.

Emotional Sensibility for a Team Member; When an entry level team member gives full attention to the job assigned, becomes the favourite of team leader, who in turn started giving more important tasks, an individual with emotional sensibility and keeping in view the long-term benefits of getting experience of wide variety of tasks, takes it in a positive way and considers it golden opportunity to learn which is the main aim of every entry level team member. Being emotionally sensible one can understand the meaning behind the words which are not said but clearly visible.

But on the other side if the same activity (extra work) is experienced by a team member with emotional instability and short-sighted ness, s/he will avoid it and be negative about any extra duty assigned, constantly reminding self of injustice inflicted upon.

Scenario; Rajnesh is working as Account Executive in DER corporation since last three years, he has shown all signs of an emotionally sensible professional, since joining of this organisation he has made his reputation of being a matured team member whose top most priority is to complete the assigned task with full dedication and sincerity, reaching to the post of Account-Executive in three years time is the result of smart & hard work.

His motto in professional life is '**Good guys perform better and infect others',** he is not only good in executing his professional responsibilities, he is 'good' for himself as well in the sense he never give ear to any criticism and negative information spread about team or organisation, neither he gave any importance to rumour spread about personal and professional life of a colleague, He very well understands that in an organisation or team we will find every kind of people, good natured or non-adjusting similarly we may find different type of organisations progressive or stagnant, as a professional our job is to give our best under available circumstances and move forward in the positive direction with out finding fault of others.

Saying 'NO' to Senior; Every senior team member expects from a junior team member that s/he will always respond by saying 'yes' to every order or request and this has been the norms of hierarchy in a professional set up. But there are some circumstances when a team member has to say 'NO' to his senior, how one should handle it, what should be the right way of saying 'NO' to a senior or refusing to accept responsibility in addition to present one without offending senior.

While refusing to accept additional responsibility one should be very polite and convey the valid reason behind non acceptance of one more project, Secondly, one must be proactive in this matter or in other words a team member must know about his capacity and reaching threshold for similar condition and prepare to take action when an additional responsibility is ordered or requested, being proactive means practising words and body language so that refusal is accepted by senior as logical not offending.

Scenario; Simi is working as a designer in a reputed garment export house, Her team leader called Simi in cabin and talked about one new project received by company and told Simi to take charge of this new project as well, Simi was prepared for this as she knew that being the best designer in company all new projects goes through her before taking concrete shape, the label of best designer has taken toll on the physical and mental health of Simi, She was over burdened due to projects which were directed towards her without thinking a second and understanding her current load of assignments. But this time Simi was prepared well in advance.

Simi told her team leader that she is already handling five projects at this point of time and will not be possible for her to take up any new assignment, it is in the interest of her and company that this project can be assigned to any other designer, so that they also learn how to handle a project independently. After giving a realty check Simi's team leader agreed to her request and called HR head to find the solution to this which might get repeated in future as well. In the beginning of the conversation Simi's team leader was little surprised but being an emotionally understanding professional and taking the right step by not allocating new project to Simi, Simi's team leader has done good job on two issues. First, she had saved Simi from getting burned out and secondly, she has saved her organisation from losing a valuable team member.

Compare Yourself; We are always reading in self-help books or articles that we should not compare ourselves with anybody else, it may be true while dealing with personal problems, because while handling personal problems an individual might attract more problems while comparing self to a financially well-off individual. Whereas in my opinion all emotionally understanding professional should compare themselves with their counterparts by observing good qualities and habits in them, because of which a team member's performance is better than others and s/he is gliding smoothly in her career.

By making a comparison, an emotionally understanding professional not only observe good qualities and habits, but by comparing with a better team member s/he tries to find out the scope of improvement and displays the urge for improvement or to be better in near future. It is advisable for all team members to have a closer look at the performance of other team members and find out the reasons for performing better than others.

This difference or reason could be poor communication skills, lack of initiative taking ability, poor time awareness', lack of leadership skills, it could be negative attitude towards nature of job or unable to manage stress related problems or going through bad relationship in personal life, it could be anything, If any professional want to excel in professional life s/he has to compare self with high performing and better professional by identifying the trigger which needs to be press to be at par or ahead of other team members.

Scenario; Hardik is working as executive (Sales) in TRE corporation, TRE corporation is manufacturing power banks for mobile phones and other electronic gadgets. Hardik's performance has been rated by his team leader as average for annual appraisal and increment purpose. Hardik felt very demotivated by this rating, whereas there is one more team member in sales team called Shrikanth whose performance has been rated as excellent for annual appraisal, Both Hardik and Shrikanth have same qualification & experience, and approximately of same age. By this rating Hardik felt dejected and remain depressed for few days, but being an emotionally understanding professional, he consoles self by telling himself that things can't go on like this I also need to perform like other star performers like Shrikanth to move forward in career, by comparing himself with Shrikanth he find himself at par with him on almost all the fronts except one front and that front is energy level, when Shrikanth comes to office he is full of energy and enthusiasm to execute the assigned jobs, Since sales job demands lot of outstation travelling, Shrikanth is always had his bags pack and ready to travel. Where as Hardik finds it difficult to travel outstation on short notice.

Having find out the reason of difference between two performances, Hardik introspects self and wanted to reach higher level of energy by making lifestyle changes, lack of which every young professional is suffering from, that is not giving due importance to healthy eating & not getting enough sleep due to using mobile phone late night, not exercising enough or having quality hobbies in the form of reading, music or cultural activities to spend their leisure time. Hardik made desired changes in his sleeping pattern and eating habits. In two months, he was able to find self with higher level of energy & focus which helps him to execute the assigned task proficiently and find appraisal rating moving from average to above average level.

Emotional Understanding for students:

Emotional understanding should be one of the most important knowledge a student must posses, Student life is in fact the beginning of journey to real world, during this journey s/he will come across so many new stops & stations which they will saw first time, to pass through these new stops and stations successfully a student must learn to accommodate a lot, some times accommodating self is positive sometimes it is negative, When accommodating or adjusting is positive everything seems to be moving in our favour, but when accommodating or adjusting is negative and moving against us we have to use emotional understanding to withstand it and overcome an adverse situation.

Emotional understanding will help a student to minimize the loss during turbulent times, it will help in maintaining positive outlook while experiencing a difficult circumstance, it will find ways to snatch victory from the jaws of defeat and help a student to find an opportunity in a challenging condition and above everything, emotional understanding will introduce us to the most important thing which nature has gifted us, known as **'LIFE'**.

Emotional understanding is very much required for a student to decide under a given circumstances, fight or flight. Every child is different in terms of social-economic background, we can't control this but as a student it is our responsibility to use our emotions, wisdom and intelligence to attain our goal by remaining focussed for which we are striving for. There is a need of orienting students about one thing i.e., to differentiate between reel world and real world, most of the students are under the false impression and influence of serials & movies available on social media.

Scenario 1; Suman has just received her senior secondary result in which she has scored 89%. Amit has reached college today in the morning after spending autumn brakes on his father's farmhouse, on reaching college his girlfriend informed him that she is braking-up. Akanksha's father scolded her for spending too much money on expensive cloths. Rakesh' s parents was very angry with him because he was spending too much time on social media which is hampering his studies.

All the names mentioned above have two things in common first, all the students belong to financially well-off families, secondly, all of them have committed suicide. How difficult it is for a parent to see his son/daughter committing this act of irresponsibility, whereas since last 18-20 years they have not faltered from their responsibility. Students have one misconception or they have never been told how much resources & time is consumed to raise them and above all students are not only the sons or daughters of their parents, they are assets of society & country. I wish if they would have emotional understanding by realising that life is not limited to marks or parents losing control over an issue, they should have been taught life skills with the help of curriculum or have been told by their parents about larger meaning of human existence.

Scenario 2; Rajneesh was sharing his room with Anuj, who belongs to rich family, one day when Anuj was away Rajneesh stole cash from his cupboard, during his master's program Neha and Deepak were dating each other, in order to fulfil materialistic needs of Neha, Deepak started dealing in illegal drugs, Sumesh who had come to this city for higher studies fell into bad company and become addicted to alcohol, during one raid of excise department he was caught with illicit liquor, has to leave his studies in middle and hospitalized for treatment & rehabilitation program.

All the names mentioned above have one thing in common that they were sent to jail as they lost their focus and forget real purpose of life & education, could not control their emotions and indulge in illegal activities or committing crime.

An emotionally understanding student would have been very much aware of the results going to jail, s/he won't be eligible for applying in government job or any other reputed organisation and h/her whole career spoiled, one of the major characteristics of emotional understanding is that it helps in doing good for a person but it helps more in preventing wrong action, because every wrong action is the result of absence of emotional understanding.

Compare or not to Compare: It is the basic nature of human being to compare self with human being for various reasons, a good student or personality knows well what is beneficial, comparison or no comparison, only an emotionally understanding student can decide in which field one has to compare and in which field one should not compare. Never compare yourself with any other student in terms of materials or branded clothes, it may be in your imagination but, it hardly makes any difference.

You can reach your destination only with hard work, knowledge and skills you developed during your educational program. The grades and impression you leave on teacher or examiner counts most. One must compare self with the student who is scoring good grades irrespective of background s/he is coming from, by comparing one may know the reason of difference between two grades and how that difference can be reduced or overcome.

Goal & Focus: A student's goal is to give their best while studying a professional programme and to be successful in that, but a student during h/her period of studies has to go through various physical and hormonal changes, not only this s/he make friends from different backgrounds of society, develop new interest and hobbies, remaining focussed becomes a big challenge, at this age it is very natural to chose pleasure which is temporary over happiness (long lasting) and develop escapist tendency, a small reason can force them to procrastinate.

Meeting these foes and considering them as friend is enough for getting off the track and losing focus, An emotionally understanding student must introspect to find out the reason of deviation from original track and correct as soon as possible, Best thing a student can do is to think about h/her parents who sacrificed a lot to provide best possible education, your parents can motivate and helps you to move towards positivity, another big reason is understanding that qualification and education is the only medium which will help you to lead a life of your choice.

Overcome adversaries or failures: During student life an individual has to face difficult situations, an emotionally understanding student needs to develop positive emotions to remain on track, these difficult conditions could be sudden loss of a family member, earning of family going down due to loss in business, Bread winner of family might lose job, any accident which might hamper a student from continuing studies.

But every student must understand that life is not perfect for anybody and is full of uncertainty, incidents discussed earlier could happen to any one in this world. Best action a student can take under these circumstances is by using understanding of emotions and remain positive, gather all the courage to fight and overcome any unwanted situation. You must get up each time you fall until you succeed, never giving up i.e., getting up ten times while falling nine times, never hesitate to try one more time with keeping success in mind.

Scenario: Akshat was very happy when he cracked JEE (Mains), he is now in the fourth year of B.Tech. programme and expecting a reputed company's offer through campus placement and hopeful of fulfilling dream of his parents. Akshat bags offer with decent package from a reputed multinational company which was having its semiconductor manufacturing unit in France, now everything depend upon completing the course.

Akshat's exam are scheduled after one week, he was moving in campus on his two wheeler, it had rained one hour before due to which his bike slipped and he suffered multiple fracture on elbow and got his knee dislocated, result of which he could not write his exams, he was feeling very depressed, after thinking a lot and overcoming his negative emotions, he made himself emotionally strong by thinking the positive side of incident that these injuries could have been more grievous and thanked God, started mentally preparing himself for next exam and to participate in campus placement drive next semester for bright future.

Emotional Excellence; After having understood emotional stability and emotional sensibility, lets move towards finer aspect of emotional understanding which is known as **emotional excellence**, earlier we have studied emotional sensibility & stability to understand the emotion of others and ourselves for managing day to day affairs of our corporate life. Now question arises what is emotional excellence.

Emotional excellence is highest form of emotional understanding in which a professional executes the assigned task in the best possible manner and bring unexpected & unmatched results due to emotional attachment and sense of belonging ness with organisation & team.

A professional with emotional excellence always wanted his team to be excel under every circumstance and give best contribution, when we are filled with emotional excellence, our sole aim is to see our team winning and to secure the honour of it what ever the price we have to pay, it could be facing hardship, working extra hours or any other option. Best part of emotional excellence in professional life is that it is interested in giving with a sense of sacrifice. in most of the emotional excellence cases it has been found that individual acted upon by taking initiative, if those team members have not acted by listening the inner voice of emotional excellence there would not have any change in their career graph or current position.

Emotionally excellent professional stood like a rock between its team and any problem troubling their organisation, they behave like shields and ready to accept any challenge be it difficult customers, an insider or enemy. A professional become passionary when its sole interest is the upliftment of team.

Scenario; In the beginning of academic session of 2021 August after five months of covid-19 pandemic it was the time for annual fee submission as we all know that covid -19 had made a negative impact on every part of society affecting almost all segments in one form or the other. our organisation received approximately 160 applications for waving off fee or delayed submission due to financial constraints, after having gone through these applications we can easily make out that only 34 application seems to be genuine, rest are taking advantage of the situation. to find out the solution of this problem we decided to write a common letter to parents of all the applicants. which is as below.

Dear Parents,

Greetings of the day,

we all are going through difficult times and facing the challenges due to covid -19, educational institute and students are two sides of same coin, institute also needs financial resources to conduct its day-to-day operations and make payments to faculty, staff and vendors for smooth functioning.

Education being sacred part in a students' life, nobody would like to earn it through false declaration and unfair means. Please submit fee in time so that we continue giving quality service and education, the absence of which might result in life long deficiency in your child's professional life. Please take appropriate decision by keeping in view your wards future.

Warm regards.

Principal

With in fortnight of sending this e-mail we received fee from 90% of the applicants, as their parents have understood the importance of right step, they have to take to secure the future of their children.

Next level of emotional excellence is displayed when a professional takes decision without any bias with whom earlier he was friends and now he is superior. this can be understood by this scenario.

Scenario; Aman & Rishabh are working as Sr. Manager (electrical) and Sr. Manager (mechanical) respectively in a manufacturing plant. They both have passed out from reputed engineering institute together and are very good friends. Last month head of their maintenance department resigned, organisation while looking from in-house replacement for the head of department role, zeroed in on Rishabh. After taking charge of Head-Maintenance, first thing Rishabh did is to call upon his friend & batchmate Aman and communicated in a very polite manner that even if I have become your senior by virtue of this promotion, but we will be working with the same sense of team spirit, as there was only one position to be filled it would have been you or me either, Aman understood the situation and promised his best to take the team to new heights.

Emotional excellence is also seen when a professional is ready to face the heat, but did not shed his responsibility as reputation and credibility of organisation is supreme.

Scenario; Kunal has just joined as customer care head in an MNC, FMCG products of his company fulfils the need for various sector of society, it was his second day in office, suddenly a person filled with anger entered his cabin and started complaining and shouting that "why you people promise those things which cannot be delivered on time", where is Amit who had promised me to deliver goods by yesterday and in turn, I have promised my supplier the same". Kunal understood the whole situation and tries to pacify things by saying that he will do his best to get the things right for him. Kunal could have easily told this guy that I have just joined and do not know anything about the deal', but displaying higher level of emotional excellence and keeping in mind the reputation of his present organisation he did not utter a single word and took full responsibility as per his position, promising the complainant best possible support.

Emotional Excellence is also exhibited by professional who resist all the temptations of earning easy money or harming their previous organisation by choosing the path of integrity and honesty in conduct.

Scenario; Rajesh is employed with a software technology firm, he had resigned from his current organisation as he got better opportunity in another organisation and serving notice period, one week before his last day he received a call from his team leader of his future company insisting him to copy data of the clients of current company and bring along with him when he comes to join, Rajesh straight away refused this stating that it is illegal and unethical practice in which he will not indulge in as he had always believed in "honesty is the best policy", hearing this statement from Rajesh his future team leader immediately disconnected the phone.

On the day of joining new organisation Rajesh was pretty nervous for the reason that how his team leader will behave as he had refused his request to steal the client's data from previous organisation, after having completed the joining formalities in HR department his team leader called him into his cabin after formal conversation he told him that he has passed the test, Rajesh was surprised as he had not appeared in any test in this organisation, his team leader reminded him of the conversation in which he told him to steal the data, if Rajesh would have agreed on to steal the data he would not have been sitting in front of him at this moment. Rajesh took a sigh of relief and thanked his parents and teachers for giving right kind of upbringing and education.

Next level of emotional understanding; is produced by sports persons & teams who gave their best and beat opponents stronger than their team, we must have read or seen numerous times that one team or an individual who was far behind in ranking came back from losing and turn the table on its opponent and pulled out a coup.

Have you ever imagined how a low-ranking sports person or team wins the tournament, it is because of emotions they used to charge themselves and motivate team members, it might be because of traditional rivalry creating do or die situation, in some case it was found that sportspersons while displaying highly charged emotional excellence some time defies the laws of science and achieve their target. this could be understood by scenarios given below.

Scenario; India was participating in its first Olympics after independence which was held at London in the year 1948 and reached final of hockey, who was the other time reaching final? It was non other than Britain who ruled our country for almost 200 plus years and was playing on their home turf. Indian team decided during team meeting that what ever happen they have to beat Britain to take sort of revenge and tell the world that we have arrived. All the players were emotionally charged as it was do or die situation for them, at one point of time when ground was wet not taking care of injuries Indian players removed their shoes to avoid slippery field, eventually India beats Britain 4-0 and clinched first Olympics gold medal after independence.

Scenario; Second incident I remember with respect to any Indian sports team displaying highest level of emotional excellence is by Indian cricket team captained by Kapil Dev which went on to win Prudential cricket world cup on 25th of June 1983. In this cricket world cup Indian team was rated very low due to India's performance in last two world cup and one day cricket, Indian team was not taken seriously leave apart considering a threat. Same thing was in the minds of team players as one of the players disclosed in an interview after winning that upon receiving the information of being selected for world cup, they consider this tour as paid holidays, but except one man who wanted to give his best performance and expected the team to follow the same. It was Kapil Dev, who motivated his men to exceed their limits and filled them with 'can do' emotions.

Kapil Dev and his men starts moving forward match by match and reached semi-final where they beat England, and on 25th of June 1983 they were in front of mighty West Indies playing final, West Indian team had won last two world cups in 1975 & 1979 and were looking for hattrick, when they saw Indian team in front of them they imagine there plans being executed to the perfection, but Kapil and his men have something different in mind, all of them were emotionally charged including those team members who were earlier thinking of this tour as paid holidays. What a miracle emotional excellence can do was clearly visible in this match, Indian was hellbent on winning this match every player knows that this is the chance to completely change the image of Indian cricket. India batting first could score moderate total of 183 only, despite of this mediocre performance There was one man i.e., captain Kapil Dev who was still thinking of winning, West Indies were bowled out for 140 only, lost the match by 43 runs.

Scenario 2; There is one more level of emotional excellence which is in my opinion is the best test which a human or a student can pass, till than we have studied emotional excellence with an outward approach in which emotions are clearly visible through body language, voice, tone or facial expressions.

There is one more type of emotional excellence which works purely on inward mode, in this form of emotional excellence emotions are not expressed, they are suppressed so as they do not disturb the process of attaining one's goal, this type of emotional excellence is a kind of safety net to avoid any unwanted thought which can waste our time and derail us from reaching goal. Guess? Who is the best person who uses emotional excellence to its best use, this type of emotional excellence is displayed by high achievers having very limited resources and minimal social support i.e. they are born in not so resourceful families but they are not deterred by their social or financial condition, they have made up their mind to achieve set goal or in other words they have decided what they want to be in life whether they want to don uniform, make their contribution by serving society, want to teach or develop something new, in every circumstances they believe in "if there is a will there is away". When we read in newspaper or on social media platform that a rickshaw puller's son has been selected in UPSC, maid's daughter has cleared IIT-JEE mains exam, a street vendor's daughter has cleared NEET exam and going to join MBBS course in a reputed college, there are numerous examples of students and individuals who overcome all their limitations and took a winning stride, it could be an athlete who practiced without proper facilities and gears won gold medal in an international event or a candidate from very meagre background cleared SSB and ready to join NDA, They all are individuals and assets of society who don't allow any condition or limitation to stop them to realise their dreams.

Now the question arises how does the emotional excellence plays the role in their success? As discussed above that this type of emotional excellence means an inward activity in which emotions are suppressed not expressed. Students in the above-mentioned category has to suppress their emotions when they have been discouraged by their near and dear ones on listening their ambition and goal, they must have been told that "you can't achieve this as it requires lot of resources." they have to keep quiet and continue their journey towards their goal, this type of emotional excellence teaches us to absorb pain and keep calm during struggle.

We can not easily imagine or feel the turbulence one is experiencing and going through, when they saw their parents doing odd jobs and working extra time so that they can support and provide the resources for their education, dream or success for which there is no surety, even when there is no guarantee of success these individuals with positive vibes in their hearts continue there journey towards their goal, coming back to the amount of pain they have to suppress when they watch helplessly while their parents doing odd jobs, but they are unable to contribute or help in reducing there misery, but they suppress their emotions keeping in view the larger interest of the future. They do not give any heed to criticism or think second time about the insult or humiliation which has been inflicted upon them, they know that every thing will be on track once they reach their goal.

Highest level of emotional excellence; is exhibited when a professional and team member is on the ground zero and amid action, he decided to disobey his seniors, because s/he is very sure that decision taken at this point of time is the right one to secure the honour of team or country, even if they have to pay the price by sacrificing their own life. Mostly this type of emotional excellence is displayed by soldiers of our armed forces on which we all are proud of.

Scenario; During India-Pakistan war of 1971, Lt. Arun Khetarpal was on top of his centurion tank named 'Famagusta' firing and manoeuvring fearlessly and not allowing the enemy to move an inch, suddenly his tank become immovable due to enemy fire he become sitting duck target for the enemy, when he communicated his position to his commanding officer who in turn ordered him to get out of the tank and take shelter till the arrival of re-enforcement. Lt. Arun did not comply with the order of his commander and decided to stay back in his tank. he replied back "my tank is not moving but my gun is working, I will not allow enemy to move forward", hanged his wireless set. During fierce battle Lt. Arun lost his life but hold on the 'fort' till re-enforcement arrived. Lt. Arun was awarded Param Vir Chakra posthumously, highest gallantry award of our country to be awarded to any soldier.

Scenario; One more real story from 1971 Indo-Pak war, which displayed emotional excellence at its best. Fighter pilot Flight Lt. Nirmal Jit Singh Sekhon was waiting in his bunker with his gears on, suddenly their was siren indicating that air base is attacked by enemy fighter jets when he came out of his bunker he saw four fighter planes approaching air base, he asked the permission to retaliate, but received negative response from his commander, ignoring the order from his commander he ran towards hanger and took his plane to sky amid heavy bombing on runway, he succeeded in taking his fighter plane in air to counter the attack, in the process he manage to hit three enemy's plane and fourth one was forced to go back, but Sekhon's plane was also hit and crashed martyring him. Flight Lt. Nirmal Jit Sekhon was awarded Param Vir Chakra posthumously, highest gallantry award of India.

Conclusion: As a human being we all are born with both type of emotions negative and positive; our efforts should be to develop ourselves to overcome emotional obstacles and learn from failures, move from cold logic to a humane mix of logic and reason. Our job as a leader should be to channelized our emotions wisely in the interest of the organization, as a team leader our emotions should work in the interest of the group, as a team member we should have emotions which can help us to grow and as a student we should use our emotions in the interest of self. To sum up in a lay man's language emotional intelligence is nothing but replacing negative thought with a positive one and acting on that thought. While dealing with others **"first**

understand than be understood". Best thing about emotional understanding unlike intelligence is that it can be improved upon by constantly working on it which clearly reflects the flexibility in human nature.

Lead Your Ship

In the last two decades there is one topic which has been the centre of thoughts & research in management world & corporate sector is leader or leadership, during industrial revolution, better machines were the sole reason for having edge over competitors, after few decades' money was also added, now it becomes combination of money and machine. Things still don't work out as desired and baffled management gurus trying to find out the solution for it, started looking here and there for meaningful & smooth process along with profit earning, now they have to look beyond money and machine (Hawthorne Studies} and (Rosy Modi providing roads and sanitation facilities for workers of Tata Steel) they keep on searching for long, suddenly they chance upon a discovery like alchemist, who was looking for treasure while sitting on the pot of 'Gold'.

Now corporate magnets zeroed on the factor which if handled sincerely can bring positive change not only in corporate sector but in their own life as well and that factor is their human asset, which is with them since the beginning of industrial revolution, with years of publications and researches they came out with two new terms 'leader' and 'leadership'.

Leader is an individual who is at the helms of affairs of an organisation, ready to lead from front, back and middle, mentally prepared to be led if required, who don the title with attitude of service and is expected to look after the needs of the organization and team members so that both grows to earn profit. It is not technology, money or raw material, it is human factor which can make a difference to any organization, success of every organization depends on its ability to introduce the concept of leadership to their manager and see them growing & turning into leaders. All of us must be reading in news that organization X was not performing well, its CEO has been replaced and within six months of joining, new CEO was able to bring down the losses. Have we ever heard that loss making organization has replaced its technical base. Technical bases are replaced for upgradation only.

    A Leader is one whom no team member would like to leave, irrespective of deteriorating condition of the organization, where as a bad manager is left in the lurch how high an organization is rising, like in a game of chess every piece has a purpose and value. Leader's action speaks the same. Leadership can be translated and interpreted in three words "**lead your ship**" that ship may be solo rowing or a yacht or it may be filled with passengers who are under your direct command or guidance, they have trusted you to reach their destination.

Scenario; When Subhash was working as team leader 10 years back, he could not understand few decisions taken by his manager, those decisions were forced on the team and as a sincere professional he was very much sure that these decisions were going to harm the organization, but could not do anything at that time, nor give them feedback neither advice, he made up his mind not to follow the footsteps of his previous manager, but ten years later when he become leader, he realizes that there was not much fault of those managers, as a manager they were not made aware of practicing leadership neither such policy and rules were encouraged by top management. Their job was limited only to fulfil the personal and organizational goal.

When Subhash took over his new assignment as head of a manufacturing unit as CEO (Chief Executive Officer), he was interested in playing the role of leader rather than manager, he called a meeting of all the head of departments and starts his first communication by conveying the message that his style of working is different from whom he took over this charge.

Subhash insisted that they should call him by his name or surname by prefixing any word showing respect, but not by his designation because he was of the view that true leaders have no title.

His next intention was to transform his team members into true leaders and tell them not to follow his orders blindly, they can ask or clarify any instructions which they have not understood properly or seems to be confusing to them and announced that he is always available for team during and after office hours for any emergency and wants to show that not only knowing the rules of leadership but want to practice them as well. As a leader he knows that things will not change if he practices the role of leader and other team members remain followers.

Why Subhash took up the role of a transformational leader? Because during his career span of 22 years, he came across two types of leadership style in practice. First was transformational and another was transactional. **Transactional Leadership:** In this type of leadership, transaction is involved. Whatever a leader does is want for something in return. In silent message he transmits that if you do this, I will do this for you. This approach is temporary in nature and is used dealing with day-to-day matter. In this leader gives in anticipation of getting back in improved manner. This type of leader runs the organisation with static mindset who is interested in numbers only, in the beginning it runs with good speed but in due course of time its speed fades away and there is chaos all-around, as every team member is interested in saving his or her job. In this case leave apart sowing fresh seeds, leaders are not being able to maintain existing trees. While practising transactional leadership style a leader is always in a fire fighting mode, means he takes steps to solve a problem when problem is standing in front with its mouth wide open.

Scenario: Ramesh is taking his team out for lunch because he comes to know that some miscommunication has taken place due to which efficiency of his team is going down. Ramesh plans to remove this miscommunication by talking to his team members in an informal way. In this way both will be happy, he and his team. Transactional leader looks for easy solution and make stop gap arrangements.

Transformational Leadership: While practising transformational style of leadership, a leader is interested in total upliftment of his team members, by bringing selfless approach in dealing with team, s/he shares experiences &, trade specialisation which gives permanent benefit to its team members and bringing positive change in organisation and its culture.

In transformational style of leadership performance is the by-product of leadership style as transformational leader is interested in giving rather than taking back and in creating positive working atmosphere where team members are contributing happily and growth seems to be long lasting. This type of leadership is done with a vision because while giving the best efforts to the present they continue to create future for self, for team members and above all future of organisation, they are more interested in long lasting success of organisation as they understand that when organisation survives for long only it will help in serving the purpose for which it was established.

One very good quality transformational leader possess is of trouble locator, by virtue of guts and vast experience s/he is able to locate trouble well before it turns into reality and inflict irreparable loss to team & organisation, it could be proactively locating a team member's burnout, toxic manager or unfit team member. Transformational leaders when move to higher ranks does not shed basic qualities for which they are promoted for, Transformational leaders can be sum up by this, **they plant** trees and know that they will not get the chance to enjoy its fruits and shadow.

Scenario; While working on a project Subhash came to know that his team requires training on an advance process which will cost good amount of money as well. Subhash immediately took decision to send three of deserving team members for training on this advance process, from the budget of the project. His step might bring down the profitability of this project, but he was interested in bringing permanent solution to this re-occurring problem in the interest of organisation, because expenses incurred on advance training will have long lasting and positive effect on Trichual (team member, team and organisation).

Immediately after one month of joining he has to appraise the performance of team members during previous year, he always took this activity very seriously, deciding about annual raise and promotion is one such activity which forms the basis of moral and motivational level of team members for next year, he very well understands that a demotivated team member cannot give h/her best while performing his duties. He is very firm on giving fair treatment to every team member irrespective of top management's personal likes and dislikes, over the years of experience he has developed the strength not to treat unequal's equally, a true leader is one who knows his job well, balance and healthy approach towards any situation or challenge, takes responsibility & initiative; deal with the fault of others as gently as own.

Leadership is one of the most intangible things in the functioning of an organization, it is the process of influencing the activities of an individual or a team towards the achievement of target in each situation where both individual as well as organization obtain the 'maximum.'

When Subhash joined the organization as CEO, He remember being coached by his senior in previous organisation who was a genuine leader and told him that one has to learn different style of leadership to handle different situations, giving way to the theory that no single style is suited best to lead, he adopts different style of leadership depending upon the need arises and takes decisions best suited for organization and team, sometimes he has to include everybody in decision making process, When he is handling an assignment with the help of middle management, he adopts **Consultative** style, he encourages team members to participate in decision making process, is open to new ideas & opinions, delegates some of the responsibilities to team members, there is free flow of communication from upward and downward, it's useful when subordinates are capable of working independently.

Scenario: Subhash wanted to re-assess the current appraisal system as he was of the view that current performance appraisal system, reviewing and appraising employee once in a year is not correct, being one of the most important activity in the career of a team member, performance appraisal should be given much needed importance, he called upon the meeting of head of departments for consultation to find a better way to appraise the team members, all HODs agreed and recommended to break present appraisal system in two parts by making it a bi-annual activity taking place in sixth and twelfth month of every calendar year, every sixth month of calendar year will be earmarked for a procedure called performance review in this performance of an employee will be reviewed jointly by reporting manager and HR department to decide about coaching, mentoring or training needs, After five months of performance review, performance will be appraised by keeping in view the progress made by team member after performance review and recommendations forwarded for promotion, demotion or increments.

Scenario; Being perplexed by number of resignations during last three months, he again called upon the meeting to discuss the matter and zeroed in to reduce working hours, he had observed that team members are spending time in office even after duty hours just to impress their seniors, he advised seniors to develop healthy work culture and encourage team members to finish the given task during office hours to save office resources.

During meeting to re-think about the number of hours, some of the employees suggested to make it four and a half day from currently five and a half day week, but few team leaders suggested that our organisation depends mostly on walk-in customers it will not be feasible for us to remain close for two days, as they were about to take decision, suddenly a hand popped up to express his views, this team member clarifies that we can have six day office and can still give our team members five day a week facility by rotating second off during week days, this will serve two purposes, first, a long pending demand of team members for five day a week will be met without having any adverse effect on revenue, secondly, with this implementation team members will get eight days off in a month instead of four days, thus saving on conveyance & personal maintenance etc. resulting in financial ease for every team member. This gentleman's advice to rotate one weekly off during week days was accepted happily by almost all team members present during meeting.

In some cases when organization cannot afford a blunder, he gave instructions like a commander leading his unit to success, while executing an important assignment and guiding in-experienced and new team members he uses **AUTOCRATIC** style in which he retains all the authority, take all the decisions and issued instructions what to do, how to do and when to do. Communication flows only from the leader; In the process he accepts all the responsibilities attached with decision.

Scenario: Subhash is looking for a new ERP system to be implemented in organisation, he formed a purchase committee to call for tender. While during a meeting to finalise the vendor for implementation of new software, purchase committee recommended the vendor who had quoted the lowest amount, but going through details of all other bidders he came across one very good vendor which had submitted its bid for project, but amount quoted was approximately 2% higher than recommended by purchase committee, Subhash took all the members of purchase committee into the confidence, zeroed on the company which was famous for quality and after sale service. In his views quality and after sale service matters most and give long lasting benefits. As head of purchase committee Subhash decided to issue purchase order in favour of vendor after assuring other committee members that he will take all accountability in case of auditors and board members asking any question.

He practices Laissez Faire; In some case he practices laissez-faire style of leadership by delegating complete responsibilities & decision-making powers to team members by showing confidence in their capability, in this style of leadership communication is free & open for all and very useful when team members need high degree of independence to perform a task or complete a project. By practicing laissez faire policy in some cases Subhash shows that he can give total independence to concern team members as and when need arises.

Scenario; When the top brass decided to market the product with the help of various platforms of social media, Subhash called the meeting of media team and conveyed the requirement of top management. During meeting and before assigning his media team to prepare a short ad film documentary to market the product. He informs the media team that there will be no interference from any department or authority in the making of documentary, Subhash always wanted to have his various teams to handle their projects independently and grow professionally.

He uses Bureaucratic style; Subhash always believes that to lead an organisation smoothly there should always be some rules, policies and regulation to be followed by every team member from top to bottom, he expects his team members to follow the same in the interest of organisation and self which are followed by leader as well, this step is taken in spite of young generation asking for more freedom from rules and regulations.

Scenario; After joining as CEO, Subhash received suggestion from HR-Head that team members are not reaching their place of work on time leading to loss for organisation and creating rift among themselves, when no action is taken against late comers, team members who were punctual earlier have also started coming late. HR-Head suggested to install punching machine on main gate to solve this problem, Subhash agreed to her suggestion and from next month onwards attendance was taken by electronic punching machine. During monthly open house discussion team members complained that they have to make a 'Q" to mark their attendance and consumes approximately five minutes daily to punch the card, after hearing this Subhash told HR-head to install separate machines inside every department, solving team members problem of lining up in 'Q' to mark their attendance.

Manager or Leader; After induction of term 'leader' in corporate world, 'manager' is considered as villain, every body started criticizing manager and wanted to be a leader, but the truth is that a good leader has to play the role of a manager side by side while leading the team, a leader is in 80% of leadership role and 20% of managerial role and interested in innovating new ways of executing given task rather than repeating old ways and wants to be fresh in his approach instead of copying the previous one, best thing a leader does to any team that s/he is interested in developing peoples and systems not in maintaining them, a leader do not like a stagnated condition whether it is a process or an individual team member and is best recognised when s/he displays dynamic mindset not only for self but for every other factor which s/he is attached with, It may be a team member, any process or organisation itself, a leader is very satisfied when s/he sees a team members moving ahead in career, reaching next level of corporate ladder by learning new things and developing themselves.

A manager doubts the ability of team members, in order to get a job done and micro manages the whole process by keeping an eye on every activity of team members, whereas a leader shows trust in place of doubt, after assigning any task a leader **macro manages** the team, macro managing a team means while assigning a new task, in the opening address s/he tells the team what is required to complete this task, what a team member will learn once the task is completed, how much important this task is for 'Trichual' (team, team member & organisation), what changes this task will bring in the professional life of a team member.

Doubt and trust have different dimension as well which is equally important, a manager doubts team member when s/he approaches h/her for activities other than related to task or official work, such as request for leave or loan etc. before entertaining an application of leave or loan a manager will first doubt the reason and ask for reason behind it, but if same application lands on the table of a leader s/he will approve it without thinking too much and look only for the entitlement & eligibility of the team member as per the HR manual.

Another aspect of doubt or trust is displayed when any unconventional condition or circumstances arises with respect to any team member, for example if a team member is displaying unusual behaviour during official hours or a team member is performing below his abilities and could not achieve the assigned target, in this case a manager will warn that team member and might issue a warning letter, but a leader will first think about the various aspects behind this team member performing below the capacity, first thought will comes to the mind of a leader that what s/he can do to improve the performance of troubled team member, a leader will try to find out if there is any organisational hurdle involved, how that hurdle can be removed and will think about personal reasons in the last. A leader generates a sense of belongingness among other team members and own every decision.

Difference between a manager and a leader is clearly visible when they assigned task and look at their team member during process of task accomplishment, a manager would like to engage team members whereas a leader would like to involve team members, difference between engagement and involvement may be understood by this description.

When we engage any team member for a task, we are solely interested in giving directions, our aim is to get the task done in the most economical & efficient way. Whereas when we involve a team member we ask h/her for input seriously, this means we implement and appreciate their contribution in decision making process, encourage them to speak about positive and negative aspects and suggesting corrective measure, involving a team member in any process has the intention of both sides getting benefitted i.e. organisation and individual, involvement also indicates a leader wants h/her team member to learn the art of brain storming for a process and pass it on to other team members as well.

Health and wellness have now become integral part of a good corporate culture, which is easily visible in the working style of a manager or a leader. For a manager health can be described in terms of physical fitness only, first thing comes to a manager's mind while discussing about health is, a gym, but when a leader thinks about concept of health, it is physical and mental both and is total wellness for a team member. A leader with adequate knowledge of wellness takes every step and decision while keeping in view the wellness of team members, most of the organisations when led by managers make health programmes which exhibits 'one size fit all' but when a wellness programme is designed by a leader for the team members of organisation, it is customised to the extent keeping in mind the age group, gender and availability of the team members in the premises. A leader not only make wellness programme but take feedback and ready to make changes if required so that it reaches almost every team member.

A manager sees his team member as a **needy** professional who is working in this organisation to earn money to fulfil his or her social responsibilities, whereas a leader sees every team member with an angle of equal importance, s/he understand that an organisation needs team member as well who can pilot the train on right track, it is responsibility of the organisation as well to look after the need of a team members so that both can meet at certain point to complete the task and where personal goal of team member and organisational goal of survival and earning profit thereafter. A leader knows that whatever s/he does in the organisation will have direct & indirect effect on society and nation.

A leader does the things right instead of right things which includes developing internal strength and he loves to be independent rather than on any support. A leader was manager earlier become leader when he chooses to evolve by finding better & unconventional ways to deal with people and situation. Leadership is visible when a managerial job is done with flavour of leader. A manager who wants to do right things to his team members will tell team members to know more about their domain and become better in this or that, whereas a leader who wants team members to know more and do better will create an atmosphere of learning by providing material in the related field or adding more books and journals in the library for the specialised domain, a leader not only take steps mentioned above for the improvement in team members but also make sure that the material or facility is utilized in the best possible manner by creating specific schedule time period for learning as well.

A leader when committed to do the things right will make all out efforts to turn h/her vision into reality, it means when s/he attended any conference or come into contact with any new concept if implemented could take h/her team one step ahead or add value to the organisation, leader will work hard for team members to have exposure to those new concepts and benefitted from it.

A manager thinks that a team member is only motivated by the financial aspects or any organisation paying higher salary in comparison to its competitors will do the trick, but with changing time a team member can not be lured by higher pay for long term commitment. A leader tries to understand what else can be done to keep team members motivated to perform efficiently and consistently and is ready to shed h/her false ego to communicate with all team members by being in touch with them to find out motivational factor along with monetary aspect and understands that human being has risen above survival mode and looking for quality life, a professional team member is writing poems, singing songs, playing various music instruments, tracking in mountains, rafting in rivers, surfing in oceans, paragliding, solo-travelling etc. along with executing professional responsibilities, a leader understands that team members wants to live a meaningful life which is not limited to earning a livelihood only, s/he is interested in exploring finer aspects of life and would like to lead a evolved one. This understanding about evolved nature of a team member pursues a leader to convince the organisation to make such policies and provide such facilities so that a team member is able to pursue h/her interest along with executing professional responsibilities.

Difference between manager and a leader could be best understood by the notion that a manager is satisfied when his orders are followed in toto and no questions are asked or in other words a manager like his team members to follow, however a leader is not contented when his orders are followed blindly and is very much comfortable while receiving back constructive feedback or suggestions for a positive change in a given task or in other words a leader is very satisfied when s/he sees team members developing and leading and not afraid of his team members rising higher,

Scenario: When Subhash used to act like a manager, he communicated while asking for a given task or report preparation. Where is the report?

When he asks as a leader giving respect will ask, please bring the report if it is ready.

In short, a manager's whole efforts are channelised towards making his organisation 'good' whereas a leader makes all out efforts to create a 'great' organisation.

Role of a leader;

Master: Leader is figurehead of the organization and everything revolves around him, Subhash as true leader takes responsibility for each and every activity going on in the organisation e.g. when his media team won an inter corporate competition, he sends team's captain to receive the award, always motivate and encourages subordinates to accomplish goals when his production team was lagging behind its target he discussed this matter with production head and came to know about few grievances of production team which he handled very smoothly and bring the production line back on track, Liaison with people outside organization is very efficiently taken by Mr. Subhash on priority basis, mostly they are bankers, investors, lenders and media persons etc. this helps him meeting out any eventuality and successful handling of any crisis. Last year when due to an accident in the factory and subsequent malafide propaganda spread by the competitor, being a proactive leader, he was able to manage this crisis with the help of connections in media fraternity.

Communicator; Subhash very keenly examines internal & external environment and keep self updated on information to be disseminated properly, a leader very well understands the importance of medium and process through which an information is to be disseminated, the recipients and outcome of that, because same information gets different response or reaction from different team members, or in other words same information is interpreted by team members as per their needs & convenience, So one has to be very careful while releasing an information, If an information lands in wrong hands it can disturb the whole atmosphere and putting a question mark on the credibility of leader.

Monitoring information should be given due importance as it is evident from the discussion that it can make or break a team, As a leader one has lot of information which needs to be released to team members, by keeping in view timing and recipient, to avoid any misunderstanding both factors should be given due importance, Sometimes as a show of superiority, leader releases an information before time to its close aids, those close aids spread it as 'grape wine' to show there closeness with the higher authority. This information could be in the form of finding of disciplinary committee in a case of team member, it could be premature announcement of promotion of a team member or a blunder done by a team member resulting in loses to organisation.

Umpire; Decision making ability is one of the key qualities which a leader is expected to posses with utmost efficiency, correct decision taken with in time frame fills the team members with confidence and guide them in right direction, it has been observed that leaders delay decisions for one reason or the other creating confusion and consuming precious time, even decision about petty things needs to be taken with in appropriate times, one needs to understand two sides of a coin.

Decision about petty things is delayed by decision maker as it is not in their priority list, when decision about small things takes more time than required, then how much time will be taken for important issues in the interest of organisation, small decisions could be about purchasing a separate printer for mechanical engineering department, or finalising conveyance rate after hike in fuel prices or it could be any other matter from which organisation is not affected much but it makes lot of difference to the end user, it is very much in the interest of organisation and self that a leader must developed a decision taking mechanism, which can decide with in given time frame.

Mr. Subhash handles disturbances very quickly and on priority basis by taking appropriate decision, once he receives a complaint from a team member about the cold food being served in the canteen, he immediately called the canteen manager, after enquiring about the whole condition he allocates more space to canteen and adequate manpower to solve the problem.

Development & Diversification; Growth and diversification is top priority in the mind of Subhash who is always busy in making future plans to expand the organisation and very much understands that he is responsible for giving decent returns on the investment made by stake holders, because with the support of these stakeholders organisation is able to receive financial support to run its whole system, their satisfaction is of utmost importance, however people friendly policies we make, these policies are useless if it is not able to make balance approach.

A leader has to make every effort to keep the organisation ahead whether it is by creating a knowledge network and devising a vision, which includes comparison of the product with other competitor's and how to be the best in segment, if already number one then how to remain best in the sector by creating an atmosphere of research, development and innovation, during last quarter business review meeting he set the target of 7% increase in revenue generation for the next financial year and 1% reduction in in overall expenditure, a leader very much understands the difference between **cost cutting and reduction in cost.**

Chief of Happiness: A leader has to be well versed in the role of human resources officer, although every organisation has its separate Human Resources Department, but it is very much required for a leader to have adequate understanding of managing human resources to run organisation smoothly and efficiently for two reasons, first, to make policies in the interest of human asset, which turns out to be in favour of organisation and secondly, not to give free run to human resources department. Recruitment and selection are one of the key functions which leader is expected to do with utmost care, Subhash is also of the view that out of the three Ms (man, machine & money) man is the most important factor who can be trained, moulded, and motivated, manage conflict. A leader in human resources personnel role can think unconventionally, Human resources department keep on making policies how to recognise achievers and give them their dues so that they continue their good performance benefiting team and organisation.

A leader can think about those underperformers who are not being able to give their best because of one reason or the other, with the experience and position s/he can remove road blocks of underperformers and bring them one level up, making exponential change in the life of those professional and in-turn benefiting the organisation and utilising the organisation's human resources in best possible and efficient way.

Next level of human resources activities a leader should involve self is to keep his team intact for longer period, i.e., a leader must make all out effort to retain team members, for a team member getting separated from organisation might be having different reasons such as family, social or personal which are out of control for a leader, but leader must ensure that no team member leaves the organisation due to poor leadership qualities or **boss syndrome**. Leader must make policies keeping in view the age group of all team members by providing them comfortable as well as challenging working atmosphere according to the need of the group and make sure that organisation must have vibrant culture satisfying the need of X, Y & Z generations. Leader must make policies which can cater the varied needs of every team member in the form of health, continuing learning & education, entertainment, socialising &

leisure, working days or hours. No organisation can stop team members from leaving it, but can minimise the attrition rate, and above all every leader must strive towards making organisation such that all team members when unable to come to office misses it.

Not interfering in personal life of team members; While going back in flashback, Subhash recalls how his head of department used to do favours by keeping the personal habits and followings in mind, being strict vegetarian and teetotaller, sitting late in the office etc. and was of the view that a team member who is having those personal preferences & habits as he is, will understand him and match his thinking. Where it is totally different now a days as there is diversified workforce which comes from different geographical, economical and religious background have totally different needs.

Qualities of a good leader; When **Subhash** came to know that one of his team members needs flexible working hours, he immediately allowed him to do so to fulfil his personal obligation, as he was interested in investing time in building relationship patiently without expecting anything in return and help people in achieving their professional goals. Secondly, when he receives a request from one of his team leaders to attend a professional course, he grants him permission for the same by ignoring the negative aspect of that person.

Subhash always recognizes individual's different need, goals & wishes, act accordingly and very well understands that one size does not fit all, lead differently under different circumstances. Whenever he saw some positive qualities in any team member, he points out immediately and encourages that individual to consolidate on that quality, he is always interested in bringing out hidden talent and capabilities of his team members by injecting great amount of enthusiasm and energy to keep motivating others, whether he is communicating on phone or giving verbal instructions he make sure that his words and voice is full of positivity.

When somebody comes to him with a suggestion or complaint Subhash was able to see his view point in all-round perspective and other's perspective as well. Leadership is not about a position, It's an attitude. Identifying challenges by making all out efforts to meet them. Builds trust through behaviour, not through position, command respect not demand respect.

Leaders must develop the strength to ask his team members "please tell me about my performance" I want to give my best, how can I improve upon and become better. A leader is one who is in favour of practicing leadership always decides in favour of organization which is eventually deciding in favour of team members keeping his or her personal interests aside.

Who can be a leader?

I am of the view that every team member can become a leader in its field and team, if we can motivate and expose them to conditions leading to act as a leader, because exhibiting leadership quality is not the job of leader only but of team members as well, secondly it is the job of leader to bring out leadership quality in team members and should not consider them as followers, by considering team members as followers a leader is committing biggest mistake of career. Everybody can be leader in his/her field from CEO to team members, students, it involves enthusiasm, initiative, leading by example, encouraging and appreciation, respect for words, knowing your job well, healthy mentality & approach, **decision taking and making**.

Deletion at leader's level: When a Leader starts its new journey after being elevated from the role of a team leader, in order to execute the responsibility of new role s/he must be ready to elevate his thinking ability and action taking to the next level as well, because a leader's job bear absolute different responsibility from that of a team leader, after assuming the role of a leader, a professional who wants to succeed in the assigned role has to open the drawing board, re-write activities and purpose of new role by acknowledging what not to do by totally deleting those activities from his list of actions, best action would be by taking a paper pencil test and erase the unwanted clutter from the past to reconstruct the path you have chosen for new destination and avoid those common mistakes which every average performing CEO has made.

Skills to be developed at leader's level ; At every level of corporate sector one needs specific skills to meet individual and organisational goals, so is the case of Leader, Leader needs to move ahead of those practices which they used to do during their previous role, one has to increase the radius of thinking and horizon, during previous role a leader's thoughts and actions were limited to benefit and save the interest of team only, now each and every employee is your team member from Janitor to vice-president, one must make policies and rules keeping in view the interest of the organisation.

Mentoring ; At leaders level, mentoring is one of the important task which a leader must perform with great deal of satisfaction and interest because mentoring is a job responsibility which is not forced or part of job description, but it is taken by a leader voluntarily in the interest of organisation and team member, it requires time & energy secondly, it is non-measurable and non-mentioned, non-mentioned means, it is not mentioned by organisation during review of one's performance, nor it is recognised by mentee at that time, both organisation and mentee thinks that mentor is doing it for its own benefit but after measuring and observing the result of mentoring, things comes out in favour of mentor who is selflessly acting in the interest of organisation.

Doing more than required; A leader becomes leader in true terms when he understands that merely doing what is required is not enough to sustain the organisation, that is the job of manager, if one wants to be a leader just achieving targets and earning profits will not establish an individual as a leader, a leader has to do more than required in terms of providing better platform for team members to grow so that all the team members are attached emotionally and socially to team & organisation, when team members observe that they are being treated as assets rather than resource, a feel good factor and sense of belongingness surrounds them and transferred to their home and society in turn. A leader must adopt management approach which along with bringing results gives lasting satisfaction to team members.

Getting into the trench; One of the most important things which gives a team member happier moment is finding his leader by his side during difficult time with the folded sleeves, when ever a team member is struggling, s/he expects seniors to guide and show the right way. Leader is not expected to be present every where, but he can easily find out where his presence will boost the morale of the individual or team. Just by asking for progress report of the project will do limited service to the organisation and team, it will be better if a leader becomes an active factor of progress report, being an active factor of progress report helps to create an atmosphere of participation, in this atmosphere leader gets out of air-conditioned cabin and get into 'trench'.

Youth fullness at leader's level. Being youthful is one of the top requirements of a leader, youthful here does not mean radiant skin and smooth joints, why I am mentioning one of the 'topmost requirement', because one has to fine tune self with the team and now a days 70-80% of a team is in the age group of 25-35 years, it is very necessary for a team to consider a leader among one of them for free flow of communication and healthy working atmosphere, A leader must be flexible in thinking so as to think like an entry level executive while talking to one and mould self as per the need of the hour when dealing with team leader.

Leadership qualities for Team Leader:

If a leader is father figure of the organization, then a team leader has to play the role of elder brother which means protecting and developing its team members with a vision and pro-action. An organisation can move ahead and remain in tune with time only if it develops leadership at every stage. An organisation must understand that if it has to survive, leadership qualities need to be spread from top to bottom. If an organisation assume that the responsibility of practising leadership is of CEO/COO only then it is on wrong track. A team leader who is in direct touch with the human assets of organisation and society in turn, all efforts of a team leader must revolve around the development of team as s/he is involved and working with future of the company, seriousness and knowledge about his role as team leader will have long lasting impact on 'Trichual'. Secondly, a team leader must remember the kind of behaviour team members like or dislike so that they can adopt or discard the practices accordingly, first by making a rapport with team members by guiding towards leading themselves, and to provide a secured working atmosphere to those who are giving their best. As a team leader one has to use less technical skills and more human skills, if your team members are doing their job happily and finding it more meaningful will result in long lasting success.

Creating Happy Hours. A team leader's job is to keep his team happy and motivated, for which an experienced team leader has to take some off beat routes to recharge team on regular basis, one of the steps is by creating happy hours during duty hours. The idea of **'happy hour'** comes into the mind of a team leader when he was sitting and enjoying his tea in his favourite corner and escaping time. He thought why it can't be done in a professional set up. Why can't we sit in the office and discuss no work during happy hour, we will be talking about only about our family, topic of interests of team members or social changes or gossip about our daily life but not work, over a cup of coffee or tea.

Skills to developed at Team leader's level. Having accepted the role of team leader there are certain skills which needs to be worked out, working independently and conflict resolving are two most important activities which a team leader must master.

A team leader is the one who has to deliver most by taking orders from top management and co-operation plus collaboration from team members, team leader is a bridge sometimes and sandwich sometimes, bridge when things are moving in right direction and sandwich when things are not moving so smoothly.

In order to excel in the desired field and perform duties & responsibilities in efficient manner a team leader must develop the art of working independently and master his skills for the desired role, which includes the most important trait that is being a thorough professional & expert in domain, being well equipped in dealing with challenges associated with domain not only gives confidence but also helps in earning the respect of team members as well, if a team leader is not able to handle the problems or challenges of domain, s/he looses credibility and many rumours plus doubts starts circulating in corridor, which makes little difficult for team members to accept orders & suggestions from team leader, and above all one has to depend on team members for execution of any task or preparation of any report. Keeping in view the above points in mind a team leader must have an edge over other team members in terms of knowledge of domain.

Second most important role a team leader has to play is of **conflict resolver,** in a team there are different types of people, some are interested in the betterment of team whereas some are interested in their own well being, few are interested in creating road blocks for others while few are knowingly or unknowingly creating road blocks for themselves, now we know that configuration of a team is very complex, it is not as simple as it is visible from outside, a team's complexity can be experienced or observed only when one is part of that team during the execution of a project.

Real problem occurs when team members are not aware that there behaviour is harming the interest of team and not allowing the team to move forward, these team players are just acting as per their 'nature', which is creating conflict among them and halting their progress, Now the role of team leader comes into picture who has to 'know' and understand the nature & approach of every team member and guide them towards right direction by using different tools of management, a team leader needs to look into conflict by different angles which may be behavioural, political, economical, institutional or sometimes social as well. It is very necessary for a team leader to handle conflict for success and smooth functioning of team with out which all other efforts go in vain.

Deletion at Team leader's Level: When a team member becomes team leader, s/he should keenly observe the changes he has to make to execute the responsibilities which comes with new role, s/he has to understand what he doesn't have to do, what he has to delete from his menu to make this journey a successful one, to complete a journey it is not necessary to move in straight line some times one has to take **U-turn** to reach the destination.

A team member after assuming the role of a team leader should delete all those actions from his working style which his previous team leader used to practice and was the reason for that team leader's average performance and downfall thereafter. It is not necessary that one becomes team leader after promotion with in current team one might have to switch job to become team leader, in that case one has to delete those misfit activities which are not in tune with the culture of present organisation, age group and demography.

Youthfulness at Team leader's level. It is great boon if team leader is blessed with the quality of youthfulness, being youthful helps a team leader to move away from rigidity to openness, youthfulness promotes burden sharing among his team members and is symbol of open mind which accepts new ideas and implement them with joint responsibility, an open mind is prone to take constructive criticism feed in a sporting manner or introduce some unconventional way of handling a difficult situation. A team leader's every effort should be to raise the level of performance of team members, for example if one of his team members is performing at the lowest level a team leader must make an effort to bring h/her to next level and create a working atmosphere to retain top level performer. A team leader's effort should be to improve and change self, his efforts should be to upgrade self from manger x to manager y. along with self s/he should make efforts to move team members upwards, from category D to category C to Category B and make every effort to retain Category A,

Scenario; Angad during daily round of his department observed that Niranjan is not looking in his usual mood, he picks up fight with any one on the drop of a hat, Angad decided to act immediately as to avoid any major loss. He called Niranjan into his office and tries to find out the reason behind his changed behaviour, if anything can be done from organization's side, When Niranjan told him that he is facing some problem from family side and could not take leave as all his leaves have been consumed, Angad counselled him and advised him to apply for advance leave, he will recommend it and even if he has to take leave without pay will result in saving his job. Angad, the team leader does not want to lose a team member whose past record was good and was trained at the expenses of organisation, Angad's timely intervention has saved one good employee from leaving the organisation, this scenario also depicts Angad's flexible approach.

Transferring knowledge and sharing Experience; A team leader should be interested in transferring the knowledge and sharing of experiences s/he had gained over the years, this will benefit as double sided sword which will cut his problems into pieces, first benefit will be he is making team members independent and commanding respect, when you make your team members less dependent on you, gives more time for improvement, innovation and learning, because his presence is not required at ground zero every time. By sharing experiences, a team leader is exposing team members to a situation well enough before they encounter it, they are ready for what could happen best or what could be the worst scenario if they take or do not take this step.

Scenario; In every job or process there is something which requires extra attention and if utmost care is not taken in that process, will result in financial loss to the organisation, there were two team leaders in billing department of a multinational giant's department, one was 'A' and another was 'B', 'A' was interested in keeping some tricky process with himself and 'B' took non-conventional and modern management process by training team members about those tricky process.

In this international billing key factor was to include taxes as per international laws and exchange rate of foreign currency at that point of time, now whenever team members of team leader 'A' require any clarification regarding billing and taxation, they rushed to the cabin of 'A', this keeps 'A' very satisfied as he sees himself as real contributor to the process. Whereas team leader 'B' knowing this tricky problem will waste lot of time, takes a proactive measure by conducting three training sessions to make team members familiar with the procedure. This resulted in availability of some extra time available for team leader 'B', which he utilises in developing self and helping seniors as and when required.

Decision Making; A leader must make his team independent of taking decision in h/her absence or other words a team leader must empower the team to take decisions about small things in h/her absence, when team becomes self reliant a lot of time is saved and trust is developed which is the most important by-product of independent decision making, best thing a team leader can do is to make team member practice mock drill in h/her presence which is the example of genuine intention of making them independent in running the show, it could be ordering any material required or seeking any help from higher management for any other unforeseen situation. Having confident and trusted team members will have dual benefit, one side is helping team members to grow into confident leaders not only for team but for whole organisation as well and another side helps in reducing the stress for the team leader by being confident that s/he has left behind a reliable team which can handle difficult situation on its own.

Punish wrong doer; As a team leader is expected to award good behaviour, he is also expected to punish wrong doer or if he is not able to punish, at least he/she should not favour or reward wrong doer. If all team members knows that any toxic or wrong doer will not be rewarded or go unpunished, they will have complete faith in the working style of team leader and follow the instructions with more enthusiasm. Not punishing the wrong doer or lingering on the decision to take appropriate action will create a rift among team members, its effect starts spoiling slowly the good work done to keep every body together.

Scenario; Here I would like to mention very true incident which really baffled me. During one of my previous assignments when a team member was not co-operating and taking leave without information, I inform my team leader about the behaviour and losses we are incurring. My boss thinks about a while and permit me to issue a written warning letter, and after four months when the result of annual appraisal was displayed, I was very sure that no increment will be given to him or he will be demoted to my utter surprise that guy was promoted to the next level, which really puts my moral to the lowest level.

Share credit as you distribute work; When we care for some body, we share most of our things and time, similarly in a corporate set up if we want to show our team that we care, we distribute work equally and when it comes to sharing credit most of the team leaders tries to take full credit for the job done, when team leaders present themselves as 'solo actor' or the only executer of target achieved. This practice pulls the team down and members started feeling demotivated.

It is not possible for every contributor to attend presentation ceremony or to be on stage, but it is the responsibility of team leader to give due recognition to its team through every possible means or mode. It may be through writing personal e-mail, giving them certificate of appreciation or having a small get together and making announcement for the same. In the absence of proper recognition team members will not be able to give their best, they won't do it intentionally but as basic human nature we need motivation to keep moving.

Leadership qualities for team member;

     When a team member entered corporate setup, how she or he wants to behave or which path s/he wants to take, decides about his future, whether s/he is interested in shortcut and easy path or correct path supported by learning & thirsty for knowledge by doing things in right way, First and foremost quality is expected from an entry level team member is to act as a leader in its domain or in other words she or he is supposed to lead self, whenever any obstacle comes in the way, s/he should take it as a learning opportunity and get its course corrected, s/he can ask self how can I improve myself as a good team member how can I remove my shortcomings in the interest of Trichual, (self, team and organisation).

Skills to be developed at team member's level; A young team member is the energy behind every organisation, without this energy organisations can not move a bit, every young team member must understand that completing the assigned task is the first step they take towards a bright career, their first step along with themselves also moves the team and organisation in forward direction. To keep this energy flowing in right direction every team member is expected to have certain skills or develop those skills for a bright future. Let us discuss those skills one by one.

Meet deadlines & produce quality work; As we all know that corporate sector runs on results and outcome of the job assigned, team member is that brick which makes the foundation of team and organisation strong. During early years of career an individual team member makes not only the foundation of team & organisation but in the process starts making foundation for self, they should give adequate importance to the responsibility assigned which is very much required for meeting deadlines and producing quality work.

All good practices, culture and policies goes into drain if the organisation is not able to earn profit and diversify, not earning profit in monetary terms will stagnate the whole system. Because money is like blood if it keeps on running in veins, every part of the organisation is revitalised, and for money to keep running every part has to perform in efficient manner and every individual has to give its best to make their team and organisation best.

Coachable and good mentee.; During the early stages of career a professional is just passed out of college and suffering from 'I know all' syndrome, which creates roadblocks in career path, all of us have some or the other drawbacks which needs to be fixed in the interest of the team and self, a team member must understand that nobody is complete and every fault or shortcoming can be overcome with the help of seniors and colleagues.

A team member must develop a positive outlook towards being corrected and coached, must listen and follow carefully what coach or mentor are saying, being coachable and good mentee opens up new avenues which may not be open to other team members, coach and mentor are senior members of the squad or group when they find any body dependable, they open up and share the recipe of successful corporate life, coach-coachee & mentor-mentee make relationship which lasts life long, as things exchanged are intangible and indestructible such as efforts, resilience, knowledge plus experience sharing etc.

Co-operative & Collaborative; A young team member can get what ever s/he wants, getting into any group of liking and connect with any team member, if she or he learns the difference between co-operation and competition and understand that in which situation he has to compete or co-operate, if one choose competition over co-operation for a particular situation, it should be the path of healthy competition only and nothing hidden approach, benefit of co-operation & collaboration is win-win situation for both i.e., who co-operates and who gets co-operation.

Co-operative team member is respected by everyone because instead of competing s/he decided to co-operate, It also indicates the presence of strength and sets the tone for future chain reaction of moving along each other rather than moving against each other, I have used word 'strength' which means one has to start by being giving co-operation before taking any favour in advance, it is a selfless activity and pro-action for any future professional need and cultivate strong relationship with team leader and other team members, building reputation of collaborator a team member sets himself apart from herd.

Deletion at Team Member's level. When in the beginning of career, every team member has been told to do this and that to move ahead on desired path, but nobody told them what not to do, what needs to be deleted from their daily routine and their thoughts, when we delete some useless activity or thought we pave the way for meaningful activities and thoughts to be added, by creating a space for positive things makes one a better professional, it could be any re-occurring negative thoughts or any un-productive habit or activity which is holding you back.

At the beginning of career, they have to delete one thing that is 'distraction', ability to distract 'Distraction' is the key in the process of growing up, one has to identify what distracts, it could be addiction to an old hobby or habit of laziness, unhealthy daily routine, it could be thoughts in your mind which is obstructing your progress or well being, delete thoughts responsible for holding you back. By deletion you make space for things which could be added for smooth sailing.

Youthfulness at Team Member's level; All team members during their early stage of professional beginning are young in terms of age, but merely by being young in terms of age is not the criteria for a young professional, one has to be young in terms of behaviour and approach towards their profession as well, being youthful also calls for applying one's own independent thinking for learning.

Being youthful can be summed up in following points. Taking joint responsibility of any mistake is the best sign of being youthful, when we are working in a team it is in our interest to be accountable as a whole team, because mistake is done by one team member but loss is born by whole team, being youthful at team member level sow the seed for future leader, owning your mistake is one of the best signs of sincerity which also indicates that a professional is interested in correcting the mistake rather than hiding it under the carpet, one more aspect of owning a mistake is ready to learn from it and not repeating it in future, which makes a team member remains young forever irrespective of age.

Being a social animal; As we all know that humans are social animal, acting as social animal during professional hours also reduces lot of working stress and create a healthy working environment for which one of the best tool is 'humour', if we can laugh with our colleagues over a silly matter or on our selves without any reason, believe me dear readers you are young irrespective of your age, this quality will bring many memorable moments during very demanding professional atmosphere.

Your ability to turn your colleagues into friends and by making healthy relationship with each other helps a professional in a long way, as most team members are of same age there is no better way but to build a healthy personal relationship by visiting each other's house, celebrating festivals, birthdays and anniversaries together, babysitting for each other's children goes a long way in making a relationship stronger, which remains alive after separation from organisation and throughout the life.

Open mindedness; A young team member should have an open mind which is ready to give and happy to take new ideas, thus doubling the assets available in the form of knowledge and expertise, doubling happens when two team members give one-one to each other it becomes two for each one, where every team member is not only giving its best possible effort but sharing its knowledge and accepting others expertise also in related field. As a young professional you will witness different scenarios and situations first time, for this either you have to give your expertise or take advice for solving or negotiating a situation, in both cases you need courage and confidence to keep your mind open like a parachute which works only when it is open.

Loyalty; A team member's first love should be h/her department, whether it is engineering, procurement, administration, Marketing or sales, you should feel proud in working for your department by making all efforts to keep the flag of your department flying high, working in the interest of department should always be the prime moto, during office hours how can I make my department better, to be in healthy competition with other teams & departments and win, if lose than prepare to fight and win in next round always keep your 'PALTAN' on top.

Initiate, innovate and spend extra time for departments progress, find different way of doing the same process efficiently, never allow anybody else to make mockery of your department, because it is due to this department you are in this organisation, make this department the shining star of organisation. Make it visible on your chest and infectious by attracting other departments to follow working for their departments, remember organisation itself is nothing, it is made up of small departments only these departments if works efficiently can bring glory and take organisation to top.

Healthy practices; Early stages of career of a team member is time to choose how you are going to live your professional life forever, by practicing positivity and living by principles followed by ethical practices, or merely keep on doing the things required for surviving in your job and spending life in the shadow of that, or by following & observing the finer aspect of life by blending it with professional life, finer aspects of human life is positivity, cheerfulness, healthy mentality, respect for knowledge and above all good behaviour, which encourages to greet & handshake with every team member whether it is in the corridor or parking.

In this case always remember one thing that honesty is still the best policy and will remain forever. During education or joining an organisation you might have been told about unfair treatment, politics or partiality going on in this organisation, but all these things are not in practice at all under one roof, there might any one of those negative things being in practice, first observe then decide, never believe in gossips, remember whoever is proficient in his task is never disturbed by any wrong practice.

Leadership qualities for students; During student life an individual has to lead nobody but self, leading self during student life means not losing the sight of your goal. Leadership can be understood & developed by students by being a keen observer and thoughtful individual, it is the way taken by an individual during studentship decide one's future, this is the time when an individual decide the path s/he is going to follow, whether s/he is inclined towards right path or the one which takes short and easy one, student must try to find meaning and character of life, once as a student you realise the importance of motivation and discipline half of your battle is won and other half by taking appropriate action to meet the desired results, this can be achieved by knowing that life is very precious and would like to spent it by accepting meaningful living and finer aspect of life, not a meagre one.

After having gone through above it must be clear that a student's journey towards being a leader or a follower begins 'now', as we and only we are responsible for our life and its effect on our loved ones and society in turn, it's advisable to unfold the mystery of life. During student time an individual has two means to deal with a situation first is through being wise and second one is through being clever. A wise choice is always full of strength and long lasting where as being clever leads to shortcut and temporary arrangements. Same can be understood by following scenario.

Scenario; Ramesh paid his full attention towards scoring more marks and prepares only 60% of syllabus as a strategic decision because he was aware of the pattern of question paper. Whereas Ajay taking wise route tries to be not selective but learn & understands maximum of the syllabus as he knows that good grades along with knowledge of the subject is equally important for a good professional career. When results were declared both Ramesh and Ajay were in the same bracket in terms of grades, but during campus placement interview things were totally different, on the basis of his knowledge Ajay was able to secure good offers from prestigious MNCs and Ramesh due to selective approach towards knowledge has to compromise in terms of offers during placement drive.

Wise choices; Students must understand that nothing happens overnight or by chance, one has to work tirelessly and with great amount of zeal for long-lasting results, anything which happens overnight or by chance is short-lived and temporary. To get things happen in desired direction one must strive towards goal with discipline and positive energy.

Coming back to clever versus wise choices, clever choices will give you temporary pleasure whereas wise choices will bring permanent happiness, one of the most important parts of student life is choosing your company **wisely** which will save you from lot of problems, helps you achieve target and realise your dream, choosing your company **cleverly** bring with itself lot of trouble resulting in wastage of time and deviation from goal. During student life one starts exploring goal of life and came to know that an individual's prime goal is to be happy and enjoy best gift of nature called 'LIFE'. If state of happiness can be achieved by merely pretending it, then everybody would be happy but to be happy one requires lot of discipline, sacrifice and sincerity towards his/her goal, as a student you are not alone, so many human aspirations are attached with it. So, use your wisdom to chose whatever action you are going to take during student life.

Own Director; By keeping in view the above it is suggested that a student must become own 'director' instead of looking here and there for guidance, one must learn to direct self towards the set goals, directing self is a learning process as we introduce ourselves to different & difficult situations, we gain confidence and prepared to handle any unknown situation, in our life there will be numerous occasions when we have to encounter a situation for the first time. **This life is a gift of nature to all of us, what we craft out of it is our return gift to nature,** this most precious gift cannot be allowed to drift aimlessly and without purpose.

Scenario; one must be reading so many articles in social media & magazines describing **'YLOO'** (you live only once) moments, it can be filling your bucket list, tasting exotic food & wines or visiting any place which others don't dare to go or doing some thing which others could not even think of doing it before. But to my astonishment 'YLOO' moment has been defined in terms of mundane and temporary things but actually it is **'WLD'** (we live daily), WLD or living daily is not a moment it is 'movement' which has permanent effect on us. leadership for students begins when they start understanding WLD and feel the preciousness and exotic flavour of life.

It is wise to be your own 'director', when we chose to be our own director, we start learning things which are important for directing self with **lights, camera & action.** light here means our inner light which we lit when we see something new or challenging situation. our inner light paved the way to see us through. and meet that challenge. Camera, yes, we have the best camera built in our body i.e., our eyes, our in-built camera should be looking for meaningful activities, or something new which we have not seen it before, always looking for something meaningful and capture it for future use. Now comes the execution part which is incomplete without action, that we have decided to do what is signalled by our 'light and camera'.

Deletion at students' level: To move ahead in life a student has been told too often to add this and that, but a student who wants to move ahead in life needs to delete few things as well which will lighten his baggage and help to move ahead in life and must understand what is holding back, it could be spending time on wasteful activity, continuing wrong habits from childhood resulting in loss of resources and relationship. Deletion of a habit is very much required as it will make space for good habit and pave the way for success. When a student decided to delete one bad habit, s/he form the base for understanding that if any change has to be made, it requires tough state of mind and sacrifice to be disciplined, without sacrifice and pain no improvement is possible.

Youthfulness at student's level.; Students are young by the chronicle age, but students also need to be young by mental age as well, flexibility of mind and in learning new concepts with interest is the key. Youthfulness at student's level means they should be like a tree flexible enough to dodge any storm, here flexibility means ability to change, as soon as you see something is not happening according to your need or harming your interest one must try to find out the correct way out.

During student life one thing which represents youthfulness is curious mind, a curious mind will look in to each new topic or theorem with the positive lens, considering it a challenge not a problem. A curious mind will turn a problem into challenge by weighing pros and cons of it and find more pros than cons, during student life one must develop curious mind which decides in favour of action by accepting the challenge, not defeated by problem. Curiosity will take you to look into new topic or theorem as stepping stone towards next level and will help you think with different angles, resulting in independent thinking which in turn gives you the eyes to see the positive side of everything. Curiosity paves the way for seeing and observing the things one step further.

Scenario; Rakesh during his teenage was very active on social media, he regularly watched so many posts, memes and reels on his social media account making mockery of education, importance of education was undermined by pop singers, actors and stand-up comedians etc. Rakesh being curious and keen observer of situation he continued observing the things sincerely, he was amazed to see that most of social media artists and influencers have performing life of approximately 5-7 years, due to cut throat competition new entrants takes over the stage and cycle keeps on moving like this, only few who were educated and taken up these professions after seriously accomplishing something in the form of education and corporate life could withstand the competition, educated professional can handle the stress of failure in a matured way and take up any other profession as per the qualification they posses, where as when un-educated fails and don't have any other option to earn a decent livelihood, resorts to drug smuggling, alcohol abuse or commits crime to remain in the fray, Having seen this situation Rakesh decided to give due importance to education irrespective of reading false and poor quality articles glorifying those short-lived careers.

Skills to be developed at students' level.

Respect for knowledge; We should always strive for up gradation of self by looking to learn something new and expanding our horizons, leaving our comfort zone behind and having interest in knowing what is happening around the world (current affairs), what is the financial deficit, export-import, foreign currency rates (economics), different culture & societies of the world (social), similarities and differences between various religions, We should always have our own viewpoint during any discussion and the courage to correct ourselves. Respect for knowledge leads from being clever to wise.

If you want me to name one thing which students should focus during their education always have respect for their education institute, teachers and peers irrespective of backgrounds they are from. Students must ask themselves, as a flag bearer of country what is expected of them, as a responsible member of society how s/he can bring change or make things better with the help of programme s/he has enrolled for.

Mock Decision Making; One very interesting thing a student can do is to develop mock decision making about activities, incidents or situations happening around, **example;** if one of the friends is not selected in college football team despite of being very good at playing football, one can think and tries to find out the reason behind his non-inclusion in team after thinking for some times you came to know that there were two contenders for centre half position but team can chose only one centre half and other player must have been better, earlier you were judging the selection committee as biased, but after thinking you came to a conclusion which has given you different angle to think.

Importance of thinking; A student must make continuous efforts to develop thinking ability, thinking is that tunnel which had hidden treasures beyond one's imagination, we don't know what we receive once we reached at the end of this tunnel, then we find out that there is no end to this charismatic tunnel which has the capacity to give us endless gifts, not in the form of precious metals but in the form of ideas how to create these precious metals, thinking will help a student to compare self with others and their conditions, ability to think is that one quality which has gifted every inventions and discoveries to this world, even if some of inventions and discoveries happened by chance but researchers & inventors were thinking and acting how to solve a problem, instead they get solution for other problem, ability to think longer than others make them stick to a problem and solve it.

When thinking is considered as a positive trait then mind is not tired by it, whereas when it is not taken as that much seriously, mind give away sooner. Thinking will not allow you to settle down for meagre results it will make you to think "when others can do this, why can't I". It will take you towards magical trio of 'when, how and why' and will make you distinguish from taking short-term benefits to more long sustaining one, by differentiating between 'glitter and gold', the most important thing 'thinking' will do is to find out the stuff required to be a leader and start preparation for it, During student life what a student can do is to understand the difference between leader or follower and decide what s/he wants to be, s/he must develop the qualities of a leader and lead self towards a bright future by start thinking like a leader and practice it.

Thinking has one more aspect, thinking in all directions means including past, present and future, it has been observed that many philosophers and researchers are propagating the theory of "living in present", which only tells you the one-third of picture, picture is completed only if we include other two-third i.e. past and future as well, because all 'three' sides of a coin called life are inter-connected and will have its full value only if past, present and future are given equal importance, learning from past, action in present and planning for future.

Importance of Preparation; Shakshi who is studying in 12th standard of CBSE board has to appear in her final exams next month, she was sitting in front of her study table and thinking about how to get best grades, she goes back to her mid-term exam by introspecting and found that few steps she has to take to improve upon her previous grades is to practice more & more on rough sheets, because during mid-term exams, main reason for her below expectation performance was her inability to produce answers on sheets in spite of knowing it, she immediately took out her rough register and started practicing theories, theorems and diagrams of different topics & subjects.

During student life one must be watching or observing the progress of few students in cultural activities, sports or studies, why few students are ahead of others and bring laurels to their team, college & parents as they get same resources in terms of time & materials and above all taught by same teachers, some students are far behind from others, only reason I can find out is that they give due importance to preparation for event or subject before participation. Winners prepare whole heartedly before entering final round, do mock activities or exercises and secured winner's podium.

Self-Discipline; Amit has taken admission in B.Tech. programme in one of the top rated institutes of country, today is the first day of the programme and institute has arranged induction class in auditorium which is going to be conducted by one of the best soft skills training institute, Mr. Kapil who is going to conduct class is well renowned faculty for the same, he during motivational lecture told many stories & incidents related to motivation and tell students how to remain focussed towards their goal and aim.

All the students were very much satisfied by the appropriate beginning of the programme, went to their hostel rooms with full of energy and positivity, started planning about current semester, making study schedule as per time-table and following it for next few days, but after few days all schedules were derailed.

Amit could not follow time-table prepared by self, he tries to find out the reason by discussing it with his teacher, his teacher sensibly discussed the matter and told him that you can be guided towards right path but you have to walk on it on your own, and for that you requires only one thing that is self-discipline. A self-disciplined student is very successful in learning and achieving the goal. Now Amit understands that motivation helps us to decide the path, but to continue walking on the desired path we need continuous dose of self-discipline.

Taking responsibility of their action. Students must take action & decision while thinking as a leader and make themselves accountable for the result, must aim high and try to reach highest level in which ever field they are interested in, dream high and think big. 'Reach for the moon, if you do not get it, you will land up on stars. Every student must know that in which ever conditions s/he is, can be improved upon from here onwards and make the impossible possible, a student may come from weak economical background, without family support or with average IQ, can realise h/her dream and achieve set target provided s/he is able to understand h/her priorities because **'Knowledge don't discriminate'.**

Scenario; During his SSB interview, Captain Manoj Pandey recipient of Param Veer Chakra (Posthumously) and one of the heroes of Kargil war, was asked by Services Selection Board interview panel 'Why you want to join army? He immediately replied that he wants to win Param Veer Chakra, and he went on to win Param Veer Chakra. Confidence level of young boy coming from small town of UP was so great that, he realised his dream at the first opportunity he got by sacrificing self.

Leaders are born or nurtured; Researches have shown that 80% of leadership growth derives from experiences on the life job, 20% can be acquired through training & study. We can turn our managers into leaders by giving them adequate training, exposure, freedom, encouragement, appreciation, responsibility etc.

One very appropriate anecdote can be mentioned here to support this theory, A delegation from a foreign country reached very famous city as part of their tour, during felicitation ceremony, head of delegation asked mayor "Can you please name few great leaders born in this city. Mayor replied back, "No great leader was born in this city, only infants are born and they become great leaders by choosing their path and achieving their goal".

Leader or Leadership; Leaders are situational effective whereas leadership is culturally specific, we should always have a culture promoting leadership qualities because an organization should take a long-term view. Leadership is an attitude and choice as you develop a positive attitude towards leader you choose to behave and act as leader

Personality

Definition; Personality of an individual is defined by how s/he behaves or react to people, things or circumstances, every individual is different from other. We all are gifted in a unique way by nature, it is our privilege to discover our own special light without comparing self with any other individual. When we compare ourself with others we not only do in-justice to ourself but also lower down our self-esteem and other achievements.

Fresh Approach; In the above paragraph I had tried to define the traditional meaning of 'Personality' in addition to the above we can consider a new approach to the definition and meaning of a good personality, In my views a good personality is one who behave well with self, I am deviating little bit from traditional or conventional definition of personality and there is a reason, having observed all the good and successful personalities, first step those great personalities took is improving by working upon self, being disciplined and doing what is liked by themselves, once you behave well with self you are attracted toward good manners, etiquettes and a disciplined life.

As a kid I along with my family used to go to watch movies in an open-air theatre near my residence in cantonment area, in movies when hero entered with a bang or get out of his car and camera showing his stylish costume and well polished shoes, was really a very thrilling experience.

When I grow up a little and hear my father's friend discussing about one of their colleague's nature and habits by acknowledging that 'he is a good personality', suddenly picture of that hero flashed in my mind who cannot do anything wrong, after few years I really came to know about the real meaning of personality.

One of the good personalities was my father and his colleagues, with whom I have spent most of leisure time, were always decently dressed and worked in favour of their organization, accepting their mistakes with open heart and ready to learn from it, solving a conflict without hurting any side, speaking when it really matters, keeping silence when words are not required, accepting their ignorance about any issue, which they are not aware of, Its not the story of my father only it is the story of everybody's father.

I was highly impressed by my team leader during my first job in corporate sector, whenever I needed guidance or support he is always there to help me, he always took responsibility of what he and his team is doing, and above all when I met my housekeeper on the floor I was highly impressed by his style of working, he always gave his hundred percent and if any staff member points out at any spot not attended by him, he immediately says sorry and rush to clean that spot. There is always a positive feeling while working with my team members every one of them is ready to help others professionally and personally, another one is always ready to submit personal benefits in the interest of team. As a keen observer and having gone through above mentioned experiences, I was able to differentiate between real heroes and reel heroes.

After having spent first thirteen years of my career in corporate sector, I joined the Indian Spinal Injuries Centre's education wing as Administrative Officer in August 2007 and came across one of the best human being and great personalities of all time and that great personality was non other than our Chairman Maj. H.P.S. Ahluwalia, Arjun Award & Padma Vibhushan award winner, taking round of the hospital on his battery driven motorized wheel chair, I was really amazed that how a person on wheel chair was able to win so many awards.

Then during my professional association of thirteen years and eight months with the institute I came to know about the very inspiring history and story of Maj. H.P.S. Ahluwalia.

Most of the incidents and stories were told by the legend himself mostly on first day of every year, as there was all-employees gathering in auditorium to start the new year with positivity and festivity. Major Ahluwalia used to tell one story every time that is how this big and one of the best hospitals was build, before telling this story he also tells us that those who have already heard this story might get bored, but this is for the new team members who have joined our organisation and to inspire them to "summit their mind". Story sounds like this Major Ahluwalia's first love was his profession (Army) and second love was mountaineering, Indian government plans an expedition to summit mount Everest in 1965, Major Ahluwalia was one of the team members of the expedition, he summited mount Everest on 29th May 1965. There were many incidents and stories told by Major Ahluwalia from formation of team to summiting mount Everest, coming back to history and story of Indian Spinal Injuries Centre taking shape and coming into picture.

Major Ahluwalia received bullet injury in his spine during October 1965 war with Pakistan and was paralyzed below waist and sent to United Kingdom for treatment during his stay, one thought keeps on recurring in his mind that, is to have similar or better treatment facility in India for the ailments related to spine as there was inadequate facility in our country for the treatment of paraplegics.

He came back to India and started thinking about how to move ahead with his plan to establish best hospital for the treatment of spinal injuries patient. He discussed the plans with one of his friends, who got the meeting fixed with Prime minister of Italy, Prime minister of Italy was convinced and provided financial support for the project which gave concrete shape to the dream project and was commissioned on First of October 1997.

Now the question arises what is great about this, everybody in this world thinks of doing something for himself and takes steps to execute the plan, but greatness about Major Ahluwalia was when he was undergoing treatment in England, he was not only fighting to survive but he was thinking of providing same quality of facility & treatment for patients to his fellow countrymen, He selflessly made efforts to realize his dream and bring this world class facility available for our country and its citizens.

One more real time story which has removed many doubts about the meaning and definition of good personality, five years back in my neighbourhood one small shop was opened by a young boy named 'Rajkumar', he has taken that 6' X 4' corner shop on rent and started selling Chinese street food chow Mein, Manchurian, chili paneer, after some times he added honey chili potatoes and fried rice to his menu, his food was very tasty, liked by whole colony, our family and particularly by my son who often used to call him and ordered the Chinese food delivered at our home, this continuous for two years and after some times it was closed down, when I asked my son about the whereabout of his 'dear friend' Rajkumar, he told me that 'Rajkumar' had gone to his native place as his family has been wiped out in continuous rain and flood few weeks back, I felt bad and express my sadness about the incident and got busy in my daily routine. Last year in December when I came back from office there was familiar smell of Chinese food on dining table, I asked my son about the source of the food in dinner, he told me that 'Rajkumar' has **come back** from his native village after one and a half year and overcoming his personal and financial losses, had opened Chinese take-away outlet in a rented shop near by our house. I could not resist meeting him to admire for his courage & faith in life and the motto "life must go on". During our meeting one more development came into the picture that he came to Delhi in search of livelihood with rupees 150/- in his pocket and start working as helper on a roadside Dhaba without any salary but only food was given in place of any monetary benefits.

My head bow down in respect to two extreme personalities displaying "never say die" spirit.

What is the need of Personality Development?

We need good personality to meet our professional and personal growth requirements and to live in harmony with ourselves, keep pace with time, realize our full potential and excel in whatever we do. As a good personality a human being play different roles to serve the assigned responsibility.

Who can have good personality?

Any individual can have good personality which s/he has to carved out from his or her nature, a good personality is chiselled out of one's nature by observing and understanding the shape and ingredients required. Anybody can have good personality irrespective of age, traits, economic, social & cultural background. Personality can be nurtured and the beauty of human life is that we can start from this very moment only a strong intention and resolution is required with Intention to improve every day bit by bit and make effort to make our lives effortless by changing ourselves from within. Best thing about human being is the ability to think, control thoughts and act accordingly.

Having a good personality takes us from being merely qualified to educated one, from being in bond to liberated one, give meaning to life, to understand finer aspect of it and to live in harmony with self & others, move from negative to positive thinking. Ready to face any challenge and see life from new approach. To attain knowledge about self and clarity about the purpose in the set of things. Intention to have good personality slowly unfolds the mystery of life which make us understand the why and how of things and our weaknesses so that we can work on it. A person intended to have good personality often ask self. How could I know, what I don't know?

While writing this book I was trying to find out the meaning and definition of good personality and what are the main ingredients of it, throughout my twenty seven years of professional experience, there is one permanent feature of good personality is presence and display of inner strength, inner strength does not come automatically with the human body one has to choose it by observing and watching it in others and our surroundings, when we observe keenly we find out how the individuals with good personality are behaving, under which situation they are reacting or ignoring, as a particular situation does not deserve their attention.

We should govern ourselves otherwise we will be governed by others or We should take care to get what we like otherwise we will be forced to like what we get.

Determinants of 'Nature'

As we all know that our nature is determined by heredity, brain, physical features. cultural, social, economic and family background, and is responsible for our behaviour, thoughts, actions, emotions, abilities, aptitude & attitude. But have you ever noticed that despite of fulfilling all the points mentioned above some individuals does not have good personality, on the other hand people from average or poor backgrounds have good to great personality? I would like to bring one thing which is common for all good personalities, that they observe and choose finer aspect of life and lead their life in a better way by choosing how to spend their time & energy, what to read, what should be the words and tone while speaking to others, how to turn adverse condition into favourable one.

Human beings need guidance to realize their purpose in life and needs carving, if they are not carved, they will grow like bushes, to turn humans into beautiful flowers they have to be nurtured with the help of knowledge, self-control, self-discipline, courage and many other qualities, as water, sunlight, soil and manure given to soil to nurture plant and bring flower to them.

Determinants of 'Personality.'

We are said to be born on two occasions, first occasion is when we came out of mother's womb and give reason of rejoice to his family & parents and second time when we decides what to do with this wonderful gift of nature called life, to give reason of being happy and rejoice to self, when we have decided how to lead life and make it meaningful, that is the moment we should celebrate our second birth, which decides how we are going to spend minutes, hours and years gifted by life. In which field we are interested in and what are the changes required to achieve set target.

Mental toughness is required to enter discomfort zone, courage and hope to find out the purpose of life, and turning impossible into possible, then my dear friend you have moved one step forward to turn yourself into a good personality, you have decided to chisel your nature and ready to get set go for your desired destination.

Whether you have decided to be a medico, an engineer, a defence personnel, a legal specialist or a sportsperson whatever you have decided to set your eyes on, you have to find an Idol from the profession you have chosen. He could be Field Marshal Sam Manekshaw or Captain Vikram Batra, if you wanted to join defence forces, Sunil Gavaskar or Kapil Dev from the field of sports. You have to know about your Idol in the given field and learn about them, how they have chiselled their nature in exchange for a good personality and turn their dreams into reality, a person with good personality gives its best in whatever they are doing.

Personality

Open mindedness is one of the most important ingredients one can develop, as it plays very important role in helping you to get a good personality carved out of your nature, for a good personality we need to be learning and experiencing new situations, which you cannot in the absence of open mindedness, a close mind is the biggest obstacle in the path of carving a good personality, close mindedness does not allow a person to experience new situation and hinders one's view to look far, become static observer and lose the shine of life, where as open mindedness helps us to explore those thing which helps to move ahead in life and opens the window to the world, This could be understood by one scenario given below. Open mindedness is not risk taking it is simply a thoughtful change in your view point which denotes flexibility.

Scenario; My son was having problem of falling hairs and was advised to have medicinal oil massage on his scalp, this age group don't like oil massage on their head, but when I told him that there is no harm in trying it and oil on your head will be applied only before sleep, simultaneously I told him about the health benefits of this process as it may not re-grow fallen hairs but it can definitely stop falling of hairs and this massage will relax your nerves and make you feel lighter, he agreed with open mindedness which resulted in very positive change, after few weeks he told me that new hairs are not coming but it had definitely stopped falling of hairs.

Open-mindedness can be understood **by one more example;** Our family always tries to pray after taking bath or at least once in a day, there is no fixed ritual, just remembering and expressing our gratitude to supreme power is considered as prayer in our home, when our son grew up we tried to pursue him to include prayer in his daily routine, for some times he avoided our advice, one day we sat together and told him there is no harm in it, you will not lose anything however you are definitely going to gain something in the form of concentration, he understood our conversation by started praying irregularly in the beginning and after sometime on regular basis.

Selecting hard choices; Positive intentions and efforts to change by **choosing hard choices** is one of the major determinants of creating good personality, because a change needs complete turnaround in thinking and taking actions thereof, this can be done only if we realised that a herculean effort is needed to achieve the desired target it could be leaving your bed early, finding time for physical activity or making efforts to remove your weaknesses or consolidating one's strengths, learning new skill to move ahead in career or learning new language as hobby.

Situational Awareness; An individual is said to have good personality if s/he learns to act according to situation, Situational awareness indicates that we are aware of what is happening around and whether we have to act, react or remain silent to it, being aware of the situation helps a professional in taking right step in dealing with situation or creating a favourable atmosphere, because acting or reacting in right or wrong manner shows true character of a professional and leaves lasting impression.

Situational awareness can be attained with the right intention and keen observing power, Intention here means one would like to take correct step in case of any situation arises, observing power means one's observation when others are handling a particular situation and mockingly deciding about the rightness of action and reaction by others, observations are not only done by juniors it has been done by seniors as well to judge juniors and take future decisions, because in most of the cases when a senior wants to know about the opinion of a junior in a particular situation, he wants to understand how s/he would have approached this situation, there are two motives behind one is to judge and the second motive is to expose junior team members to that situation and preparing them for future roles.

Scenario; Raman is holding the position of General Manager in ABC network Ltd. his organisation manufactures networking equipment, Raman's style of knowing, judging and developing his team members is quite unique, for every different & difficult situation he called a meeting of his team or talk to them individually and ask them what they would have done in this situation. His sole aim is to develop independent thinking in their team members, he does not like herd mentality, being a progressive professional he like any challenge or situation should be approached from all the directions and best suitable solution considered & implemented with every team member getting exposure to that situation. His main interest is making his team members expressing their views in front of their seniors, with due respect to them. When a junior's suggestion or point of view is accepted or even taken for consideration it further motivates all others to think independently and avoid herd mentality.

Understanding and developing inner strength; What is inner strength? Inner strength can be said to be an invisible light which glows in the mind of an individual professional and used to take decisions and seek guidance for self, getting into muddy water and exiting from it. But before that a professional need to understand the inner strength and develop it, in the first step any individual will think of negative aspect of any situation or people, but after some introspection inner strength help you to turn negativity into positivity.

A person with good personality is Intellectually open. Person who had wide range of interests & flexible in his beliefs, tend to creative, curious and willing to accept new ideas, not rigid, dull or imaginative. Inner strength will see good in other peoples and propel you to grab that good quality and steps for introspection.

An individual having good personality is stable and adjusting, seldom loses his emotional balance, give value to others & their opinions and show positive side of their nature and behaviour. exhibits confidence and effect when executing any task. Avoid being nervous, self-doubting, confused or anxious. Inner strength will make you push towards making desirable changes for achieving one's goal. A professional with good personality is sociable and extrovert, this quality makes them comfortable and friendly with others rather than being shy, unassertive or withdrawn.

Agreeableness is another quality which makes good personality, Agreeable people gave importance in maintaining harmony by giving importance to other's opinions as well, being tactful and considerate they spread warmth rather than being cold & rude. Inner strength will make you strong enough to avoid useless fights and arguments. A professional with good personality is filled with conscientiousness, set goals for themselves, and pursue it persistently with planful, disciplined & achievement-oriented approach rather than being careless, irresponsible or impulsive.

In professional life, there are five factors which determines a good personality, they are **Self Esteem, Self Efficacy, Locus of control, Beliefs and Values**. These five factors are very helpful in shaping individual's professional life and career path. These factors are not visible from outside like well toned physique or branded dress neither these five factors can be purchased form any showroom or online portal but can be developed only with continuous introspection and positive intention.

Self Esteem; It's a belief about one's own worth based on an overall self-evaluation and the degree of liking an individual has for self. Individual with high self-esteem tend to view themselves as worthwhile, capable and acceptable, in contrast to those with low self-esteem tend to have trouble dealing with others, view themselves in negative terms and are hampered by self-doubts. Adequate level of self esteem is required to perform at highest level of corporate set up, because only a professional having balanced self-esteem will understand that others also have self-esteem and should be dealt accordingly, everyone of us reaches balanced level of self-esteem after certain period of life & career, by negotiating many speed breakers and road blocks.

Self Efficacy; Self-efficacy means a person's opinion about self that s/he will be able to deal with any situation when it arises, Self-efficacy and performance are cyclically related with each other. Self-efficacy of a professional decides its performance and which in turn decides Self-efficacy, Self-efficacy is very vital for a professional for career growth as it helps in learning new things and make a professional achievement oriented. It is organisation's responsibility to introduce their team members to the concept of Self-efficacy, which will enhance their performance and helps them grow in their career path.

Locus of Control; Locus of control can be referred as an individual's opinion about what controls him or her and what they can control or in other words some professionals think that they are responsible for what is happening to them, whereas some professionals thinks that their activities are controlled by chance or luck. Professionals or individuals who think they are responsible for what is happening to them seems to posses internal locus of control whereas second type of professional who thinks that their activities are controlled by fate or luck, posses external locus of control, now it is very much clear that understanding & knowledge of locus of control plays very important role in professional's performance in organisation only those professionals succeeds in completion of their task and duties who have internal locus of control, take initiative and make efforts to make deciding factors favourable, whereas it is not so in the case of professionals having external locus of control.

Beliefs; Beliefs are through which a professional perceived a particular aspect of life, it is also determined mainly by culture, religion and family upbringing. In other words, beliefs may be defined as assumptions we make about ourselves, team members and organisation, beliefs help us in shaping our thoughts and actions which leads us to the most important part of professional life i.e., decision making, to be a positive and successful professional we have to take and make decisions about self, team members & organisation and act accordingly.

Values; Values may be considered those yardsticks which helps a professional evaluates and decides the steps to be taken in every aspect of life and profession. One very good thing about 'Values' is that it is mostly positive in nature, with the help of values we come to know about the meaning of successful life. For **Example,** if we consider our neighbour very successful, as he is having all the material stuff of modern life, from swanky car to luxurious villa, but when we come to know that government authorities are raiding his offices and homes to investigate tax evasion. We immediately shift our perception of successful life.

Personality for Leader;

Self Esteem; A leader with high self-esteem is able to take independent decisions, set higher goals for self and team, high level of self esteem helps in maintaining healthy relationship with team members, which in turn helps in executing most of the task at the highest level of a professional setup, as most of the actions are completed at CEO's level is through healthy relationship, most of the problem solving takes place with the help of healthy relationship with different levels of professionals in the organisation.

Scenario; Nikita is CEO of a mid-cap manufacturing unit which is engage in producing gas burners, last week workers of the factory went on strike for few demands, Nikita was thinking how to solve this problem, as management was not in a mood to give any concessions to workers, they think that by giving more concessions, labour union will ask for more, but Nikita was of the view that management should reconsider their stand as their will be no financial burden by accepting the demand for some change in reporting time rule, it will be win-win situation for both sides, at this point of time management is in strong position, but time may flip and labour union might be in a stronger position to bargain for more, at that time our giving gesture might remind labour union to co-operate. Nikita having adequate level of self esteem understands that second party also have self esteem and should be deal accordingly.

Self-Efficacy; A leader must have the confidence and knowledge that they can do and guide in most of the tasks involved in the process by standing with & behind team. High level of self-efficacy is expected from head of the organisation because with the changing time and technological advancements, every moment a new challenge might erupt or expected to apply different style of dealing, Secondly, non display of high level of self-efficacy affects the reputation of the leader and ability to impress the team and self.

Scenario; Kalyani, who is working as General Manager of a textile production unit in Haryana, this unit is doing very well in terms of profit and demand of the product was exceeding the supply, Top management was very happy with leadership capability of Kalyani, Kalyani's production unit has to depend on good quality yarn from other vendors, some times best quality yarn is not available so they have to compromise on quality or stop the production in the middle.

Kalyani was always thinking of how to solve the problem of irregular supply of quality yarn, idea of having own unit of producing quality yarn came to her mind and she suggested to top management to set our own yarn production plant for self-reliance, Kalyani was ready to carry the responsibility of setting up the plant from initial stage to commissioning, She called her team and informed about the new development, started delegating her present responsibilities and her deputy being a very intelligent and efficient professional expressed happiness over the new project, by sharing the new responsibilities.

Locus of control; It is very important for a leader to have internal locus of control as s/he is responsible for every action going on in the organisation, secondly, a leader with internal locus of control takes calculated risk which is very much required for the success & growth of the organisation. Internal locus of control gives leader a special type of satisfaction.

Scenario; Shailesh while getting out of his house had a flat tyre and don't have stepney repaired when tyre of his car got punctured last time, he took a cab to office in a hurry and leaving important project report in the car left behind, this project report was to be discussed with his general manager, he got disturbed due to ongoing chain of incidents, but Shailesh having internal locus of control went to wash room, washed his face, containing and telling self, "I will not allow any external circumstances to derail my plan". He calls his General Manager and tells him about the incident, requesting him to postpone the meeting for tomorrow. General Manager was little upset with this but he is working with Shailesh since last three years and Shailesh has not made this type of excuse before, so he agreed to the request of Shailesh by re-scheduling the meeting.

Belief; A leader at this stage of career understands the meaning of beliefs and has already practiced it during his entire career successfully, now his capability lies in understanding the beliefs of his team members for taking appropriate decisions, in my views a leader must have positive belief that honesty is always the best policy. A true belief and practicing it, sets good example while dealing with team members.

Scenario; For displaying honesty Shailesh does not have to talk big, he simply does it by setting example by never using offices resources for personal use, such as peon or housekeeping staff, whenever he uses driver along with office vehicle during leaves and holidays for personal use, he informs accounts department for deducting appropriate amount from his salary and same process was followed for using courier, photocopying and printing services. Being honest with your organisation has two benefits, one it stops misuse of organisation's resources, and secondly, it sets team members free of guilt as team members have to print their children's homework, question papers and assignment, now they can use offices photocopy or printing resources at a subsides cost and without any guilt, otherwise they have to go to market after office hours to get those photocopies and printouts thus saving lot of time and energy.

Values; Values are should do behaviour, two best values a leader can have, is dynamic mindset and ethical leadership, as a father figure it is expected from a leader to give equal treatment to team members. A role displayed with values is far more effective in long term rather than getting small benefits for short term gains. Whatever a leader does and exhibits is passed down to the lowest level of organisation. A leader is the one who has to practice dynamic mindset value and spread the message of mindset value across the hierarchy, not only spread the message but conduct a fair audit to find out the gap to fill it with dynamic mindset, knowledge and training.

Scenario; Ankit is working as CEO of DCF corporation, whenever he has to hire a new team member, he looks for dynamic mindset, he knows that having dynamic mindset is one of those qualities in any professional which can take him to new heights, Ankit very much understands that dynamic mindset is not only true in terms of human beings but in terms of organisations as well. This prompted him to introduce practices of modern management related to development of organisation & team.

Second value which he practices is 'Ethical Leadership', in my views ethical leadership may be defined as when a leader is able to listen to positive suggestion and corrections in positive way, being a student of dynamic mindset, Ankit very much understands that if he wants to grow his team and organisation he should not allow 'Boss Syndrome' to come near him, which states that 'Boss is always right'. He understands that his organisation's growth depends very much on knowledge and talent of his team and their constructive feedback is very much required for smooth and flawless functioning, Ethical leadership is also about equal distribution of credit along with equal distribution of work.

Personality for Team Leader;

Self-esteem; High self-esteem helps a team leader to take decisions confidently in favour of organisation and not influenced by any other distracting factor. A professional can take right decisions only if s/he knows the strength and weaknesses of self, a team leader's interest is creating better working atmosphere for self and his team, sometimes s/he succeeds, sometimes do not, but never loses the sight of goal, another benefit of balanced self-esteem is positive outlook towards any situation, understanding the importance of it with in the radius of team.

Scenario; Ankita is working as team leader (mechanical) in a manufacturing unit producing agricultural machineries, her deputy manager who was associated with them since last two & a half years has submitted his resignation, HR department has shortlisted few candidates and send the list to Ankita for recommendations and forwarding the name to General Manager for finalisation the right candidate, Ankita was very much impressed by profile of David and she wanted David in her team, but there was one problem despite of being younger and less experienced in his field, David was more qualified than her.

In first instance Ankita don't want to forward David's name to General Manager for final call, but after one day she gave second thought to it and her balanced self esteem prompted her to take right decision, she thought it is better to have more qualified professional to move the team in forward direction, as it will infuse fresh approach & knowledge in field. Ankita questions herself, why she is feeling threatened?" She told self that she has reached the position of team leader in a span of ten years of professional life on the basis of her ability only, induction of David will be a positive step to strengthen the team, after lunch she received a call from General Manager to finalise the candidate for post of Deputy team leader, General Manager asked her the same question about David, but Ankita told him about her preference, after getting go ahead from her, General Manager send his recommendation to HR department for finalising David's name for vacant post of Deputy team leader (Mechanical).

Self-efficacy; With high level of self-efficacy a team leader is confident of executing any task coming his way whether it is first time or every time. Self-Efficacy is that tool which gives a team leader the support in handling day to day challenges and helps a professional to succeed under trying conditions, Self-efficacy can be attained by being open to various types of experiences and knowledge, when a professional with lot of courage venture into the unchartered arenas and get out of it successfully gives h/her the confidence of dealing with it and with the attitude of "Come what may come". I will be victorious.

Scenario; Sonali is working with ABC communications as IT head, her department's responsibility is to provide IT support and developing software for smooth and better working of organisation, she has been associated with this organisation since last three years and widely respected for his knowledge & professionalism. Sonali has been observing since last one year, outcome and performance of freshers has not been up to the mark, Sonali takes out some time to understand the reason and finds her assumption was right, senior team members are not guiding freshers properly in learning the required skill to perform better,

Sonali was thinking how to handle this situation and find out the solution for this basic human problem, she does not want to give direct orders to senior team members, after lot of brain storming with HR department, she prepares a mentor & coach programme. In this programme every senior team member is teamed up with one fresher who will be known as 'buddy' and assigned task to coach fresh team member along with their professional responsibility, these coaching can be measured in term of tasks and result of this programme was integrated with performance appraisal of both i.e. trainee and trainer, Sonali herself took the role of mentor, this initiative of coaching and mentoring programme brought good results by taking the efficiency and productivity to desired level.

Locus of Control; With internal locus of control a team leader becomes quite confident and do not hesitate to allow other team members to take initiative, prepare proactively, believes in allowing juniors to take initiative and allowing them to explore different angles of doing the same process, and is considered as one of the best actions a team leader can take with a notion "main hoon na".

Scenario; One more real incident I would like to share with all of you from my previous organisation, lecture on general subjects were conducted by regular faculties where as few specialised subjects were taught by visiting faculties, one of the special subjects which was taught by visiting faculty is 'Research Methodology and Biostatistics', faculties have to visit affiliating university to evaluate the answer sheets for respective subjects they have taught.

Visiting faculty of 'Research Methodology' expressed her inability to visit university to evaluate answer sheets due to some personal reasons, non-evaluation of answer sheets will withheld the result of students, one of my colleagues who was the head of the department of a specialised stream took the matter in her hand, she get the question paper form library, prepare key of the question paper and reached university to evaluate the answer sheets, internal locus of control of this regular faculty helped everybody from student to university by getting the results declared well with in time.

Scenario 2; Arvind is working as team leader (marketing) in a multinational organisation and has developed internal locus of control after spending twelve years in corporate world and is always in control of the outcome of decisions taken by him and backed his team to take decisions, taking responsibility not only for moral reasons but for setting up professional standards as well, moving one step ahead he very well understands that in any process or procedure improvement or innovation can be done only if we fully own, understand and remain 'attached' with it and observe it very minutely and can find merits and de-merits in it, which helps us removing de-merits and improving merits.

  Arvind's company was engaged in manufacturing toys, during the closure of quarterly marketing report Arvind observed that two type of toys were not getting repeat orders from retailers, when he contacted retailers in person, they confirm the data but unable to give the satisfactory reason behind lack of demand for these two toys, Arvind wanted to find out the reason behind this to improve the sales of those two toys, those two toys were made for the children aged between 3-5 years.

  Luckily Arvind's two daughters were in the same age bracket, he took these two toys home and gave to his daughters, along with their other regular toys, at first they were happy to find new toy but in few minutes they started playing with their old toys leaving new toys, Arvind picked those toys for little longer and started playing like kids during this playful exercise he find out that due to faulty design it was difficult and painful for children to hold them for long. Arvind reported the detail of his playful exercise to his seniors, seniors were very happy to see the extent Arvind had gone to bring the results and appreciated Arvind's effort to control the outcome.

Belief; A team leader must develop those beliefs which helps to get the best out of his team, a team leader is the bridge between management & team, some times he has to apply negative belief for the best outcome and keep team in learning mode, best positive belief a team leader can have is "if I takes care of team members, they will reply back with same intensity and behaviour".

Scenario; Vijay, while working with his team always take care of his team like a senior without compromising on professional standard, during one incident when annual inspection was scheduled, Arvind fell ill and could not prepare for annual inspection by government authorities, his team realises the gravity of the situation and started preparing for the inspection by applying themselves more than hundred percent, resulting in the successful conduct of inspection.

When Arvind joined back after recovery his CEO congratulated him on successful conduct of inspection, on this Arvind says "I have not done anything "it was my team in my absence". CEO replied back "Arvind you were not present physically but your team was working for you and repaying back assuming that you are present in the office, you have reaped what you have sowed".

Values; Values are chosen among certain alternatives, two best values for a team leader can be loyalty and dependability, because most of the team members have just come out of college and looking for something meaningful, having value as loyalty makes a professional to obey the instructions in total, and second meaning of loyalty is that till the time of any team member is working with the organisation s/he is expected to be loyal during that duration, Dependability means an individual does what he says and have respect for words, since a team leader is glue between top management and team, H/her words are marked by both sides, being a dependable professional is a sign of good personality.

Scenario; Simi is working as team leader in corporate communication department of a large multinational organisation, dependable for both sides i.e. for seniors and juniors equally, Dependability means your team can depend on you to take decisions and action, if result is positive your team members will take credit if it's negative they will try to find out on whom they can shed the responsibility.

Simi's organization is in the process of hosting quarterly meeting of officials from the rank of assistant manager and above on 28th day of next month, Simi requested one of her team members to send a common e-mail to designation of assistant managers and above in this regard, after two days Simi receives a call from General Manager regarding the mistake made by her team member, in hurry he mentioned 'Managers' in place of 'assistant managers', first information e-mail was sent under the caption of 'Corporate Communication Department' XYZ corporation Ltd., now the correction mail will be sent by Mrs. Simi Khurana, General Manager (Corporate-Communications), XYZ Ltd. Simi being a dependable team leader owns the mistake of her team member and corrected it.

Personality for team member;

Self-esteem; What is the key word of self-esteem? Key word of self-esteem is worthiness, and who else need it most, it is young team member who has just passed out from a B-School and trying to find out the ways to handle complexity of corporate world, by dealing with confusion of directions to move, there are two main factors which knowingly or unknowingly paves the way towards high self esteem and expresses 'worthiness' in terms of young team members, one of these two factors is sense of belongingness and second one is "I am equal to every other team member of my level, not more nor less", without any complex.

With this balanced level of self-esteem an individual team member can set higher goals for self, able to handle any conflict successfully, absorb any adverse or difficult working condition, as sense of belongingness with the organisation helps a team member to ward off any negative feeling towards place of work and understands that every organisation has it pros & cons and one has to learn to see the brighter side of it and make it more brighter with the help of three Es which are education, enthusiasm and experience.

Scenario; Nirmal who has done his Masters in law has joined as intern (legal) in one of the biggest law firm of the country, after completion of internship and keeping in view his performance Nirmal was offered regular appointment which he accepted happily, Nirmal being from a well to do family and his team leader who is seven years senior to him is from a middle income group family and reached this position on his own by completing his education with the help of scholarships and educational loan.

Nirmal always looked down at his team leader Alok for this oblivious reason, In one of the assignments Nirmal did blunder for which company has to pay hefty amount, but instead of blaming Nirmal, Alok came ahead and shared the responsibility , this incidence changed the outlook of Nirmal towards his team leader, and his self esteem comes down to balanced level, after this he comes to understand that team members can be judged only on the basis of their performance and qualities.

Self-efficacy; An individual team member with high level of self-efficacy is bound to have a successful career and good personality, because in the initial stages of career s/he should be able to learn and take new assignments with confidence. One very good thing about self-efficacy is that it can be build and improved upon, there are two tools for building high self-efficacy.

These two tools are observing others and monitoring one's thoughts, by observing other professionals having self-efficacy, we also prepares self for new assignment with confidence by watching closely what steps s/he takes to tackle the first exposure to new challenge, second thing which makes high level of self-efficacy is the first thought or emotion which comes into your mind, it may be negative or positive both are right for you, one may be wondering how negative or positive both may be right for situation, that is the beauty of emotion or thought, if we think that we will be able to accomplish the task, we will accomplish the task or if we think we won't be able to accomplish the task then we won't be able to complete the task. This is the reason why we should be always positive and affirm to high level of self-efficacy in our professional field.

Scenario; After completing her M. Pharma from a reputed pharmacy college, Karan Preet joined a large pharmaceutical company as Medical Representative, she was doing well in her field, in the meantime company decided to setup one more unit and approached Karan Preet to join R & D department of new unit attitude and inclination towards research and development. Having received the offer, she gave her consent to join R & D department of new production unit, as she has high self-efficacy, she became star of the unit and utilises her knowledge in the interest of organisation and career growth of self as well.

Locus of Control; A team member with internal locus of control performs better and know that they are responsible if something went wrong and this mistake will be corrected by learning right approach and procedure. When a team member understands the meaning of locus of control starts taking h/her life and career in positive direction.

Scenario; Rajesh has just joined as trainee in a multinational setup, during his studies he very clearly understand the difference between external locus of control & internal locus of control, he promised self to always have internal locus of control. Within the eight months of joining, he was assigned to work on new software for assembly line, he works very diligently on it but when time comes to implement it he couldn't do it successfully, after one month management decided to put advance software in place for which Rajesh had volunteered by making a presentation about what went wrong last time, what are the lessons learned this time and the modification or improvement done in previous software, after looking at the presentation, top management decided to give one more chance to him which he successfully turns into a mile stone by converting failure into success.

Belief; A team member who is just out of campus and joined corporate sector, must test beliefs which s/he has developed over a period of time and be ready to change them if required, one may be wondering that beliefs can be adjusted or altered. Yes, a dynamic mind when steps into the corporate sector should adjust pre-conceived beliefs for the betterment of team and professional life, as we know that beliefs are important to react to what is happening around, team member should have firm belief in the say. "Work is worship" and will be successful only if s/he follows it with sincerity and interest.

Scenario; a fresher or a trainee team member should have firm belief that at his level doing the assigned task sincerely is the only requirement to move ahead in life professionally. Akshat has just joined a multinational organization as trainee, his parents & teachers had advised him to be sincere towards his job. Adhering to their advice he started performing his duties with great deal of interest, leaving his work of place only if required, result of his sincere work was seen with in six months of joining and he was considered for regular employment role whereas five other trainees who have joined with him were given extended probation period.

Values; When we choose a value and know the consequences of it, a team member should have values such as adaptability and Integrity. These values will help a long way in surviving in corporate set up where s/he is a cub in new jungle. In the beginning of the career following the value of adaptability is one of the most sensible value any probationer or trainee can have, embracing adaptability not only gives you an edge but also gives you strength in any trying circumstances.

In the beginning of career what ever you put in the foundation stone will take concrete shape and form the basis for a wonderful professional life, my sincere advice to the beginners is to choose your values and stick to it, by developing the capacity to change it as well if it is guiding you towards wrong path, take U-turn and start moving in that right direction which you think will take you towards your goal, having values makes you understand that 'life' is more important than career, one can be successful without values, but for a wonderful life and great career one has to choose certain values and abide by them, or in other words having values helps us to take a stand with clarity and live a meaningful life.

Adaptability here means different meaning, in general adaptability is related to adapting self to new weather condition or adjusting to new group of friends, or it could be making changes in daily routine when transiting from work from home to hybrid work schedule. But when adaptability is taken into bigger meaning, it indicates changing values for 'Trichual'.

Scenario; Nikhil, has been working with a software giant since last one year, it was his first job he wanted to learn everything from project management to adjusting in office atmosphere, since last few days Nikhil was little puzzled because of the behaviour of one of the senior team member, taking advantage of seniority he don't contribute much towards execution of project, only dictates what to be done and make other team members feel low, due to his toxic behaviour all other team members are getting disturbed which is eventually leading to delay in project.

Since childhood Nikhil was told not to complaint as complaining is considered negative habit and he had maintained this habit of not complaining for small things and adjust accordingly to be comfortable in every situation, but this situation is totally different, it is the question of reputation of team and organisation.

Nikhil decided to change his value of never complaining and reported this matter in the form of formal complaint to project manager through formal channel, Project Manager being an experienced professional sensed the reason behind various delays in deadlines took appropriate action to bring the project back on track. Nikhil also felt a sigh of relief by using his value for productive reason in the interest of team and organisation.

Personality for students;

Self-esteem; Knowledge and understanding of self-esteem is essential for students, because students must keep themselves in high self-esteem, with the high self-esteem they will be able to handle stress or any other untoward incident during student life and does not deviate from goal. It is during student life that one starts taking decisions about self, and develop relationship with others, balance level of high-esteem helps a student to take right decision, during student life one has to understand that s/he can compete with any one of class mates and learn to say 'NO' with confidence, when you learn to say 'no' with a valid reason, you display independent thinking which stops you from being the part of herd.

Scenario; Archana is studying in third year of B.Tech. (Electronics) in one of the top-rated institutes, she was not able to get the same grades as she used to get during school time, she was trying to find out the reason behind it, after having given a honest thought she came to know the reason, those who got the admission in B.Tech. programme are the ones who had topped in their respective schools.

Archana now realised that she has to compete with toppers of the school and merely being doing average effort will not show the desired result, she has to increase the rate of efforts, Secondly, she was always in the habit of saying 'Yes' to the demands of the group, whether it is late night outing just to pass time or bunking lectures, she has observed that if she had said 'NO' on few occasions she would have saved lot of resources in terms of time and money, Now Archana decided to say 'NO' to any unjust demand of group, immediately she got a chance to test her resolution of saying 'NO', she heard a knock on her door as usual there was Sakshi asking for her books just before exams, as Sakshi always prefers spending money on dresses rather than on books. Archana clearly said 'NO' to Saakshi's demand and saved self from a probable problem.

Self-efficacy; An individual with high level of self-efficacy is confident of executing any task, for students it may be working on new subject related assignment, participating in inter-house debate for first time, co-ordinating for annual day etc. Students who want to have successful career and above all a meaningful life, must understand self-efficacy as a pillar for strong foundation. Having high level of self-efficacy will help you to approach difficult task with positivity. Self-efficacy builds resilience and helps setting up goals and find the process to achieve it.

Scenario; We used to give assignment to final year of masters level students to teach first year students, one of our students named 'Kajal' came to me and told that she has been assigned the topic to teach first year students is 'Research Methodology and Biostatistics' in which she has failed last year and has to appear in 'back paper' to clear the course, I told her that this topic is given intentionally to overcome the fear of this particular subject, still there are two weeks time in scheduled lecture, please give adequate time to prepare it and keep it on your priority list.

I once again told her that we all are 'with you', these words gave her confidence and she started preparing for her 'micro teaching' class with great zeal and came out of the lecture hall with victory sign. It is very necessary for students to start understanding the concept of self-efficacy, as this will help them to face the challenges of new life when they venture into corporate world.

Locus of Control; Internal locus of control help students in a very positive way as they held themselves responsible for their overall success or failure, if any deficiency arises, they know that they are responsible for it and can take corrective measure to overcome it.

Scenario 1; When Simi joined a professional institute to pursue her MBA, she got disturbed by the opinion of her group, on every step they told her that she is not good at this or that, but Simi having internal locus of control, stopped paying heed to their opinion and understands that no human being is perfect, she posses all the required qualities to complete the course by remaining focussed on her studies this indicates that students have to develop internal locus of control so as not to get confused or disturbed by others opinion about themselves .

Scenario 2; Rajat is pursuing his B.Tech. (Computer Science) from a prestigious institute but he is unable to secure good grades in his first semester due to reason not known to him, suddenly he receives a call from his room mate to go to a new movie and knowing the nature of Rajat who never refused, has already purchased tickets for the show, Rajat immediately left everything and reached movie theatre.

One evening Rajat was not in good mood and want to spend some time in recreational activities, he asked his roommate to accompany him to nearby mall for dinner, but his room mate straight away refused by telling him that he has to prepare for tomorrow's class test. Rajat immediately came to know what is wrong with his studies, his life is controlled by others and he is not able to say 'NO' to others whereas others have their priorities set right and takes decision as per situation. Rajat immediately decided to change his manner of response and stop pleasing others by always saying 'Yes'.

Belief; Student must believe that education which s/he is getting is the best available as per their ability and resources available, there is no point comparing his course or institute to any other course or institute. Students must harbour a firm belief that their parents & teachers are more experienced, knowledgeable and well wishers, their advice or guidance may not be liked by us but their sole intention is always our betterment and students must remove the misconception that they were born approximately 25 years ago, they can't understand our point of view, every human being goes through similar stages of evolution during life span.

There may be big technological gap between two generations, but human brain and mind functions similarly for family, Childrens and other fellow human beings which is caring and positive. Students must understand that we will definitely get something from the guidance and advices of our parents & teachers, not because the age difference but because of the reason that they have gone through same experience when they were students few decades back.

Scenario; Madhavi took admission in a management institute to pursue her masters in data analytics, whenever she is with her friends, she hears her friends having low opinion about their institute in comparison to other institutes which are ranked higher, During one casual outing when most of the group members were present, Madhavi stated her point of view that we should stop criticising our institute, because of this institute only we will achieve success in future personally & professionally, which is standing tall for all of us and there is no point comparing it with other institutes, an institute is not known by his building or infrastructure, it is known by the laurels brought by students wo are studying here, on hearing this all group members decided to work hard towards their studies, resulting in the most placements in a top multinational company.

Values; Student life is the best time to understand, decide and settle for higher values, values settled during student life makes long lasting impact on the life, which indirectly affects surroundings and society. Student must aspire for higher level of values without compromising. Two best values for students are independence and purpose.

Students should value independence most, independence not in wearing different type of clothes, not in selecting which food to order, but taking independent decisions such as which project to work on, which book to purchase, taking measures to save money. They should avoid going with herd and decide what is right for them and with in their means. Students must value accountability, what they have come here for, what are the expectations from them, what will be the impact of their result on family and themselves. It is value for accountability which acts as a change agent for society and self, there should be all out effort to be accountable in every condition.

Purpose; A student having thoughtful personality knows about the purpose of what s/he is doing whether it is life or education, as a student we have to find the purpose about our action, life is the most precious gift of nature and its purpose can be fulfilled with the help of good qualification and education, to find out the purpose one must question self, why I am doing this? what will be the effect of it on my life and other's lives related to me and in this process one must ignite the process of moving from being useful to purposeful, usefulness basically confined to an individual or utmost to family, where as being purposeful is choosing larger canvas to paint which is extended to society and nation, being purposeful we know the importance of our duties and consciousness surrounds feeling us proud.

While taking lectures on management topics, I often asked students one question " Why you have joined this course?" believe me 90% of the them were clueless. most of them were NEET aspirants, when they did not get admission in 'MBBS' programme, they chose the programme which is closest to medical programme i.e., paramedical science (Physiotherapy and Occupational therapy) and pursuing it half heartedly to earn their livelihood, to be useful to themselves & their families by earning livelihood.

During my tenure I suffered from frozen shoulder and was treated by one of our students who was about to complete his course, after being treated successfully, I told that student about his wonderful profession because it brings smile on the face of a person who was writhing in pain few days back, after listening my compliments he was so happy and told me that nobody has communicated with him in this manner. I wish somebody should have told them about the purpose of studying this programme what changes they can bring in to the life of others and themselves if they pursue this course whole heartedly.

Scenario; Shikha was passing by an under-construction building, she stops and asked a labourer, what are you doing? he replied back "nothing, just earning my livelihood". when she asked the same question to another labourer. he replied "I am constructing a very strong and beautiful building which will be better than all other buildings in the city". The two approaches towards their job made all the difference in being useful and purposeful.

Scenario; Mr. C.J. Kurian was managing director of 'Amul', the famous milk co-operative revolution, one day his grandson come to see him in his office, in a playful mood the guard with the big moustache standing outside the office did not allow his grandson to enter but after few attempts, he was allowed to go inside to meet his grand father. when Mr. Kurian asked his grandson what he want to become in his life, his grandson immediately answer "I want to be security guard'. on hearing this Mr. Kurian said to him ' be a security guard but be the best security guard in this world".

Nature or Nurture; Question arises whether nature (genetic endowment) or nurture (environmental influences) determines personality, findings are best expressed in the ratio of 40:60 i.e., 40% genetics and 60% environmental influences, it shows that we can have good personality by continuous effort and making desired changes in our behaviour.

Conclusion; Beauty of human life is that it can be corrected or changed at any point of time in life by changing ourselves we can become the change we want to see, and it should be our duty to have a great personality in the interest of self, family, society and nation. Gratitude is the biggest thing you can do, be grateful to your teachers, elders and parents. Experience the blessings around you, there are so many things which others do not have, count them, stay blessed and be grateful.

De-Stressing

Ashok is sitting in his cabin feeling little uneasy as he has to prepare a report which his team leader has asked for, he was trying to procrastinate the task but his 'uneasiness' is not allowing him to do so and constantly reminding him of pending task , suddenly a thought came to his mind that whole team depends on him for this report and team will be let down if did not follow the time frame for this important submission, he had two more tasks lined up to complete, now he has to decide which task he should take up first, after completing the task he went over his thought process and tries to find that one factor which had helped him not only this time but every time to complete the task in given time, he zeroed in on that **uneasiness** which was constantly pushing him from inside to take action and finish the assigned task, now he realised that in professional working atmosphere it is called 'STRESS'.

Ankita is roaming in the corridor of her office without any reason, every other team member was occupied with work but why she is not at her desk, in fact even she also does not know the reason behind her aimlessly roaming in corridor, Ankita has been assigned a task by her team leader which seems very difficult to her, this type of disturbance is also called 'STRESS'.

Stress can be termed as double-edged sword, one of its edges is fitted with positive stress and second side is fitted with negative stress, for executing any given task we have to take stress in our stride, only then we will generate adequate amount of energy, by using this energy we can execute what we have been told to do. As a student or employee, we have to daily cope with tests or projects etc. Due to increased competition and for delivery of better quality of work in less time leads to a condition in which a professional pressurizes self to do more with the same level of resources is called "stress".

Stress triggers one of the two basic reactions fight or flight, Physiologically, this stress response is a biochemical "passing gear" involving hormonal changes that mobilize the body for extraordinary physical & mental demands.

Types of stress; Mainly there are two types of stress, positive or negative, Positive stress means the type of stress which prompt us to complete our task and get our belts tighten is known as **Eustress.** Whereas state of negative stress robed us of all our productivity and send us in to state of dumbness, we are not able to take small decision is called **Distress.** It's reason maybe sudden financial problem or heavy workload resulting in sadness, display of anger, anxiety and nervousness.

One more type of stress is caused due to hyperactivity to meet deadlines or eleventh-hour rush, it is called **Hyper Stress.** Another kind of stress is opposite to hyper stress and caused due to less than optimum activity is known as **Hypo Stress.** More often this is experienced by person who is out of job or whose capability is underutilized, while experiencing hypo stress an individual thinks that s/he has the capability to produce more but don't have the opportunity to do so. Now it is very clear that optimal amount of stress is very much necessary to keep the fire burning, without stress everything will become stand still.

Application; It is very important for managers to understand and learn about occupational or professional stress and factors leading to it, knowledge of stress will help them in managing team & team members in a better way. Stress is inevitable, efforts need to be directed at managing stress, not at somehow escaping it altogether. What will happen if there is no stress? few types of stresses have positive consequences as well, are integral part of human life and cannot be avoided but it can be managed in one's favour.

Having in-depth knowledge of 'STRESS' helps a leader, team leader, team member and student to identify the reason, type of stress and find out the solution to reduce it by making balance for optimal utilisation of its human asset, there is one very particular thing about stress is that, it does not allow the person whom it is troubling to speak up and seek help, it confuses the person and that individual is unable to distinguish between pressure and stress. Stress steals the ability to think rationally, seek help and keeps on rotating in the vicious circle.

If the team leader is unable to identify the above factors i.e. type and reason, s/he will not be able to reduce the stress level of a team member and improve team's performance by bringing relief to particular individual, a relieved individual becomes more valuable member of the organisation and well equipped to handle the same situation if it happens again, now we have come to know that how much it is necessary for a professional or an individual to understand the definition and meaning of 'Stress' to handle it properly, it is like having a knowledge of difficult curves and hair-pin bends while driving in a hilly terrain, in a hilly terrain to make driving easy and safer, various sign boards are placed before every probable danger which helps a driver to negotiate those dangers safely. Similarly, a team leader and individual professional must be able to identify different warning signs for smoother functioning of team.

Causes; We have discussed about the various types of stresses, now we will discuss different causes of stress. As a social animal all individuals and professionals come from different backgrounds economically, academically or socially, cause of stress will be different for each of them, there is no certainty about what causes stress to whom or in other words we can never be sure that a professional from a particular background will experience stress due to a particular cause, a professional or individual coming from weak economical background may be stressed due to organisational cause or a professional coming from academically sound background may found himself stressed due to individual cause or an individual coming from strong social back ground may be stressed due to group cause or vice-versa.

We can overcome or minimise the effect of any negative activity only if we know what causes it and make efforts to hit at the root of the cause but stress is one thing which cannot be eradicated totally some amount of stress will always be there to push us to reach our goal or keep us away from reaching our goal, as per industry standards stress may be caused by organisation, other than organisation, individual or group.

Extra-organizational stressor – Social or technological changes & family Problems are one of the main causes which gave rise to stress outside organization, another reason can be re-location to an unwanted place where an individual has to re-settle self in terms of accommodation, children's education and neighbourhood which consumes lot of time & energy and even after that one is not sure of getting things of choice, economical, residential and community conditions also generates stress due to poor economic condition which forces an individual to live in lower standard of residential and community conditions. It is very much clear from the above description of extra organisational factors which causes stress, we can easily find out that these causes can not be removed instantly, once we have come to know that we could not control causes, what should be our next step.

We all are best creature of nature and have immense possibilities, we should learn to adapt and adjust our selves as per requirement of the causes. Question might be arising in our mind is this stress happening first time to some body in life, if we go down memory lane of our professional or personal life we will remember that there were many colleagues who had suffered from stress due to extra organisational factors it may be social, personal or technical, stretching further we will remember that how some team members have over come it and some team members have succumb to it, resulting in deteriorating performance, only difference between these two individual, that is winner and loser is their ability to adapt to the cause of stress.

Minimising Extra-Organisational Stress; We can minimise extra organisational stress by two steps, first by identifying it and secondly by recognising it. We must be able to make clear distinction between identifying and recognising. Identifying here means the cause' which may be social, personal or technical and recognising here means type of stress. Eu-stress, du-stress, distress, hyper or hypo, when an individual feels that her personal or professional life is going off the track, s/he must apply brakes and start finding the way out. While suffering from extra-organisational stress one is alone and only the sufferer can take himself out of this situation, nobody else.

Organizational stressor – Organizational stressor are those type of stress which happens due to factors while executing job responsibility, among the most infamous organizational stressor is high stress job role in which a team member has to put more efforts than his capabilities or which requires going beyond physical and mental boundaries, in this type of stress an employee cannot take rest and has to be always on his tows, meeting targets, attending future customers, poor working conditions, poor infrastructure or organizational politics etc. are main reason for this.

One point is to be noted down that extra organizational stressor and organizational stressor are inter connected means if anybody is suffering from organizational stressor, she or he will have effect of this stress on his personal life as well and vice-versa. If a professional suddenly started experiencing stress during normal routine and unable to execute the given task smoothly is the indication that s/he is suffering from extra-organisational stress and its effect is very much visible while performing routine duties in organisation. Burnout is one of the biggest problems which happens due to organisational stress.

Minimising Organisational Stress; It is the responsibility of leader to have in-depth knowledge about stress and the various causes of it, one very important aspect of this disturbance should be known to a leader i.e. inter relation of organisational and extra-organisational stressors, every team member is directly connected to society and its output in any form will have direct consequences on various aspects of society or in other words knowingly or unknowingly h/her actions are affecting society while being indirectly linked to it. A head of the organisation must spend substantial amount of time in knowing about the behaviour of team members and any change is happening in their nature or behaviour due to work pressure.

Leader's inability to gauge the impact of distress on team members will result in loss to the organisation either in the form of productivity or individual itself, loosing an individual due to distress will have very negative effect on society and individual will suffer from extra-organisational stress as well, leading to vicious circle.

Team Stressors – Absence of team 'we-ness' also results in high level of stress for a team member, while working in group every team member expects support from other team members and want related conflicts to be solved amicably, when it does not happen few team members who are sensitive and depend on group for their professional & emotional requirement experience high level of stress, chose flight mode to escape. A team consists of members coming from different specialisation and temperaments, so a team leader has to be very understanding to minimise the effect of team stressors.

Biggest team stressor has been found to be 'Ego', an ego mindset thinks that s/he is the most important team member or some team members are under impression that without them team cannot move an inch. Leader must identify this misunderstanding and remove it by directly confronting the trouble creators.

Minimising Team-Stressor; A leader must understand and have fundamental knowledge how to handle & minimise team stress, in my views one thing which can help a leader to reduce team stressor is healthy communication with team members and encourage them to practice the same.

Having proper communication with team members will help a leader to clarify their respective positions and remove confusion if there is any which will bring clarity and help team members to execute their respective duties. A team leader must encourage free flow of communication among team members so that they can sort out petty differences on their own, when team members learn the art of proper communication and started solving their problems on their own, develop confidence among them which takes the team's and individual's performance to next level, communication helps an individual who was earlier finding difficult to gel with others get along easily after removing self doubts.

Individual or Personal Stressors – One of the biggest individual stressors is role conflict and ambiguity in which one has to take job not suitable to their qualification or aptitude but accepted it just for the sake of earning livelihood, Self-concept can also be about not being able to perform efficiently there are few qualities required to be a good employee. An individual finds self in hyper or hypo stress due to one reason or the other, stress to an individual may be due to many reasons, most of the reasons are under our control, but very few reasons are beyond our control.

Effect; Every individual has different reaction to different stress conditions, because of social, economic, education, physical, mental background and emotional strength, some professionals are able to handle external stressor successfully and some professionals are successful in handling organizational stressor which depends on present circumstances. For example; a trainee will absorb stress positively in the interest of his job and career, whereas a middle level executive will absorb stress as he has to execute his social responsibilities, a senior professional who had no personal or family responsibility left will react to high level of stress will prefer life over job.

Scenario; If we take a pot of boiling water and put a spoon of coffee in it, coffee's aroma will spread freshness around you, again take a fresh pot of boiling water and put some potatoes in it, potatoes will get boiled and anybody can mash them, again take a boiling water and put some eggs into it they become hard boiled. It is like this every individual will react differently to same condition. By this example we can learn that we should make and develop ourselves in such a way that no condition can derail us from our original path. Under 'boiling' conditions either we should be spreading aroma or become so hard that no one can break us, in no condition we should become vegetable, allowing anyone to mash or cut us.

Reason of Stress for leader;

After opening his eyes during a journey John looked at his watch and assume that he will land at airport in two hours from now and within an hour of landing will reach office to attend a meeting where he will discuss about the preparations for delegation which is coming to check quality of the product for export order, if everything goes as per plan he has to order new machine for enhancing production capacity of manufacturing unit, For an outside observer these activities seem to be very hype, but for John it is very life consuming as he is feeling very tired at this point of time. He was thinking about the holiday plans as he wants to spend some time with his family and want to attend a wedding ceremony of his friend's daughter, but due to his professional commitments he was unable to do so.

When he got his first job after completing his MBA, he was very happy and think that he will be doing **this job for living but now he his living for the job,** since last twenty years his internal condition has not changed except the position and power, words like freedom, happiness and relations seems to be far distant and beyond visual range.

John has reached that stage of life where he can honestly introspect about the reasons for this condition and take decision accordingly as there is lot of life left to enjoy and celebrate. When he started analysing as evolved individual, he was able to point out those mistakes which he did knowingly or unknowingly and were against the basic rules of professionalism, he admitted following reasons for stress which he could have avoided.

Not Delegating routine tasks; Delegating is one professional quality which every leader must practice, as like other normal managers who suffers from 'I can do all' syndrome, which does not allow managers to become leaders, only those managers who change their working style in order to become leader chose the path of delegation which is laced with dual benefit.

It empowers team members to learn a new process which develops trust between the two, simultaneously it lessens the burden of leader for routine tasks, leader can utilise available time for more important tasks. A manager is afraid of delegating due to the reason of letting a secret out and might lower his status in team, where as leader having broader outlook, can act in the interest of team and organisation, a leader can go back to the time by recalling the struggle when he joined corporate world as trainee and there was nobody who can mentor him, he doesn't want to happen this thing to young team members.

Scenario; When John was out of station, he could not find any reliable team member who can be instructed to make preparation for upcoming events. He remembers those training sessions on which company spend lakhs of rupees and trainer used to talk about delegating, he simply ignored this as myth and thought he can do everything on his own, but today he considered delegating as integral part of senior's professional life. If he had delegated some part of his professional responsibility to his team mates, he would have been enjoying this wonderful trip and food which is being served as per his choice, but his mental condition is not fair enough to do that, he is continuously thinking about the piled up 'to do list' once he joins back office.

Quantity not Quality; We all know that quality is always better than quantity, those teams and organisations move far ahead of their competitors who prefers quality setting apart winner from loser, Despite of knowing that quality is always better than quantity, or in other words for a successful organisation Quality of its product is the sole guarantor of beating any competition and remain afloat in the market during every tough time, earn good name and revenue, but when it produces cheaper goods, equipment or material in the name of cost cutting, it cuts the organisation in two ways, one it needs to be repaired many times which involves money & time and on other side spare parts are not easily available and very soon that equipment become obsolete. When an organisation thinks of taking cost cutting measures, this measure cuts everything except cost, instead of cost cutting an organisation must resort to reduction in cost.

Scenario; When we read medal tally of various countries participating in Olympics, Asiad or Commonwealth games, country which had won one gold medal is ranked above all those countries who have won fifty silver or bronze medal, remember one gold medal is far above than many silver or bronze medals. It has been observed that in many organisations or educational institutes equipment are purchased only to fulfil regulatory requirements, whereas by spending some more amount it could be utilised for the purpose of imparting knowledge as well, throughout his career John had looked for quantity instead of quality, which resulted in time loss, undue stress to team members and leading the organisation towards to down fall.

Not developing quality human assets; Human assets are the most valuable component for any organisation and are flag bearer of it, one needs to continuously strengthen those hands who holds the flag. Strengthening of hands can be in the form of living in tune with the time, training on latest topics or modules, allowing team members to have **'knowledge time'**, knowledge time is that small portion of daily routine when a professional is encouraged to read or write about new researches and developments in his or her area of expertise & domain, encouraging team members to get some new stuff out of it, if that stuff is beneficial in improving the performance and efficiency of the team it can be implemented.

Scenario; John goes few years back and remember how he rejected few candidates who were more qualified to him, because of fear that they will take his place and his importance will not remain same in the hierarchy, in every ten-fifteen year desired qualification for a job keeps on changing but quality of talent remain same. As we all know during our parent's time in 1950s high school was considered a good qualification and after that it keeps on rising, few years back Ph.D. was not so common qualification, but it is not same now? Including talent in team should be the main aim and priority of a leader, only talent can withstand the storm generated by ever changing business scenario, because talent does not only means being a successful professional, a talented professional can adjust and develop self with the ever-changing professional atmosphere and remain productive for team and organisation.

Scenario; Why all developed countries encourage developing country's talented professionals like doctors, engineers, IT experts and scientists to settle in their countries and make policies, working & professional atmosphere to attract talent irrespective of their origin, all of us know that these countries face so much opposition from their own citizens because of these policies and practices, but they still follow it and don't stop practising these policies because of the result it shows, we know that almost every fortune 500 company have talented Indians as their team members, on board or as CEO. Somebody has rightly said "If you are the most intelligent person in a room, then you are in wrong company".

Not promoting open door and open communication policy. Communication is the key for any organisation and team to remain gelled whereas lack of proper and suitable style of communication will scatter team members by confusing and not allowing them to take quick decisions for efficient & smooth working, secondly, having closed door policy will create distrust among team members, Open door and open communication policy will encourage team members to express themselves at the best available opportunity, but every team member should be confident that s/he will be heard at the first available opportunity, this confidence encourages team members to think about the betterment of organisation and innovations which can benefit the process to take their product to next level, It has been clearly evident from world history that all the advancement whether it is social, technological or scientific took place with the help of suggestions or view points brought on table at appropriate time, as after certain time best suggestion become useless, as either we don't have energy & time available to make best use of it.

Scenario; John remembers that how he avoided meeting team members who are below manager rank and feel discomfort while talking to them in open and if any lower rank team member crosses his path in corridor or parking, he avoids them or keep communication to the minimum, this practice has put him into category of unprofessional and unapproachable leader, result of which he has to depend on group heads feedback only to take decision and other team members did not have any say during any problem solving, challenging meeting session or conflict resolving conversation, annual appraisal activities. This limited communication policy of John as CEO has put him back into the category of 'Manager' from 'Leader'.

Reason of stress for Team Leaders;

Ashutosh is associated with the DRT corporation as team leader, he is not feeling good about his team because of its poor performance and three of his team members have applied for leave at the same time due to ill health, as a forty year old professional he was unable to think properly and could not find out the reason behind team's poor performance even his performance is not up to the mark since last few weeks, he wants to take a break from office to have rest by spending some time with his family and join back fresh & rejuvenated to solve this crisis which he wanted to do without losing any time to minimize the loss, As his intention was very pure to solve the ongoing problem, after introspecting self he could find out few reasons which have led to this condition.

Procrastinating about solving internal team problems; Procrastinating to solve any dispute of team members or delaying any decision will result in uneasiness which might turn into unrest and disturbs the harmony of working atmosphere, for a decision taker it might not be of that importance, but for two parties involved in conflict or dispute and both of them thinks that they are correct, an outcome of decision will help them to settle down and concentrate on their respective jobs, this will also set the trend for future decision taking and making mechanism, if the decision making is quick then team member will rely on it and report matters for decision making, if decision making mechanism is improper then team members will decide among them selves resulting in groupism which again is chain reaction for re-occurring disputes and conflicts.

Scenario; Ashutosh don't spend time on complaints received regarding unethical behaviour of a team member or mis-behave of a toxic team member, smooth functioning and cohesiveness is the most important requirement for outstanding performance of team, but Ashutosh did not pay much attention to this as he thought about this complaints as normal, his failure in dealing with these complaints has two effects, one it has adverse effect on the working atmosphere in the group secondly, he has to face allegation of taking sides of those against whom complaints were pending. So, in order to avoid toxic atmosphere taking over team, a balanced decision taking mechanism must be developed and put in place, as we all know that "Justice delayed is justice denied".

Not giving feedback on the performance; What is the most important need of a team member executing h/her task efficiently? Which is one thing a student looks for after writing exams? Which is one thing which a professional looks for after completing a task? Answer to all the above three questions is 'Feedback'.

Feedback is that catalyst which can continue the chain reaction of tasks in positive way, requirement of team members have changed, when they are putting in so much efforts in the form of energy & knowledge, they don't want to continue in dark and want to know how they are doing, any improvement or modification is needed for efficient use of time and resources, constructive feedback not only saves time and valuable resources as well and fills a team members with pride and feels that some body is taking interest in them, self pride is very much required for continued motivation and interest in tasks.

Scenario; Ashutosh never gave any feedback to team members during their job nor he told them about the importance of job they are doing, in the absence of both the above points team members keep on moving in the dark and all the shortcomings comes into picture when they have completed their task, team members would have appreciated if any improvement, modifications or their shortcomings were told to them in the middle of the task, which could have saved them lot of time and resources as well. His one-liner was "First complete the given task then come to me". His negative attitude towards giving feedback has resulted in loss of many manhours and precious resources.

Not identifying high stress job roles; A team leader needs to identify high stress role and job allocation must be done as per proficiency of the team member, but this is common practice which sets apart a leader from manager, a leader identifies high stress jobs and take special care of those performing it by putting extra efforts and channelising their energy, knowledge and experience, when a team member gives 110% s/he expects special treatment from team leader and team in recognition of services which keeps the team in winning mode.

Scenario; Ashutosh did not identify high stress job roles, so he does not deal with them accordingly, he is under impression that all job roles carry equal amount of stress for which team members are getting awarded & rewarded as per their performance but things are not like this, some job roles in the team carries high level of stress and team members doing it expects their seniors to acknowledge it and reward them in proportion. Ashutosh should have identified those roles and rotated them among other team members also in order to give them feel of same, Ashutosh could not feel the pulse of changing times and act accordingly.

Not coaching & mentoring for team building and, on the job learning; Coaching and mentoring are those two pillars on which a team leader builds and moves team, coaching helps young generation to become better professional and mentoring helps a professional to come close to team leader, coaching fills young team members with confidence that they don't have to run here & there to learn about their trade practice, team leader is here to guide and help them learn tricks of the trades, where as mentoring will help a professional to open up to mentor personally which helps in solving lot of emotional or behavioural problems if there is any, when you come close to your team leader you are interested in doing good for your team, which might be passing information about toxic or selfish team member who is hell bent on harming the interest of organisation.

Scenario; When Ashutosh was introduced to mentoring and coaching classes by human resources department, with the aim of passing it on to every team member, he did not took them seriously, it was in his mind that he was never mentored or coached he learned all the skills required to complete the task without anybody's help, but over the time things have changed a lot with more research and exposure new ways have been found to do the activities in a better manner. Completely changing the way what is expected from team leader, a team leader who wants to have minimal of stress has to be in tune with the time for the progress of team members and self. Coaching and mentoring is one path through which a team leader can reduce the stress level of self and team members.

Not knowing about the family of the team members; Knowing about the family of team members should be one of the important functions of any team leader, now a days social fabric and family support has become very fragile, an individual looks for these things out side family and organisation is the only place where s/he can take cover to have peaceful solution or moments to recover till the ordeal is over. If a leader can take interest and know about the family of team members and their problems only then s/he can act accordingly to help them remove or reduce the stress they are facing if any.

Scenario; Ashutosh as team leader has to go through medium level of stress due to one more reason, as he don't take any interest in knowing about the family of his team members, resulting in some wrong allocation of job responsibilities, there is very fine line between interfering in the personal life of team member and knowing about the family of a team member.

A team leader who wants to reduce stress for himself has to minimize the stress of its team members as well, whether it originates from the organization or outside organization as there is direct co-relation of team member's stress and team leader's stress, it can be done through get togethers, celebrating festivals, through casual conversation or through developed trust.

Reason of stress for individual team member; Aniket has joined a multinational organization few months back through campus placement drive, since last few weeks he was not feeling comfortable. For a professional who has just started his career, it is very necessary to get comfortable and adjust to the culture & atmosphere of a corporate setup as they have a long journey ahead which they have to take on their own. But due to one or the other following reason they are unable to adjust and build confidence for their next responsibility.

Sense of Job insecurity; Number one reason of stress for a fresher in corporate sector is sense of insecurity about job, through media, social media or family surroundings they have heard numerous stories about impermanence of job in private sector, it is very much true that job loss in any private sector takes less time as compared to government sector job, but it is also true that there are immense opportunity available in private sector, private sector is the biggest employer of country, one very good thing about private sector is that if we are executing our responsibility properly, nobody dares to touch us, because both of us need each other to complete the cycle. Most of the job losses are due to product becoming obsolete, and the beauty of private sector is that it is very flexible and give importance to talent rather than rules and regulations,

Scenario; Shashank is working as executive commercial in RTY corporation, presently he is going through medium level of stress due to an invisible reason, despite of executing job responsibilities in a decent way he is afraid of losing his job due to perception generated by social media in the form reels and memes in which jobs in private sector is perceived as horrible, where as the truth is totally different, if there are job losses, there are job creations as well, take everything as challenge not problem and keep smiling under every circumstances, network yourself well, keep your savings more than your expenses, to meet any uncertainty, If any individual is giving 100% in any organisation s/he should not be afraid of losing job.

Mismatch between qualification and job responsibilities; One of the prominent reason of stress for a team member is mismatch between qualification, aptitude and job, in some cases a professional accepted those job offers which were not suitable as per their aptitude, in the beginning they thought that they will be able to sail through but in a specialized professional world it is very much necessary for attitude to match aptitude for a stress free career or to handle stress smoothly, as we all know that an individual's professional career expands around 20-25 years, it's very difficult to spend this period working without choice of our own or doing job which becomes daily struggle.

Scenario; Kriti has just joined a multinational corporate setup and got selected through campus placement after completing her B.Tech. in computer science, she has opted for B.Tech. (Computer Science) under the pressure of her parents who want her to be part of IT revolution going around the world, but Kriti wants to pursue her career in advertising & mass communication.

She was very uncomfortable during few first weeks at her place of work, she felt as if her life is getting out of her hands, because she can easily imagine about spending next 25-30 years with this discomfort, she started finding ways to get out of this mess, which was imposed by the choice of her parents. She knows that there is always second chance, third chance or fourth chance till we don't accept defeat, she continues working as software engineer till she had saved enough money to meet the course expenses to realise her dream, took admission in Masters programme with mass communication as major subject.

Lack of Psychological Hardiness.; A team member invites stress due to lack of psychological hardiness because s/he has already made a rosy picture about the profession, which does not match their expectations when they took the job, refuse to adjust to work culture and requirements of profession, sometimes it happens because when an individual does not get job of the level of their qualification or take job too personally. When we get out of our comfort zone, we need some amount of psychological hardiness or in raw words a team member should have hard skin to avoid taking everything too personally, lack of psychological hardiness makes young team member feels like every action or word is directed towards them and responsible for everything revolving around h/her. Where as an entry level team member must concentrate on what he is responsible for, deviating from this will attract stress.

Scenario; Sashi is associated with MD's office since last three years as executive secretary, Managing highest office of an organisation is not an easy task, Sashi is doing her job with great deal of efficiency, but in doing this she is suffering through high level of stress, because every other team member who want to have a word with MD, is higher in rank to Sashi and want his job to be done on priority basis, it is not possible for Sashi to do the things as per their convenience because MD's decision is final what to do and when to do and in the process senior team members some times loses control, for which Sashi has to bear the brunt of it, as a soft skinned human being she feels very bad and get disturbed for without any fault of her.

She was thinking of getting a solution for this problem, she looked around and observe the behaviour of other team members and found that no other team member is that much emotionally weak and soft skinned as she is, all other team member get along with themselves normally after few minutes of heated exchanged of words or being scolded by seniors, now she has found the solution of her problem i.e., ignoring &

avoiding negative conversations & matters which is very much required for healthy working atmosphere and herself.

No training and guidance from senior team member; An organization distribute stress when they don't make policy for training and guiding its new entrants, most of the organisations have policy of on the job training, which keeps the team member confused, seniors also feel threatened with the presence of new entrants in team, as new entrants are fresh and beaming with energy, There should be unwritten communication with in the organisation that giving support to freshers will be considered as positive move, every organization must have system, give time and responsibility to senior team members to guide freshers, this will act as dual benefit, one, it will save time & resources whereas by second side, we can help reduce stress for new team members which help them to get assimilated in the team.

Scenario; Kamal has joined a new organisation after three years of job in a reputed organisation and found that working culture here is totally different from the previous one, as he was not getting enough support from seniors to execute his job, but one thing he realises that it is only fortnight since he joined, it his responsibility also to try and get the support of seniors, he must take initiative & steps to develop those qualities which help him getting closer to senior team member and shun those habits which hinders from learning.

He realised that after all seniors are also human beings and like any other human being they also need respect & attention, there are certain requirements which needs to be fulfilled to open up with seniors, For this proficiency in soft skills helps a lot, a young team member who is interested in getting the support & co-operation of seniors must be good in time awareness, communication skills, emotional sensibility etc., developing these skills will make one likeable among seniors and will leave long lasting impressions by paving the way towards solution to lot of problems.

Not learning from mistakes. A good professional must take initiative to replace the tag 'I am the best' with 'I am the best learner'. In the beginning of career, we all make mistakes but problem occurs when we keep on repeating mistakes, due to learning helplessness we can't overcome the negative attitude, resulting in the low performance, one of the biggest reasons for stress is unable to learn from previous mistakes. It is not necessary that mistake occur only in the process one is responsible for, mistake could occur in communicating or co-ordinating, when we take it lightly it is bound to happen again, it is our duty and professional responsibility that we don't repeat a mistake or loose resources of organisation due to carelessness, it is better to have a diary in which we can note down day's important activities, which includes those mistakes as well, these underlined activities powered an individual to remember those mistakes and improve upon.

Scenario 1; Ramit has just joined a reputed multinational company involved in manufacturing premium bakery products catering to the need of high-end costumers. Ramit has topped in his MBA (Marketing) programme, having some sort of superiority complex, he looks at other team members as inferiors and finds his senior team members as old fashioned as they follow professional dress code and wear informal dress only on Friday, it almost took a week's time for seniors to convince Ramit to follow official guide lines on dress code.

Ramit thinks that he knows everything in this world or in other words he suffers from 'I know all syndrome' which results in paying less attention to the instruction of seniors, missing important steps of the process thus committing mistakes and repeating them, repeating mistakes puts a professional in the wrong book of seniors and self, because nobody has time & resources to work upon one thing again and again. After his turbulent stay of six months when Ramit's appraisal for completing probation was processed, all his seniors have recommended to extend the probation period by another six months.

One has to develop keen observing power to observe other team member's mistake as well and learn from it, do a mock exercise by observing what should have been done? in place of what is being done? This curiosity will help you explore and experience new options for improved version of self.

Not trying new things. Nothing new can be learn by working on same process and system for long time, repetition makes job monotonous and boring, resulting in loss of interest towards professional duties and stress formation for self & team. When a professional losses interest in his trade, it is not only organisation suffers which has spend lot of resources on training of individual, but it is nation & society's loss as well, when a well educated and trained professional losses interest in job due to high level of stress, Organisations & teams are now a days making every effort to keep negative stress at minimum and interest of team members intact by encouraging them to try new things with in the affordable parameters.

A trainee when pressed into service need to learn fast and adjust with the team, sometimes they have to execute new task to make things happen which requires to learn few things for which they don't have aptitude or not have educational background, but they have to learn it and execute it thereafter which need lot of efforts but it is a must for a successful tenure with the team, by accomplishing a new task or gaining knowledge in a new field gives a team member great deal of confidence.

Not understanding company's culture. A professional has to have basic understanding of different types of culture in corporate setup, by understanding the culture of organisation, one is able to minimise the negative stress because she or he has it's own built-in culture, which is the gift of family upbringing, some pre-conceived notions and style of life s/he wants to live, principles to follow, but sometimes reality is far away from imagination, having face to face encounter with mismatch culture fills a professional with negative stress.

Every organization or company has specific culture through which things move, functions & operate. There are specific individuals through which one can reach out to seniors, in every organization there are credit distributers around whom power revolves, to fit into it and to be successful in an organization, one has to understand and read those signs. In most of the organizations there are two power centres, especially in family-owned business setup, one is formal and second is informal, formal power is the one which is designated officially by management.

There may be one more power centre which is informal, s/he might not hold formal designation but has equal say in decision making, s/he may be close relative of top management or a professional associated with organisation since inception or very high skilled and knowledgeable professional whose contribution to revenue is substantial. So, an individual must understand this and make every effort to strike balance between the two.

Reason of stress for students;

Shalini has taken admission in one of the best institutes of the state but due to one reason or the other she is unable to score good marks in the first sessional exams, she tries to find out what is holding her back, why she has not been able to attain her goal and unable to fill the gap between reality & imagination which is the practical aspect and right way to lead a successful student life.

Not learning to say "NO"; Since childhood we have been told that we should always say 'Yes' to any request or demand made by others, because saying 'No' has always been considered as bad manners or rude behaviour, but with changing times and challenging circumstances, it is very necessary for a student to know when to say 'no'.

As a student, we are little shy to ask for something and a bit hesitant to say 'NO' to any unwanted request which led us to some unpleasant circumstances and create misunderstanding, A student is expected to say 'Yes' to every demand raise by their seniors and peers, it may be attending party instead of completing assignments or giving loan to friend for anything but not for study purpose, there are so many other things to which a student should say 'NO', but could not, resulting in emotional hazard.

Scenario; Gagan is studying B.Arch. from a reputed institute away from his hometown and living in hostel, he has inherited good qualities like helping anyone who is in need, but in hostel fellow students are taking advantage of good nature of Gagan, when ever fellow students need something in the form of money, books or any other material first name comes to their mind is Gagan, because of his good nature Gagan is facing lot of problem, and there is only one reason behind his problem is his inability to say 'NO',

De-Stressing

Gagan is of two opinions whether he should continue his good nature of helping others or save self from getting disturbed and losing peace of mind, his main aim is to pass this programme with good grades, if helping others is creating a problem in the way of his goal he should immediately stop helping others, his notion of helping others took a U-turn, when he saw a friend whom he had helped financially was partying other night in a fine dining restaurant along with his gang, this has shaken Gagan from inside, forcing him to think that he was not helping others but in fact he is being used by fellow students, Keeping in view the demanding student life It is very necessary for a student to learn to say 'No' , Saying 'Yes' in place of 'No' is a bigger problem than earning a label of good guy, and will derail your planning to be good at studies, by losing time, resources and 'real' friends in the process.

Not asking for help and guidance. What will others say if I seek help from my seniors and fellow students, will not they think that I do not know this or that, does not it expose me in front of my friends, won't they take advantage of my weakness. A student who is new to a professional programme is hesitant & shy to ask for help and not aware of the benefits of asking for help and guidance, we have to bend a little and put our best foot forward to get some precious advice & help in the process. Learning to ask for support also shows your intention to do things in best possible way to achieve the desired results and meeting targets. Another benefit of seeking help from seniors is that it will make long term relationship, provided this help is only related to academics only not for any other matter related to any type of pleasure.

Scenario; Tripti who is doing her BJMC (Bachelor's of Journalism and Mass Communication) programme from a private institute and want to be content developer in the field of media, During professional course, Tripti found that she is little bit hesitant to speak fluently on the prepared topics, she wanted to find out the reason and make a course correction for the same, she decided to take help from one of her classmate in this matter, but that classmate could not help her.

Tripti did not lose heart and with lot of courage she approached her faculty to solve this problem, faculty was very happy to see the positive approach of Tripti to overcome her shortcoming and guided her properly to solve the problem, As a student one must understand that during student life nobody is perfect or knows everything, student life is a learning platform, one student may be good in studies but non-supportive to others in daily matters, those who are good in sports or co-curricular activities suffers from superiority complex, a good student who is interested in moving ahead is a keen observer and ready to look within and don't hesitate to seek help in the matter in which s/he lacks proficiency. Seeking help is a sign of inner strength and thirst for improvement.

Not accepting reality; All students have some dreams and targets which are nursed since childhood, which trade is best suitable for me, is it medicine, management, engineering, law, teaching or Information Technology, but between this we must keep a reality check about ourselves, there is a chance we may not be fit for what we are dreaming for, or there are more talented and capable individuals vouching for those positions or rankings, there is fair chance of not getting you had worked for or dreamed about, but that does not mean you lose interest in life or career and become disheartened, to avoid negative stress we have to learn to accept what we got, give your hundred percent to your second choice and become number one in that.

Scenario; During school time Raman Preet had dreamt of joining civil services, she made a rosy picture about her ability which was far from reality, after stipulated number of attempts she could not qualify UPSC and she has to settle for junior position but was unable to accept the truth and every day she make herself feel bad for not being making it to the civil services, giving undue negative stress to self, one day she was sitting in her office thinking about unnecessary stress, she says to herself that nothing can change the fact that she cannot become a civil servant in this life, why can't she gave 110% percent to what she is right now and excel in this very position.

Not letting go, Not forgiving; If one of your friends humiliates you in front of group members without any fault of yours or you have gone through a bad day, your thoughts keep on revolving about those incident or humiliation, with all the efforts you could not take that incident out of mind, asking yourself so many unreasonable questions leading to high level of stress thereby putting question mark on your ability as rational thinker.

One has to learn how to be comfortable with self, not to be upset on trivial issues, a student must channelise all thoughts to be at peace with self, s/he must not lose sight of goal due to petty reasons and must understand that priority at this point of time is to forget and let go this untoward incident or humiliation, this is not permanent mark on you, to avoid stress overtaking one must get rid of it sooner and move ahead.

Scenario; Simran who comes from family of average financial background, is doing her M.B.B.S. from a reputed institute on the basis of rank secured through NEET exam, Simran posses every good quality of an excellent student except one and that is she can not let go any incident which had produced negative emotions for her, she constantly keep thinking about that incident only, one bad incident is enough to keep her off the track whole week, during an unofficial gathering one of the peers indirectly commented about the average financial status of Simran.

That friend does not speak any thing directly to her but Simran took it personally and got disturbed by this incident which happened few days before final exams and was reflected in the marks scored by her. Even after exams Simran was constantly thinking about that, when matter went out of control, she decided to meet college counsellor, counsellor told her that if she wanted to lead a good professional and personal life, she has to learn how to overcome these type of situations which will be re-occurring in a student's life, how long we can keep pondering over these petty issues and lose peace of mind, secondly some times those statements are not directed towards us and it is our perception only which puts us into trouble, Counsellor told Simran to forget that incidence and forgive that individual in the larger interest of nobody but self. Simran thanked counsellor for guiding her in the right direction.

Thinking with closed mind; One of the top reason for students is accepting and listening what ever their mind says, but the truth is that mind says so many things which may be related or not related with us, A student is expected to learn with open mind and develop the instinct which can solve day-to-day problems by keeping every point and circumstance in mind and able to delete useless and unrelated thoughts which unnecessarily consumes lot of energy, time and are misguiding, as the future of our country it is very important for students to channelise their energy and thoughts in the right direction.

Scenario; Himanshu was doing Bachelor's degree in civil engineering, he has chosen this stream (Civil) because he comes from family background of builders and his father also wanted to have him professionally qualified to take over family business in a better way and introduce modern technology in the trade. In the beginning of the programme Himanshu was very much interested in learning the art of civil engineering, but after second year his friends who have taken admission in other streams such as computer science, electrical or mechanical, teased him constantly by telling him that only the applicants having low rank opt for civil engineering.

This teasing created confusion in the mind of Himanshu, who lost track of his studies and interest in the civil branch of engineering. When his father noted down trend in Himanshu's grade, He decided to have a talk with him, during open and frank conversation he came to understand whole scenario. He told Himanshu that every individual and their need in this world is different from others, every human being takes decision about their future keeping in mind the circumstances and resources available, one should never compare with anybody else in this matter. Secondly, one very positive aspect of Himanshu pursuing Civil Engineering is that he doesn't have to look any where else for job, he has well settled family business which he is expected to take to next level by learning and applying latest trend and technology of civil engineering, whereas his friends have to queue in front of companies coming for campus placement. After positive conversation with his father Himanshu once again started pursuing his course with great deal of enthusiasm and completed it with one of the best ever rank scored in civil branch of engineering.

Not owning their mistakes; Stress level for any student will start rising when they take decisions by keeping only themselves in mind and not owning their mistakes, every student is bound to make mistakes during journey of learning process called life, Stress is minimised when a student makes practice of owning their mistakes which is sign of strength, and brings clarity about next step to be taken, not knowing what needs to be done and start looking here & there for a escape goat, it has been observed that students blame their parents, teachers, relatives or educational set-up for their problems or poor grades, they want to change these static factors, not looking within, even if those factors are responsible for stress, but nothing can be done about them, so it is better to adjust and act accordingly.

Scenario; Shubham is pursuing bachelor's degree in physiotherapy from a reputed institute in capital, he always wanted to be a doctor and tried to crack NEET exam after completing 10+2 exam, in first attempt he could not get admission in M.B.B.S. programme, so he decided to give it one more chance next year, he had full one year to prepare for it, even then he could not qualify for M.B.B.S. programme, reason being that he thought as he had missed admission in the programme last year by 12 marks only, will cover it by preparing in the last four months, so he keep on spending most of the time on social media & binge watching on OTT platforms and did not gave any heed to the point that he will not only be competing with last years students but also with the freshers who had just cleared their 10+2 exam and are more hungry to get admission in M.B.B.S. programme. For this he continued blaming parents, atmosphere of his house or sometimes whole society and coaching institutes.

While sitting in the canteen of his physiotherapy institute Shubham introspect self and tried to find out the reason for his failure to clear NEET examination, he finds nobody else but himself responsible for the debacle, if he had worked hard and given heed to his parent's & teacher's advice not to be overconfident in this matter and concentrate only on studies during gap year. After taking admission in physiotherapy programme, he wanted to give hundred percent while studying it and to be one of the best physiotherapists.

Managing Stress; A team member undergoing heavy stress is unable to execute assigned responsibilities in a proper manner, leading to poor work performance and interpersonal relationship, these two factors lead to absenteeism and sudden change in habits such as preferring isolation, poor eye contact and non-worthy feeling.

We have to find out the reason of stress, to take preventive and proactive measures by understanding our body rhythms, scheduling priorities and time awareness. delegating tasks to others. making time for leisure. focusing on one thing at a time. requesting others for help. There are few techniques through which we can relax, giving our mind and body much needed rest, with the help of few relaxation techniques like meditation, deep breath, massage and exercise. Physical fitness is the key, take proper care of your body and make it strong. Exercise regularly, remain hydrated, move towards tranquil mind, take Balanced Diet, avoid alcohol, tobacco and smoking.

Conclusion; After having gone through above read, we know that 'A' side of sword called stress is laced with energy, enthusiasm and positivity which helps in overcoming speed breakers of success. Where as 'B' side of sword is laced with procrastination, inaction and excuses. It is up to us which side we want to use. When we chose 'A' side which always results in positive side of life, where as if we chose 'B' side its result will be hazy and of no use by the time it arrives.

Building a Winning Team

I was an important member of cricket team during my college time, we were up against last year champions in the final match of inter-college tournament. Our team and coach met on a road side tea stall to discuss the strategy to win the match as our coach and captain was not very comfortable in facing number one team, but we were aware of their weakness & strengths and hopeful of winning the match, during the match I was able to grab the wicket of their star batsman when he had scored only 11 runs, this wicket puts them under tremendous pressure resulted in losing the match and we were new inter-college champions for the year 1991.

After celebrations, I was really happy and thought that I am responsible for this historic win because I took the prize wicket of their star performer otherwise, we would have lost the match, but during celebrations our coach did not mention my name separately, he simply said in a matured way that "I really appreciate that every team member has given his 100%, executed the assigned job to the perfection and played his role superbly." I was really very disappointed and discuss the matter with my father, my father told me that in a team all members make equal efforts to achieve the goal once the goal is achieved whole team is praised and given credit for, not a single performer and you took the wicket of star batsman with the help of that fielder who took the catch."

When I joined a multinational company as a trainee after completing my professional course, I was really very happy and eager to show my abilities as a professional and win laurels from day one, I was interested in leading others, but in due course of time I learned that at this point of career I don't have the experience and position to lead others but I have to lead self and become a reliable team member by directing all my knowledge & energy to achieve the goals of the team. During one project my performance was best as considered by self but in fact all team members had performed well and given their best to achieve the target, from there onwards I understood that a real professional or sportsman performs and surpass his previous best not to impress others but to self.

I was highly impressed by working style of my team leader whom I joined one month back for new project, as I was going to my cubicle after taking lunch, suddenly I heard my name from behind and stopped immediately and saw my new project head calling me, I thought it might be regarding some discussion about the status of the project or any new addition or correction in the project, but I was astonished to hear him talking about the day-night one day match between India and Australia, our discussion went like this.

Team Leader; What a fantastic match it was.

Me; Yes Sir, but we lost the match.

Team leader; So, what? We played well and fought till last over. Hopefully we will do better in next match.

After completing the conversation, we both went to our respective work of place, one thing kept me happy that I have met a team leader who was discussing other than official things. Next time I was sitting in the cafeteria with my group, again my team leader joined us with a cup of coffee in his hand, we become little suspicious and thought he came looking for us to reprimand us for some mistake in the project but he started the discussion about adventure sports and encouraged us to do paragliding or biking as he was also member of biking group of the city. Our team was really happy the way he connects with members. We were discussing the matter after few days and thought how much extra efforts our new team leader has to make in order to know about hobbies and interest of our team members, be it through social media or reading their personal files.

After eight years of job, when I become team leader and my whole responsibilities came upside down, because as a team leader my self interest takes back seat and the interest of my team always comes first. At this point of my career, I have to guide & lead a team. Sometimes I have to use carrot and sometimes I have to use stick.

While assuming the responsibilities of team leader I was very happy and a thought came into my mind that now I will sit in the cabin and order only what is to be done, but after few days this style of leading a team went hay wire as I could not understand what's going on, when going back into earlier days of my career and recall my first boss who used to lead the team by jumping in to the trench and soiling his hands with grease, than I get out of my cabin and start following the same practice leading my team towards success. I have learned that each and every team member is equally important and the success of team depends upon every team member giving its 100%.

I remember an incident about my friend who was serving the Indian Air Force as fighter pilot, during a regular sortie his plane developed a snag and he ejected successfully and after recovering from this accident, first thing my friend did is to meet the team who packed his parachute. This incident reminds me that every member of team is equally important from parachute packer to air traffic controller.

Today morning while sitting in the office with some free time, last twenty-eight years flash backed in front of my eyes, When I stepped into this corporate world as student and reached to the post of CEO, I remember transition of society and corporate world from individualism to team spirit. Twenty years back while receiving any award or trophy celebrities, actors and sports person always delivered thankyou note without mentioning their team members, but things have taken a U-turn and importance of team has been realized by giving it equal importance.

Need & Benefits of Team; All inventions and discoveries in this world are done by teams, no project or achievement is done by single person although when a single person is called on stage, first word comes from h/her mouth is 'team', whether its Nobel prize winner scientist or writer, Oscar winner director, actor & actress or winning team's captain of any sport or game spraying a shower of champagne, now it's very clear that nobody can achieve a goal alone. We need a bunch of capable people as team to execute a task.

Formation of team helps in improving organizational performance, since team consists of several specialists from their respective fields it increases productivity, minimizes wastage and reduces errors by continuously helping each other and keeping a check by not allowing the things going out of hand as it's not individual's loss, it is loss for whole team.

Every team member is known by its team's name. when "we work as team" or "we decided to work as team", there is very fine line between above two phrases, in first phrase, we are working as a team means we are doing or executing our assigned task and rest will follow we are not bothered about goal accomplishment, but when we 'decided' to work as a team, we take full responsibility by connecting ourselves to goal accomplishment, in this we are not only concern with executing our task, we are happy to help others to excel in their task in the interest and growth of team, When we decided to work as a team we forget differences and gel to provide quality services whether we are in IT sector, hospitality, services or in any other field, no sector can grow by encouraging individual laurels. Quality and customer services reaches new heights with the individual working as a proud member of team not as an individual.

    A team member who has 'decided' to be a team member does not hesitate to describe real condition to team leader and team members, so as to avoid any loss occurring to team due to h/her, Secondly, they do not hesitate to ask for help to mend this and get out of it with minimal loss. Now the question arises why a team member who has 'decided' to be a part of team is so confident of getting help at the time of distress, answer lies in h/her confidence because s/he had also helped another team member to get out of a problem by sparing extra time and energy. When we have cushion or backing of a team, our stress level becomes low and we feel comfortable & confident in the company of each other, this comfortable and confidence help us to execute our task with ease thus increasing our output and making us proficient in our job.

    A sense of dignity prevails when we are part of a team which is continuously winning, exceeded its limitations and performed beyond the expectations of their seniors or top management it may be winning a bid, completing a project on time or developing an improved product gives us opportunity to relate to team in a dignified manner, a sense of pride is always carried along with trophy as physical award or trophy is kept in cup-board but its presence is always felt on chest and shoulders of the members of winning team.

    Self-control is one more by product which is the result of winning team, as part of winning team we not only carry the pride but also reputation of the team which requires lot of self-control, one has to be extra careful for not bringing bad name, a single bad incident is remembered for long time, not only in the name of the individual who committed the blunder, but it also remain associated with the team, so as a team member if you don't want to bring bad name to your team, take extra precaution while speaking, listening and execution while in office or public.

Another wonderful feature of a great team is that keeps the team member motivated thus creating a positive work environment, which in turn reduces and counter biggest problem of now a day i.e. high attrition rate, professional organizations are making all out efforts to retain talented team members, all are looking for greener pastures irrespective of thinking what organisation has done for them, team members are also social animal who looks for cosy & healthy working atmosphere, if they are comfortable with the flock it is less likely that they look for new nest, it is very important for organizations to strengthen their teams by using every possible resources available to retain talent.

A team when it is good and tries everything to be best by working smart, hard & intelligently, becomes apple of eye of the seniors and come closer to decision makers & top management, this is the best reward a team can fetch by working hard and clinching their goals, when a team is closer to decision makers, it helps them to get the things out of the way which helps them further to enhance their performance by triggering the chain reaction.

It is very important for a team to excel in its domain and an individual has to move from merely a team member to "I have decided to be a team member" because being a team member comes automatically whereas decision to be a team member is taken happily & willingly which leads to **Organizational Enhancement** and is the ultimate aim of a sincere professional in the interest of self as well.

Team winners for a leader;

Demonstrate Character & Competence; A leader has to demonstrate character and competence with a clear vision and must have competence in his or her domain to win the confidence of team members. Character is tested when an organization is not doing well and failing to achieve its set goals or asking for change to keep in tune with the time.

What steps a leader takes to stream line the organization and make it bounce back, inject positive vibes in team, the type of communication, how he motivates the team members. Is he able to tell them, you are not merely bread winners for your family but you are bread winners for this organization as well, when any problem is faced by family, all family members get together to overcome it, similarly when our organisation is going through rough phase, only we as a team member can make a turn around and bring it back into green, correcting our mistakes and start journey with a fresh out look into the future as rising sun. Character is also demonstrated when a leader has enough strength to take tough decisions in favour of team and keeping the interest of the organization as supreme. A leader if want to establish his credibility should refrain from using words like this "I don't know anything, go and get it done".

Ability to motivate and inspire team members; Motivation and inspiration is that fuel which generates power in a human being, as human beings we all need an outside push to give our best. Question arises who will take responsibility of getting the best out of team members, it is leader's job to keep its team members motivated and inspired, as discussed above team members needs outer push so that they can give their best, team members are not machines sometimes they lose focus, sometimes they lack interest, sometimes they do not have mental or physical energy, to bring them back on track a leader has to take adequate steps.

Key to motivating and inspiring for a leader is to go back into 'flash back' and remember how she or he got back on track and produced best performance. It does not mean that most of the team members are demotivated, but they are unable to find the right track to reach their destination or common goal of team. A leader must encourage & develop culture and dynamic mindset of its organisation so as team members are left with no room for anything but to remain motivated. It could be done by maintaining proper channels of communication, setting examples and giving proper recognition by practicing fair play policy.

Best words you can say to a team member, not what he is doing best right now, but what s/he is capable of doing next, an individual is motivated when they listen about the immense possibilities s/he is filled with. Secondly, there is hardly any team member who is demotivated or lack the energy or will to move ahead in life, if a leader thinks there are many team members who are not enthusiastic or lack energy to execute the given task, watch them closely when they are engaged in the activities which interests them, when they are walking in corridor after duty time or when they are in the company of their friends, it is leader's job to find the reason and remove the obstacle from their path, a leader must try to find out the answer to the question, 'What is holding them?

Participative Leadership & Shared Responsibility. While leading team a leader is team member as well and has to be an active participant during action, to make team members realize that they are also leader in themselves and is always standing in front of them when anything goes wrong and 'behind' when everything is moving smoothly. With the appropriate action and communication team members needs to be reminded continuously, that I (leader) am responsible for everything happening here, if all of you gives your best every time, you share my leadership and in turn I will share your responsibility.

Scenario; When Dr. APJ Abdul Kalam was working as project director in ISRO to put satellite in to orbit, but in its first attempt he could not succeed, ISRO has to face media persons during a press conference, head of ISRO Dr. Satish Dhawan told Dr. Kalam that I will address the press conference to tell what went wrong in putting the satellite into orbit. In the second attempt when ISRO was successful in putting the satellite into orbit, Dr. Satish Dhawan put Dr. Kalam in forefront and tell him to address the press.

Cohesiveness or Sense of we-ness; To accept self among and equal to team members is the most difficult task for a leader, A manager becomes leader if s/he put h/her foot in team member's shoes, since a leader is the most experienced and professionally qualified individual of team, it is natural for h/her to consider self superior to rest of the team and have controlled arrogance so that no team member takes undue advantage.

There are certain circumstances and moments during task execution when, a leader has to be like other team members, for dual advantage, first, when a leader bring self to the level of team members, it fills the team members with confidence as they understand that their leader is getting down to their level to give them guidance and confidence, another side helps in executing the task in a very congenial atmosphere, generating faith in leader and style of leadership. This cohesiveness does not come easily one has to learn to move from being 'I' to 'WE', a leader who wish to move from 'I' to 'WE' has to shed so many colours and skins, it requires inner strength and positive intention to do good, secondly, equally difficult journey is travelling back from 'WE' to 'I' and continuously keep on rotating as per the situation.

Clear Vision & Clear Performance Goal; Best thing a leader can do to develop culture of excellence and make no compromise with it, a clear vision has to be formed that there will be no compromise on quality, a clear message has to be sent to all the stake holders that our ultimate goal is the success of organisation which depends upon every team member giving its best, our survival depends upon the success of organisation and every team member is expected to keep up with the desired pace, any team member getting behind will be helped to be part of winning team but no lethargic ness or carelessness will be tolerated at any level. There might come a situation that few team members getting upset with leader's strictness, but truth is that most of the team members like this professionalism by happily accepting the challenge.

Leader needs to have clarity in directing team and set transparent performance goals for a successful organisation, a leader cannot have 'please all' policy and must set those goals which are achievable & measurable, by keeping in view the ability, strength and weakness of team members, when targets and goals are set rationally and team members are successful in meeting those targets, they want to reach next level by accepting higher targets. A leader must encourage brain storming about where we are, where we want to go and how we will reach there, who will be the flag bearer for the same, all these discussions should be openly discussed with the strength, to remove weaknesses and take constructive feedback.

Problem Solving; A leader's job is very lonely and most of its time & energy is consumed in problem solving, as head of the organisation she or he is responsible for everything whether it is good or bad, in day-to-day activity she or he comes across many problems which might include sudden shortage of raw material, a talented team member leaving the organisation or sudden break down of assembly line, a leader has to deal with many such problems.

A leader is mostly known and remembered for approach towards solving a problem and taking proactive action so that the problem is not repeated, leader's approach is mostly appreciated when s/he involves all the team members concern to sit down and encourage brain storming about it, most successful leaders have the ability to respect ideas, opinion and suggestions to reach consensus. When every team member is heard and their opinion & suggestions considered, thus paving the way for best team build.

Problem solving is also taken as example how a team gels, best thing a leader can about a problem is to turn it into a challenge and motivate team members to find out the solution. Once a problem is identified, all energy should be channelled to solve it rather than lingering it, sometimes a problem is not from the domain of the leader, a leader must accept that there is no harm in getting out of the way and leaving the experts to take decision regarding this situation.

Strength and ability to step back; When we are unable to move forward or stuck in a traffic jam or travelling on a road which is very risky and the whole caravan might be lost in continuing the journey, a wise and insightful leader will take a U-turn to save the team, because wellbeing of team and self is the prime motive of leader, a leader will not hesitate to take U-turn to keep team on winning track, where as a manager who is interested in personal glory will not take a U-turn and continue on wrong path even if it endangers the very existence of team or self.

A professional who was appointed as head of organisation due to competency in domain, but under h/her leadership organization's performance is going down, lot of rumours and gossips started spreading in the corridor about the capability and competency of head, and the worst thing which happens during this, head who was best in domain could not give required output due to this interruption, which again become a question mark on the head's reputation simultaneously resulting in the loss to the organisation. This can be understood by **example**; Sachin Tendulkar and Virat Kohli are among India's top cricket player during the peak of their careers they were given the responsibility to lead India, as we all know that they were not successful as captain, they both surrendered their captaincy and step down, but knowing that they are valuable part of team India, they offered to remain part of team, their decision to continue to be part of team bore good fruits, as they made good contribution and helped Indian team in winning many championships.

A leader understands that ego is the biggest hindrance in a professional's life, and the flexibility to move forward and backward is the key for a successful career and utilizing h/her ability to the best.

Discovery for & by leader; Leader's job is to discover a purpose for his team and various methods to be in tune with the world so that s/he can take his team ahead. Leader has reached a stage where he is able to discover new skills in team members to take his team & organization to new heights. Leader must have in his mind to attain and enjoy finer aspects of life, try to reach stage of self-realization by developing the capability to see beyond revenue generation and cost cutting, giving financial & non-financial entities same importance and preferences. Develops caring attitude prefer knowledge & education over qualification and interested more in giving. Let us discuss them one by one.

Silver Quality: Any new discovery in self gives confidence. (For self), When a leader discovers that she or he possesses certain qualities which are the core of action and is able to steer team in the right direction. Secondly, when team becomes aware of these qualities all team members are filled with confidence and knows that they can depend on their leader as and when the need arises, a quality which is known to self and other team members creates a bridge of dependability, which in turn gives birth to positive culture.

Scenario; A leader's **silver quality** may be good decision making, A good decision-making leader is a boon for any organisation as every team member knows that whatever decision a leader takes will ultimately leads to betterment for organisation and team members, even if in the beginning it look tough but in due course of time it is in the larger interest of team.

When a leader assigns you a project which requires lot of travelling and energy consuming because s/he knows that you are the one who is best suitable for the job, since you are going to execute this type of project first time, but you are not sure whether you will be able to perform the assigned duties, but after completion of the project you discovered that you are more energetic than you had ever thought of. Successful completion of task was your confidence on the decision-making ability of your leader.

Golden Quality; Any new discovery in others generates trust. (For others). There are certain qualities which you have mastered or developed over a period of your career, they become part of your professional life and it is very normal for you or in other words when you display these qualities there is no sense of specialness, but for others it is really astonishing.

Scenario; Abhishek is leader of XYZ corporation, over the career span of approximately twenty years Abhishek has developed the quality of taking initiative in every task which is assigned to him, team members were really astonished and happy to see that when during an assignment one of his team members fell ill, leaving them short of strength, but he was confident that our team will complete this assignment with in given time frame because of his adaptive and organized response. Your exemplary performance makes other team members astonished as they discovered that you can achieve your target with the given resources without complaining about it.

Diamond Quality; Any new discovery in self gives us confidence. (For team). There are few qualities which we are aware of during our professional activities or career, this diamond quality is very close to our heart and give us edge over others. When as a leader we discover that we have one more quality which we have not used it till date.

Scenario; Abhishek while working as CEO of XYZ corporation was well established and successful, during a top management meeting one of the Directors during tea interval casually discussed that as per diversification plans management is thinking of setting up a steel plant in addition to their present pharmaceutical operations and looking for a professional who can handle this new set-up. Abhishek after thinking for a while told the Director that being from technical back ground he considers himself best for the above-mentioned new assignment and his first assignment in corporate sector was setting up of a new plant from erection to commissioning of 100% export-oriented unit of terry towels. On listening this Director gave him appointment to meet him for further discussion.

Platinum Quality; A new Quality developed for the success of self and team. When we came to know about few qualities, which we as a leader must possess for the successful role. We identify and start working to master that quality by learning, unlearning and relearning at any stage of life or career shows that learning is a lifelong activity and age has nothing to do with it, our sole interest is the betterment of self and team by finding out what needs to be learned for smooth functioning.

Scenario; it is not only discovery about any new qualities, for a leader which may be absent to perform well in newly acquired role, when a leader lacks one or two qualities which are very much required for. It is h/her responsibility to identify, learn and utilize these qualities.

When two departments of organisation were in conflict due to professional reasons Abhishek look into the matter and resolve the issue to avoid further aggravation of problem, it was first time in his professional life span that Abhishek had handled such issue, but he accepted the challenge, studied and prepared self to meet it and was successfully able to resolve the issue with the help of newly acquired skill & quality known as negotiation & mediation, before pressing himself into new task Abhishek has to do lot of homework by identifying & understanding the qualities required to deal with the matter, he felt a sigh of relief and contented by adding one more feather in his cap, which he posses and seniors also came to know about one more quality on which they can depend on him if such situation arises again.

Barrier in building winning team by leader.

Credibility of Leader; If we want to point out barrier in a leaders' way which stops him or her from being recognised as leader, which may be past performance, not having respect for words, unprofessional attitude or weak emotional understanding. Leading a winning team requires lot of qualities and above all intention to sacrifice personal interests for the benefit of team.

Team Winners for Team Leader;

When I became team leader after ten years of job, I think about the types of teams I have led and participated as an active member by giving my best, good thing is that I was part of many other teams also while executing the responsibilities of my primary team, my first exposure to be member of an **Advice team** which was expected to give its recommendations to management about recreation & welfare activities for employees, how to expediate the process of handling their grievances or how to reduce the time span for decision taking mechanism for a grievance.

This exercise I have to do it while working regularly with my **Production team** which was responsible for day-to-day functioning and maintenance of plant, as in-charge of maintenance team, we have to coordinate a lot with other departments and always on our tows for dealing with any emergency if occurs. As our organisation is earning fair amount of profit, higher management decided to set up one more unit to meet the increasing demand.

I was appointed a member of **Project team** to give my recommendations as technical competent professional and have to co-ordinate with functional specialist of other departments such as civil engineering, finance, and logistics etc. with the dedicated and well-coordinated efforts of our team we were able to execute the project in given time.

Our management decided to celebrate it by constituting an **Action team,** which was responsible for conducting motor bike rally from Headquarters (Bombay) to manufacturing unit (Pune) and inter department sports meet as a team building exercise.

Building Winning Team by Team Leader;

Providing supportive environment.; Team leader's job is to create an atmosphere where all team members can thrive and move towards giving their best, in a supportive atmosphere all team members feel themselves not only a member but part of the team as well, a part however small is equally important to complete the whole process, with the smallest part missing no team can move ahead, team leader's job is to see that this support reaches to the smallest of part, be it is electrician, guard, house keeper driver or another team member involved in providing support to team.

Heading a team is very lonely and delicate job, one part giving away leads to the whole chain getting disturbed. Team leader's job will be less stressful if he or she is able to understand the need of all parts of his garden who bears fruit as per the need of the plant, in fact group leader is a gardener who is to provide food (understanding), light (love) and water (Trust) to its team, this keeps the garden green even during summer season by conserving energy throughout the year.

Foster Team Work & Co-operation; As a matured team leader, one must foster an element of co-operation among team members, but it has been found that in order to hush up and fasten the project execution, they encourage competition in the team and failed to understand that competition is between opponents or rivals but not between team members, competition moves faster than cooperation for some time only and is short lived, it crumbles and start moving at snail's pace or sometimes it starts moving backwards as infighting takes place among team members to grab number one position.

Co-operation means integrated efforts to achieve a pre decided goal and fulfils the inter-personal need of team where as competition fulfils an individuals need. Now the question arises how we will recognize or award co-operation, for that we have to device an efficient system, so that competition is replaced by co-operation and its result is spread to whole team by recognising and appreciating co-operators, rewarded and mentioned during team meetings. Co-operation creates permanent bond between team members as element of adjustment and giving in the process

Scenario; Rashmi was heading a project and whole team was doing good except two team members being very impatient, they want everything to be done in seconds actually their speed was much more than the average team member, this condition of rate busting by two team members is putting all other team members under stress and these two rates busting team members were getting arrogant day by day. Rashmi discussed the matter with these two team members, introduce them to the importance of co-operation and the benefits of being co-operative. When these team members start their journey on co-operative mode bringing tremendous turnaround in the behaviour of fellow team members and liked by everybody in team. For a team leader it's very necessary to develop co-operation as a tool for smooth functioning of team.

Conflict Management; If a team leader wants to win the confidence of team members and direct team towards attaining the pre set goal, s/he has to be very proficient in dealing with conflict with in time. A team consists of members coming from different educational, social, economic background, gender, personality, aptitude and attitude, a conflict among them is bound to happen. A team leader's job becomes more complex when s/he sees team deviating from its goal to satisfying self-ego or in other words team members are consuming their energy to win over each other rather than making a winning combination to achieve the goal. Internal conflict drains the team of its positive energy. To keep the team together and free of any conflict a team leader must be very proactive in tackling this menace of internal conflict by understanding the nature and complexes of every team member.

Conflict does not only occur among individuals but between groups with in team, and most interestingly sometimes it is unconscious act by individual or group who do not understand or are not aware of the result of their actions, in other words team members or groups are working hard to achieve common goal, but actually they are heading or involved in satisfying their ego knowingly or unknowingly. Conflict can be resolved with the help of proper communication and taking the team members back on track by making them realize their priorities and giving them pep talk about importance for their careers, differentiating between ego satisfying or achieving team's objective.

Develop Trust in others/Fair Treatment; Trust is that gel which joins every team member, motivates them to help each other and move together in a rhythm. Team members having trust on their leaders understand that whatever a leader is doing will be in the interest of 'Trichual' i.e., team member, team and organisation. Team members will refrain from giving their best if they are not treated fairly. A team leader has to respect his or her words this time and every time.

Scenario; This scenario is a typical for lockdown and work from home case, Sakshi is working in a multinational company and is always visible on her desktop screen during online meetings, but since last few meetings Sakshi is not visible on screen as an active contributor, neither her online official status is showing "out of office", every other team member start whispering about the favours granted by team leader to Sakshi.

Sunita's company was about to introduce a new software and Sakshi was entrusted to test this software before final launch, but team leader (Sunita) has not taken into confidence other team members before taking out Sakshi from routine work and neither it was communicated before putting her to testing job. This lack of communication created a kind of distrust among team members which led to lot of confusion and wastage of precious time & energy. If team leader has communicated his action properly, could have saved Sunita from allegation of favouritism.

When to pull or release the string; Building and keeping a team intact is a mammoth task which requires lot of skills, a team leader should not always play the role of goodie-goodie and must have the ability to take decision as per situation. A team leader is superior & senior to other team members and is accountable for every thing happening good or bad which gives h/her the right to do the right for the right.

A team leader is expected to pull up underperforming team members by telling them clearly what is expected of them, before pulling up a team member, team leader must gather all the facts so that team member does not feel that s/he has been targeted without any reason or on any false complaints.

A team leader should not hesitate to take adequate action against faltering team member but also turn that team member towards accepting the challenge of change and improvement, by doing this team leader will win the confidence of team members. Winning the confidence of team is more important than any other thing which could happen to a team leader, once you have won the confidence of your team members, they will understand that whatever our team leader is doing is for our benefit and they will not hesitate to follow orders.

Unearthing hidden qualities of team members; Remember when you take out winter cloths and find few hundred rupees left in the pocket of jacket you wore on the last day of the winter, if finding few hundred rupees, which will be spend in one or two outing to mall or movie, gives us immense pleasure.

Can we imagine how much happiness and joy we will be adding to a team member's life if we discover some qualities or positive traits which s/he is not aware of, unearthing hidden qualities in one of our team member has dual benefits first, when a team member is told about an additional quality which she or he possess, knows that him or her work has been observed, Secondly when an additional feather is added in the cap of an individual team member which is going to remain with him lifelong and bring great change in his or her career.

Ability to discover hidden ability is the best trait a team leader can have, it is like excavating an individual for positive reasons, in the mutual interest of team and team members, extracting hidden qualities creates an atmosphere of development and progress which fills a team member, having average capacity with self-confidence as s/he starts thinking that there must have been some other hidden qualities in me and will surface at appropriate time.

Discovery for & by Team Leader; A team leader should have burning desire to move from his present stage i.e., from surviving in his job to discover the purpose of his job. Purpose of his job might be to create a team which is one of the best in field or to bring positive changes in the professional and personal life of team members, instead of doing right things, s/he is motivated to do the things right. Team Leader has to discover intention, selflessness and an eye for detail among team members once a quality is discovered same should be conveyed. Discovering some new qualities for self which has the power to take him from manager to leadership role.

Silver Quality: Any new discovery in self gives us confidence. (For self), When a team leader is able to discover some positive qualities in self and able to practice it consistently, other team members knowing this quality of their team leader, approaches h/her without any hesitation in matter related to the unhidden skill of their team leader.

Scenario; Ankit was working as team leader and knows that he is accepting, whenever a new task is allotted, he accepts it with positive mindset or if any new team member joins in he welcomes h/her with open heart. During project execution one of the important processes went wrong, Ankit took that task into his hand by jumping into trench and corrected it with in no time, his senior called him into his cabin and labelled him as Mr. dependable. When one of the team members left in the middle of the project, Ankit took additional responsibility by learning new skills and did not allow the absence of left team member felt on the project.

Golden Quality; Any new discovery in others generates trust. (For others). Along with looking for new qualities in self, a team leader has to take team members to next level of thinking and action, by motivating them and creating an atmosphere where team members are encouraged to expose themselves to other than routine tasks. When a team member is engaged in other than routine activity, they have to apply different approach to come out of the challenge successfully.

Scenario; Ankit was working in his office when he receives a call from family member of one of his team members informing him about the accident this team member has met with, he immediately called other team members and started chalking out plan to help the injured team member. Ankit told other team members what steps needs to be taken, but to his utter dismay one of the team members who used to keep silence on other trivial matters has already reached hospital, met the family of injured team member and started chalking out plan for next step to be taken. After this incident Ankit was very happy to see this team member taking initiative, called her and informed the positive side of taking initiative in this matter.

Diamond Quality; Any new discovery in self & others. (For team). As we all know that a Diamond is used as collection in the form of precious gem stone and secondly, it is used in industry for making tools in cutting industry. In the same way a diamond quality is used for discovering and removing unwanted negative quality which might become obstacle in one's career path. A team leader's job become easier and his team's speed increases when s/he develops **'Diamond Quality'** in terms of self and team members.

Scenario; Dheeraj called his deputy and enquire about the selection of a team member who is to be send to attend training program next month. His deputy recommended the name of Satish, whom he finds fit for two qualities one, his knowledge & interest in marketing and second eagerness to accept new challenges, Dheeraj appreciated the observing power of his deputy, but he added that while recommending the name of Satish, mentioned positive qualities only but failed to observe one negative quality which he had observed while working with Satish, that his soft skills are not up to the mark as it should be of a good professional looking for making a career in 'Marketing'.

Dheeraj told his deputy to kindly inform Satish about this short coming which needs to be improved. There is still one month left for the conference and things can be improved upon, it is not only the professional's competence but organization's reputation is also at stake. Satish after coming back from conference thanked his team leader Dheeraj for pointing out negative quality and giving him chance to improve upon due to which he was able to attend conference and learn new development in the field of marketing.

Platinum Quality; A new Quality developed in the interest of life & goal. For a team leader it is not only discovering hidden qualities in self but developing something new or which is the need of the hour to propagate the team's winning agenda, a team leader who is interested in learning new skills is very positive sign and takes team to new heights. Secondly, by setting the example of learning a new skill at this point of career also motivates other team members to be in tune with the time and ready to learn new skills whenever required.

Scenario; Neeraj is working as Team Leader in ADG corporation, his company is having stores in all the four metro cities of country, since last six months he was feeling little uneasy because company's operation has gone online by using best software in practice, Neeraj being not computer friendly is finding it difficult to cope with it.

Last week one of the team members by mistake gave wrong information to Neeraj, which Neeraj passed on to Head Office, resulted in loss to organisation due to wrong decision taken on the basis of that report, he introspects and thought if he would have double checked the data provided by team member, the damage would have been avoided.

He dared going near computer leave alone fetching information from software. After thinking a lot Neeraj requested the IT team to include his name for training in the operating software. After spending challenging time with IT department, he was able to learn how to operate software. Now he was able to check every report & data provided to him by his subordinates, while sitting in cafeteria he was remembering training time, when other young participants were able to understand and operate steps involved in first attempt but he become proficient in those steps after two or three attempts did not lose heart and came out victorious.

Barriers in building winning team for Team Leader;

One of the biggest hurdles in building a winning team is when team members started thinking a like, in other words team started following 'Yes Man' syndrome which also means that team started blindly following instruction not giving a second thought or without using their intellect and experience. this drawback stops a team from developing into a winning one, and remain a surviving one. It is the responsibility of team leader to develop every individual team member into a curious and questioning one, only then one can build an innovative and progressive team.

Best thing a team leader can do is by asking wrong questions and make individual team member realise that it is nor in their neither in the interest of the team to blindly follow the instructions, they have to understand that with the alert mind and using their common sense any improvement in the process can be made.

Scenario; John was working as a project leader, during one meeting he finalised a particular software for the project, next day one of his junior team member Shikar met John and introduced him a better software which will be more suitable for the entire process and he frankly told John that he discussed the purchase of software with his friends outside of the team. On enquiring about the software John too found this software better than the one he intended to purchase, John was feeling very contended as practice of open house discussion in the team bore fruits and always stated that "My words are not final, there is always room for improvement at the top". This policy of open house discussion has fetched John many suggestions which were the source of better execution of steps and improvement in the process.

Team winners for Team Member;

Building winning 'self'; Team members are young pillars on which a team stands and move towards its goal, These raw young team members which I called pillars has the biggest responsibility on their shoulders for taking their team forward and in the process bring shine for themselves, best thing a team member can do in the interest of team and self i.e., build a **winning self** in other words managing self appropriately, growing into a better and stronger pillar in turn making their teams better and stronger.

Building winning self will make things happen and some pillars will grow downwards to become **(foundation)** of the team, some grow horizontally to become wall **(cover)** and some grow upwards to become roof **(protection),** in short, we can say that young team member's responsibility is to grow in such a manner that all areas are covered, team is strengthened and examples are set. When a team member decided to build self by keeping in view the needs of the team s/he not only help a team in winning, but becomes foundation, wall and roof for self which is the goal of a sincere professional.

Praise each other; "Hi Ranveer, you have done a wonderful job yesterday during meeting with our clients which removed their doubts and helped us to win the contract, you have done your homework well, professionals like you are the foundation of our team". Who in this world of dying skill of praising each other does not want to hear from a fellow team member. Real praise gives a team member confidence that hard work is not going in vain and s/he is on right track.

Instead of thinking about its own action and performance, an individual team members must learn to praise their colleagues by continuously pointing out good in them, imagine how much joy we feel when somebody praises us and the amount of energy it generates, similarly we can make our team members joyful and energized by praising them. Praise is very powerful tool it shows that one is thinking not about self only but take interest in other's wellbeing as well. It is like honey being poured into someone's ear and expecting to turn that honey coming out of mouth in the form of words, setting up chain reaction.

Self-evaluation and Goal Setting; No team member can move ahead in his career if s/he do not have the will and intention to critically evaluate performance and adjust self as per the need of the team. What a wonderful way it would be if we start evaluating by giving honest feedback to ourselves instead of waiting for it to be done by others, it will be of immense importance if we can learn to examine work done by ourselves on the parameters and standard set by organisation. After doing fair self-evaluation we can move to goal setting and adjust individual goals in co-ordination with team, a team member has to set goal as per need of the team and professional requirement. Because only that team members can win which gives importance to the goal set by organisation and can become diamond members of the team by aligning their goals with the organisation & team.

High self-expectation; One of the best ways to perform well in your job is to expect best performance or have high expectations from self, in other words we can attract best performance when we told our inner self that "I am going to do better this time and every time" it works like magic, create wonders and will definitely help in surpassing your previous performance.

Now the question arises can we surpass our previous performance every time, performance does not only mean visible results or which can be measured, it can be more patient, better focused, utilizing energy judiciously or well-planned efforts. Benefits of high self-expectation results in bit-by-bit improvement and give us tremendous joy once we start achieving set goals. When a professional has high self-expectation, it challenges and compare self with other high performers and thinks that when others can achieve this milestone, 'Why can't I?' another individual might have any advantage or edge, but that does not mean that I can't achieve this milestone, it might take little longer than the one who has an edge over it or in an advantageous position.

Trying our hands at something new; We are very much excited while watching a suspense thriller movie because we are not sure what will happen next who will do what, whether our guess will come out right or we have to hold our head in sheer disappointment. If we want, we can have same level of excitement by trying our hands at something new which requires lot of courage, but this effort will not go in vain and its result will surely come out as per your expectations i.e., you will learn something new, your excitement and joy will know no bounds.

There is no greater achievement than learning something new or doing same activity with new approach. So, if you want to be important part of your team, you need to keep on thinking and finding time to do something new, as discussed above one of the two things will happen either you will achieve what you have aimed for or you will learn something new which is going to remain with you forever. As a team member, one must take a note of role, consider self as an important pearl of the whole process.

Self-Motivation; Motive for action, motivated people are internally driven, they don't wait for things to happen they make things happen as they are go-getters. They understand that objective of feedback is to correct, not to punish. Self-motivated persons take everything in their stride and willing to overcome their problems, they are solution focused and their motto of success is not the absence of problem but overcoming it. Self motivation helps a professional to be independent of out side motivation which may be in the form of example or training which remain in mind only for few days, but being self motivated a professional is full of energy & positivity every moment while performing the assigned task leading to success.

Scenario; Srinivasan is working with a multinational organization since last fourteen years and observed since last few weeks that he had lost the urge for coming to office, position for which he had worked so hard to reach, does not attract him anymore. For few days he kept on pushing self to reach office but on one morning he could not get up from bed to reach office, he tries to find out the reason but in vain, next day he gathers courage and reached office but could not concentrate on work; after suffering for few days, He discussed the matter with his wife and best friend, both advised him to meet a specialist to get it diagnosed. Counsellor listens to his narration carefully and after three sittings he diagnosed him with burnout and advised him to take proper rest and change of place for a fortnight.

Discovery for team member; Discovering qualities in each other should be the primary goal of every team member, when a team member joins corporate team as a fresher s/he is not aware what it requires to be best. As a team member who is just out of college and in first job or may be second has to discover qualities among his peers and group, once we start discovering new qualities and skills in self or in other team members it becomes very interesting activity and good exercise which keeps the things moving and avoid stagnation, it is very important to look for discovery of new qualities and skills for the given reasons.

Silver Quality: Any new discovery in self gives us confidence. (For self). A team member having intention to succeed in field of expertise does not know much what lies ahead, s/he needs to unfold and acquaint self with the qualities required by diving deep into inner self and become keen observer of actions by continuous improvement. During this process when they find a strong and positive quality discovered in self which helps in executing their responsibility, filling them with confidence by continuing their quest for new discovery continues.

Scenario; Neeraj is a sincere team member working with CVB corporation since last two years, his report card in professional term can be graded in good category, that's why after successful completion of probation period he was elevated to the post of 'Executive Commercial', When he was transferred to a new department and this job responsibility requires lot of energy and independent handling of situation, he came to discover that he can handle a department independently which requires mix of youth and maturity, earlier he was associated as team member only, making aware of his qualities by his team leader who also knew that Neeraj possess those qualities and was happy to put the right person in the right place.

Gold Quality; Any new discovery in others generates trust. (For others). A team moves on trust which is generated when team members know each other well professionally & personally by taking genuine interest in each others success and upliftment. It would be a wonderful gift if we as individual team member gives a gift to other team members, which is permanent in nature i.e., discovering a hidden quality which has surfaced while working together. This permanent gift is going to live with the team member forever and create a life time bond.

Scenario; When Ashok was looking for a team member who can handle new department (data analytics), Ashok's organisation was into manufacturing FMCG, with the introduction of data analysis as a new tool for enhancing the prospect of business, first name come to his mind was Sandhya who is the most smart working team member available at present, Ashok discussed the matter with team and propose the name of Sandhya, but Sandhya intervened in between and requested Ashok to reconsider her nomination and instead give charge of new department to her colleague named Sushmita who is working with her since two & a half years, along with wonderful analytical skills she is aptly qualified with the specialized degree in statistics, on hearing this Ashok changed his mind and thank Sandhya for her selfless observation, after the meeting Sushmita also thanked Sandhya from the bottom of her heart for proposing her name

Diamond Quality; Any new discovery in self & others (For team). A diamond as discussed earlier, can serve two purpose one is its shine which puts it in the category of valuable stone and second quality is being the hardest natural thing on earth, is used in cutting tools to shape the hardest of metals, similarly a team member possessing '**Diamond Qualities**' may observe other team members keenly and discover or pointing out negative quality and help to remove that negative quality with the diamond cutting tool in hand.

Scenario; Akshay is Team leader of ZXS organisation, His organisation is involved production and export of specialized paper used in printing of currency notes. When Anshika saw her senior Akshay roaming around here and there without any purpose, she asked him the reason for the same, Akshay and Anshika are working together since last seven years and Anshika is only two years junior to Akshay in other words they have a very good professional relationship, Akshay tell her that top management has assigned him the confidential task of restructuring the department and he is looking for a trusted aid to execute this thankless job.

Anshika told Akshay if he thinks right, she is ready to help him as she is the senior most of all other team members and can keep the processed information up to her until it is officially announced. Akshay was ok with the proposal of Anshika but he told her that it is time bound programme and Anshika has the habit of taking leaves casually, he told her that she cannot take any leave till the submission of report and won't be allowed to go out of office during office hours till the completion of report, Anshika thanked Akshay for pointing out her negative side and she vowed to remove this short coming not only for this task but every project she will undertake in near future.

Platinum Quality; This Quality is developed in the interest of our life and goal. Platinum is one of the costliest and valuable metal on this earth, valuable in the sense that even if anyone has the money available to buy it, Platinum is not available in abundance, so is the case of **Platinum Quality**, this quality is unearthed from the personality of a professional when it's a matter of survival for that professional or in other words a platinum quality is earned by a professional when it becomes almost necessary to learn or earn that quality or perish, for an individual team member it could be change in attitude towards required in any matter or improvement in communication skills to be a successful team member or working towards better time awareness.

Scenario; After attending a training programme Abhay and his team leader Amanjeet resumes office, Amanjeet told Abhay to prepare a report & presentation to be shared with all other team members in the interest of the organization and optimizing the expenditure incurred on training programme. In the beginning Amanjeet was little apprehensive about assigning this task to Abhay. But when Abhay presented the report & training ppts, he himself was surprised when everybody congratulated him and praised his efforts. Whereas his boss in front of everybody titled him as very good observer and organized professional. It was Abhay's first presentation which he handled meticulously by working on his communication skills and above all his interest was to share & distribute the knowledge and experience gained during conference.

Barriers in building winning self.

Invisible Career Path: As a professional all of us join a team or decide to be a team member in search of only thing, that is self. 'Self' here means what s/he is capable of achieving and making the most of life given by nature. A professional expects clarity in path which is going to take h/her on the road to success and fulfilling dream, those goals can only be achieved only if that professional is able to visualize the path on which s/he has to travel

In the absence of that path a professional loses focus and start wandering like a ship without ruder, confusion prevails if there is no career path visible, a professional want to know h/her destination if s/he has to give her 100%. it is very important for a team to have visible career path for all of team members to avoid losing focus and purpose, which is very much required for smooth sailing of team. Since team members who are new to corporate set-up are the most affected by the invisibility of the career path, for them it's like a ship which had 'Sirened' to start its journey but don't know it's destination, wasting time & energy, second thing which is mentionable here is that it is not loss of that individual but of whole team and of nation as well.

Changing Goals and Objectives. Frequent changes in objectives and goals keep the team member confused, which also reflects poor planning on the part of organisation and is indication of messy working style. As we all know that "well begun is half done", frequent changes in plans also indicates that we are unprepared & half-baked to start something new. Every professional would like to work in a team or organisation which gives proper importance to first function of management, making life easy for every team member. Frequent changes in plans sends a team in to vicious circle of instability.

Scenario: Rekha and Sashi were working on a component of a new project and steadily progressing towards their goal, suddenly they receive an e-mail from project head that due to some emergent conditions, Sashi has been transferred to another project and will be replaced by Sumit in two days' time. It was so simple for project head to order a transfer but he could not understand the disturbance incurred due to this step, how much time new member will take to start working as a team is a matter of question.

Secondly, when a team member is replaced without proper training and counselling, will disturb the progress of the project, here we have to understand the difference between training and counselling. Training is for specific trade which is to be used in project, where as counselling is introducing a team member about the working culture & atmosphere of project so that team member can bring required change and adjustment to be a valuable part of it

Scenario: Neeraj was very happy today as he was inducted into a project team to develop a new product, he and his team started working on the new project, it has been since a fortnight they were moving forward, suddenly on the recommendation of sales and marketing team the specification of the product was changed, now they have to start everything from scratch and devote themselves to develop product on new specifications, resulting in re-allocation of physical and human assets. Poor planning and hurrying of project led to confusion and loss of credibility for higher authorities.

Loafing; One of the biggest barriers in building a winning team is erected when a team member started looking downwards instead of looking forward thus loosing sight of goal and started giving preferences to survival instead of development or resilience. It happens when s/he starts following team member with lowest productivity, Same can be understood by story given below.

Scenario; There was a king who was little worried about dwindling state of affairs of his kingdom, he decided to take help from a saint, saint understood the matter and advise the king to do as he told. Upon reaching his kingdom back the king ordered his solders to dig a well and ordered all the citizens of the kingdom to fill this well with milk by tomorrow morning by contributing one pot from every family, after hearing this head of every family followed the order of king. When king went to inspect the well, he was shocked to find that well is filled with water instead of milk, now he understood the whole scenario, every family head of the kingdom has poured a pot of water instead of milk, assuming that a pot of water will mix well with thousands of pots of milk and nobody will know that s/he has poured a pot of water instead of milk.

Non-recognition of Team Work; Team has just finished a project and delivered it on time, during submission the project head had shown to the higher authorities as if he had done all the work related to project and other team members were spectators only. Toughest mindset to break in a team is feeling of 'I', where an individual is recognized instead of whole team, productivity of other team members comes to stand still if they are bypassed while receiving their dues in the form of credits, when a team has accomplished the given target is indication that every team member has executed the responsibility assigned, but it is a fact that some team members job is more important, but that important job cannot be completed without the help of less important team members. It is like asking which of the five fingers are most important while making a punch.

Team Winners for students.

Students must learn the art of team work during their education and understand that nothing can be achieved alone, all of us have to take help and support from someone else to realise our dreams, however intelligent, hardworking and resourceful we are, there is only one thing which makes us vulnerable i.e., being human, no human being is complete and everybody has something unique, during student life we undergoes two types of education one is formal and another one is informal.

Students during their formal education has to team up with teachers, seniors and classmates to achieve the desired grades, they should always try to extract maximum from them and learn various ways to work with them and came out as winning team member. During informal education they have to learn how to incorporate friends, relatives and family members in their life, because these team members are equally important to execute the task and instrumental in achieving one's goal, they give us guidance and comfort when we are confused or in need of some solace due to some difficult situation, these team members who become our part during informal education comes into picture and take us out of the difficult situation when required.

Team members whether they are acquainted during formal education or informal education plays very important role in a student's life, on one side they introduce us to the world on the other side they help us to handle challenges arising out of it, So it is always better to understand that whether it's professional life or personal life having a good team is very important, how you choose to be a team member and which team member you choose to be with self or in other words "You are known by the company you keep".

Praising Each Other. In this world there is one hidden treasure which everybody loves to receive but least interested in giving, and to everybody's amazement this treasure is available with everybody and it can be shared without any financial burden, in other words it is available in abundance with every human being and very surprisingly is the scarcest material floating on this earth, can you name it. No, because we all are very miser in using this element called 'praise'. Praising is that material which can be used in manufacturing good team members and get the best out of them.

Every human being would like to be praised but reluctant to praise others, praising is two-way highway if we have to travel on it without any hurdle, we have to give it first and then take it. Students must take the road of praising and appreciating team members to establish positive relationship as praise has immense power to change one gloomy face into a smiling one. Praise is scarce but very powerful tool which can solve a problem without saying much, it can mend broken relationship, or motivate a team member who is feeling low, can remove a confusion which is obstructing team's progress. Despite of being free flowing element it is quite heavy, because very few team member can pick it up and throw towards other team members to lighten the atmosphere, it is advisable to develop the courage to throw praise towards other team members first to start chain reaction.

Comparing self-performance and goal setting; A student must keep track record of performance whether it is personal or professional, positive side of tracking self performance is beneficial because we have the power to move forward by correcting our actions and make continuous improvement. It is very positive step if we learn how to compare our performance with others and know where we stand, when we learn to critically evaluate our performance with absolute honesty accompanied by appropriate action will able to find answer to these questions. What is the reason that I am not being able to do it, where as I have mental and physical strength equal to anybody. Why I have not able to channelize these strengths in the desired direction for optimum results.

What is the connection between comparing and improving performance has to do with winning team, we all wants to be teamed with individuals who has performed at our level or better than us, nobody wants to be team-up with the individuals who is having grades below us, as we all know that winning team is configuration of individual team who are capable of executing the assigned task in the best possible way so that overall performance of team is rated at number one or in other words, a team will win only if every team member contributes its best and align its performance as per need of the target, but a team is made up of different individuals having different attitude and aptitude, many times whole effort of team goes in vain due to lack-lustre performance of a single team member. If a team wants to win or achieve its target with all the team members crossing finish line in best possible time, even a single team member is left behind is considered loss.

By comparing we comes to know where we are and where we have to go, what changes we have to bring, at student level importance of comparison and setting goal afterwards can take our team to winning podium. There are many activities apart from studies which helps in becoming better human being and requires team work, although studies also require team work, main contribution coming from student, teacher and family members. Other activities like sports, cultural and NCC or NSS also helps us in learning how to build a winning team and be a part of it.

Exceeding your limits. Exceeding your limit has different meaning in different fields, but if a student has decided to be a good team member, exceeding your limit can be in the field of time spent for studies, it could be improvement in any field which requires better performance or it could be overcoming fear of studying a subject for which we do not have the desired aptitude.

Building a Winning Team

Student who is studying four hours in a day suddenly realizes that this duration is not enough, making required changes to increase the number of hours to study is also exceeding its limit, a professional team member realizes that s/he gets tired or lose focus after five hours of work, finding out the problem or reason and making efforts to remain attentive during full duty hours is also exceeding its limit or a sports person who runs 100 meter race in twelve seconds practicing harder to complete it in eleven seconds is also exceeding its limit. this positive intention will make you a good team member with formal and informal team.

Being a good team member will help you gain attention, support and affection during student life from all corners of institution and family, as a student we can achieve whatever we want to do, during our college days, any improvement comes when we push ourself to beyond the limits set by self, remember word 'ourself' when a limit is drawn by ourselves, only we can erase that limit and exceed it. As we all know that a winning team needs and expects continuous improvement and growth from its team members, a team consists of team members who represents three types of category A, B, & C. or in other words it can be interpreted into rate busters, medium performers and chisellers, if we want our team to remain ahead of other teams, we have to be ahead of ourselves, means we must have the intention and will to surpass our previous performance to turn our team into winning one. Keeping status quo will only stagnate and stop the desired progress. for a winning team exceeding its limit means all three categories of performers need to push themselves little hard and try to meet next level of team members. C must try to meet the standard set by B, B of A and you must be wondering what A should do, A must improve upon self and raise the bar. In this way all categories of team members will exceed its limit.

Now the question arises when an individual or student exceeds its limit, how other team members are benefited, student's team & team members are benefited by getting motivated to see improved version of that individual and try to follow the footsteps, this also gives happiness to informal team members as well. It is not only matter of giving happiness to others, when we as a student decided to exceed our limit, we are the biggest beneficiary of this change which is going to have permanent impression on our career and life.

Scenario; Akhilesh is studying B.Tech. program in one of the prestigious institutions of the city, but he was unable to do well in physics. When he discussed the matter with his team (Faculty), they advised him to increase his study time and devote added time to remove his weakness and understand what is pulling him back whether it is theory, numerical or practical, once he identifies this thing, he had zeroed in on his problem which can be sorted out with persistent application, when Akhilesh was not performing well his team members formal & informal were very anxious about his future and feeling low, but Akhilesh taking responsibility of his professional course and career brought happiness in the life of its team members.

Discovery for Students; Student life is the beginning of foundation on which every other pillar of life will stand on and this is the time when a student is introduced to various qualities which are required for smooth sailing in career, we may call it discovery, because most of the qualities spur up this period of life. Be it how to communicate with elders, meaning of respect and how it is paid to seniors, how to avoid distraction to achieve the desired goal, how to identify negative or positive stress and handling them accordingly, where to use hard skills or soft skills and so on.

Silver Quality: Any new discovery in self gives us confidence. (For self). When we as student discovers any new quality and use it repeatedly with success, gives us confidence and strength to move ahead towards goal successfully, any addition in the form of new quality discovered is boon to self. Discovering silver quality paves, the way for a chain reaction and others qualities starts surfacing as well, when a student discovers a new quality in self, s/he thinks that other team members must be having some qualities which have not surfaced yet.

Scenario; When school administration was looking for a extrovert and wise student who can be the captain for group of students going to attend inter-state youth summit, Aakash applied for the position of captain knowing that he possess all the qualities required to head the contingent, panel responsible for selection of the captain was also of the view that Aakash's extrovert qualities will keep the communication between group members open and as he approaches every situation very wisely by keeping all the pros and cons in mind by overcoming emotions, Most of the students has to live in another city or hostel for higher studies and they find it difficult to adjust for two reasons one is negative and another is positive. For positive reason s/he has to overcome emotions and concentrate on studies leaving behind comfort of their houses. For negative reason they have to discover strength in themselves so as not to fall into bad company.

Gold Quality; Any new discovery in others generates trust. (For others). When we look at others with interest and curiosity or in other words along with self we give importance to peers as well, in the process we identify **golden qualities** in peers, and tell them about those hidden qualities which they are not aware of, it is like having gold kept in idle state in a secret drawer and not using it to gain the momentum for a successful student life and career there after.

Scenario; Simran was preparing to leave the canteen after lunch when she was called by the vice-principal who informed her that keeping in view her sincerity and co-ordinating capability in mind she has been appointed as 'captain of green house', Simran felt little surprised to hear that. Because she never thought about qualities she possesses and makes her eligible for this position but her seniors and teachers were aware of her capabilities, she thought she was just following the instructions of her seniors and teachers which resulted in this notable achievement.

Diamond Quality; Any new discovery in self & others. (For team). Diamond's shine increases when it is used for removing unwanted and negative things, Same is correct about diamond qualities during student life whereas on has to find out not only good qualities in self and others, but negative qualities in self and others so as to get rid of those negative qualities with in time and strengthen those positive qualities so as to make life more beautiful and meaningful.

Scenario; School was celebrating its golden jubilee year, lot of cultural, sports and extra-curricular activities were planned, one of the main attractions of celebration was cricket tournament between four houses of colleges.

Sakshi approached sports head and wanted to add one more feature to the tournament that is '**running commentary**', when sports head wanted to know the name of commentator, Sakshi offered her services for the same, who saw her with astonishment and ask about her knowledge of cricket & Hindi language, not getting satisfactory response from Sakshi, Sports head told her to prepare self and asked her to appear for test one week before the start of inter-house tournament, Sakshi came to know that she has to improve a lot on those two factors to be proficient in Hindi language commentary, She thanked school's sports head for correcting and guiding her towards right direction and throughout the tournament Sakshi receives loads of applaud from spectators and team members. One very positive thing happens in the life of Sakshi that she took cricket commentary in Hindi as profession.

Platinum Quality; This Quality is developed in the interest of our life and goal. Platinum is very precious metal which is found & refined with very complex scientific process, Same is the case with Platinum Qualities, these qualities are not with any student in the beginning of their life but when it is found that this platinum quality in the form of aptitude, attitude or interest is missing which is very much required to be a good student and for leading a wonderful life. Every student must churn life to add this **Platinum Quality** in to his cap by leaving no stone turned however difficult it may be. Platinum quality should be very dear to a student and its team comprising of teachers, family and friends.

Scenario; Neeraj who was from middle class family joined a prestigious college with the help of his grades in entrance exam and is interested in doing his studies sincerely and take active part in college activities which resulted in his excellent performance during the course, neither college administration nor Neeraj was aware that simply focusing on his studies and not getting distracted by the image which OTT serials and movies projected of students and professional institutions.

During introduction and induction programme conducted by college it was conveyed to every student that the key to successful completion of this course is to remain focussed by fending off distractions by identifying it, because this period of higher studies is not only the golden period of one's life but also demands responsibility, every body in this world don't get this opportunity, at this point of life "time is life". Words of counsellor had deep impact on Neeraj who after reaching his hostel room, immediately make a list of potential distractions and how to avoid them.

Barriers in Team Building By students;

Unclear goals and Objectives; It will be difficult for students to be part of winning team if they are not clear about their goals and objectives, at this stage of life students are full of confusion & doubts as they have to take every step with utmost care and positive approach by eliminating doubts and find a crystal-clear road to proceed towards successful life.

Scenario: Subhash has just passed his 12th grades with 87%, in spite of getting good marks he is not clear which course to pursue or which field to take to be a good professional, this indecision is putting him under lot of stress after exploring many options he has taken admission in B.Tech. (Mechanical) for which he was least suitable for, resulting in failure in first year and loss of financials. This scenario could have been avoided if knowing his indecisiveness, instead of following his friends he had listen to the combination of brain and mind or have taken the help of professional services available.

Conclusion; Building winning team is an effort realised bit by bit, if somebody ask me what will be your preference while building winning team journey or destination, my reply will always be that I shall prefer good **company.**

Time Awareness

When I was doing my bachelors from one of the reputed private institute of capital, I used to prepare time table one month before the commencement of exams and try to stick to it, but to my surprise my preparations was not matching with the time or number of hours set aside for the studies I got confused and disturbed due to this mismatch, in spite of giving full importance to the activity, results were nowhere near my expectations, I sat down and introspect my activities of the day and I found out that I was continuing with my physical activities like gym and jogging leaving me with less energy to concentrate and do that extra bit to grasp the knowledge and practice to reproduce topics.

To understand something new we must have combination of physical and mental energy which helps us to concentrate on the subject. It was my low energy level which was obstructing me to perform well in my studies, after having pin pointed the reason, I corrected the daily schedule by eliminating the gym from my daily routine for the time being resulted in successfully clearing the exams with good grades.

A similar case happened with my friend who was studying with me in the same institute, he discussed the matter with me while sipping a cup of tea in canteen, I told him to introspect his daily routine and find out the difference between the two and meet me tomorrow, because having gone through the same situation few days back I was in a position to help him out and as a friend it is my responsibility as well to share his worries, after giving a thought he told me that last month he fell ill and during his hospitalization doctor advised him to reduce weight, so he started dieting, he was full of energy before doctor's advice but after taking dieting he lacks energy to concentrate on studies, dieting was right thing to do but timing was wrong as exams were near and one needs adequate amount of energy, so just a small discussion and right step at right time my friend was able to utilize his time for the right purpose.

Scenario; Suman is working as a mid-level executive in a multinational organization, since last few weeks she is unable to give her best, because of this she become very demotivated and resulted in revolving in vicious circle of non-performance, she was unable to find out the reason behind this it seems as she has lost her professional mark somewhere else, after observing Suman for few days her project leader intervened, called Suman over a cup of coffee and told her to take two days leave for introspecting herself, when Suman joined back and informed her team leader she is constantly thinking about one of her colleagues who is promoted ahead of her, she thinks that her colleague being promoted ahead of her is not a fair decision taken by top management, but her project leader clears the confusion and informed the reason behind her colleague's promotion, after removal of confusion, Suman started working with double zeal.

After completing my graduation, I took admission in one of the prestigious B-School, there was a class schedule on time management, look at the catastrophe I reached late in the class annoying the trainer, trainer gave me hundred rupees note and told me to go market to buy those lost fifteen minutes from a shop. I felt very bad and told the trainer that nobody can buy back lost time, after few minutes he turn towards me and ask how I will achieve my goal, I replied that, I will learn time management and time saving techniques, on hearing this he again told me in tough voice that nobody can manage time one has to manage self with respect to time, about time saving he told me that time cannot be saved in a jar or in a bank account, time can be either **utilised or wasted.**

It is very much clear from above examples that equal amount of time is available to each of us, but it requires right amount of energy, positive attitude, clear direction and discipline to utilise it to the full.

Time Chain. All our activities are interlinked from waking up in the morning and going to bed in the night. If we falter in one activity its effect is visible on other activities and individuals as well, with whom we are associated. We must know when to loosen up and when to be strict with self and others to utilise time. If we respect time, it will respect us in return. Time awareness refers to utilizing time effectively so that right time is allocated to the right activity.

Scenario; When Subhash made an appointment with Tarun to see him at 10.00 a.m. He could not reach on scheduled time and was late by half an hour, in turn Tarun has to re-scheduled his meeting with Amit, in turn Amit has to rescheduled his meeting with Kamal, now it is clearly evident from above sequences that initial disturbance of half an hour resulted in approximately three hours of loss in total.

Objective; Objective & need of being aware of the most precious invisible matter available on earth which is free, equally distributed and available to all human being who are born on this earth, one more very good thing about time is that it is inexhaustible or in other words it will never be out of stock for any new human arriving on this earth, another very interesting thing about time is that no one has to give application to receive it, it is credited into one's life with the first breath we take.

Despite such favourable qualities and credentials, if you ask **'time'** about its grievances, it will tell you that despite having those qualities and credentials and being hugely beneficial to mankind "I am the most disrespected, taken for granted and wasted commodity in this universe, "I Would like to be more useful to mankind". In this connection only human race can take initiative to utilize me properly".

To understand how we can utilize our quota of time and realize our full potential as everybody in this world gets 24 hours in a day. Why is that some people achieve more with the available time? It's a myth that we manage time, truth is that we manage ourselves with respect to time. It's a myth that we save time truth is that we utilize present moment which is given to all of us equally by nature. It's a myth that we waste time but that is not possible, we waste ourselves.

Awareness of time should be one of the most important activities of professional and personal life of an individual, in this age of cut throat competition with almost equal resources available to every individual, time awareness is key to effective functioning. When we use time judicially & efficiently, we increase our output with respect to time and remain ahead of our competitors.

Time awareness is also key to happy family & personal life, during career path a professional want to divide his time between family and office to have good work-life balance. Because a life cannot be said complete if we excel in professional field only leaving behind our family, this will cast a shadow on individual and ultimately leads to dissatisfaction. By utilizing time efficiently, we can increase our career prospects and opportunities in life.

Getting Organised & beating Time-Cheaters; Best thing a professional can do is to be aware of time-cheaters and find out the way to defeat them, for a professional it is always a race against time however hard s/he tries there is never enough time to execute given task, to have breather between task execution identify time-cheaters and beat them which is the key for proper utilization of time.

Time Awareness

Time awareness helps us in better planning for setting up of goals & objectives, meeting deadlines, helps in delegation of responsibilities while prioritizing our activities by spending our time on right activity. Poor planning cheats you lot of time, a to do list for today and tomorrow will help by remembering the tasks to be done on personal and professional front. Keep a diary with you for noting down important points. Identifying distractions, take appropriate step to stay focussed and set your priorities. Don't procrastinate, identify habits which consumes extra time.

Biggest challenge a professional or a student faces in proper utilising of time is their cluttered desk or unorganised work place where s/he has to spend minutes to locate the document, equipment or tools, which could have taken few seconds, it is not only correct in the case for physical things, it is correct for soft files as well, it has been observed that a professional who has prepared a very good report, but when boss asked for it, s/he keeps on juggling with the laptop to locate the soft file, it happens because after preparing report s/he has not transferred it to the appropriate folder. Decluttering is not only applicable to physical things it is applicable to our soft systems also, regularly declutter and clean your soft systems and update it with advance software to have proper utilisation of time.

Better communication, clear instructions, listening carefully because clear communication and appropriate way is one of the biggest time utilisers, we have to be very attentive while giving or receiving instructions, a small miscommunication might lead to mistakes or repetition of task, which not only waste time but is the reason for misunderstanding & confusion as well, Seniors and subordinates are advised not to hesitate to ask again to remove any doubt if any. Listening and asking, two very important pillars of communication must be given adequate importance to beat the time cheaters.

Taking proper care of health is also a big boon and best time utilizer, a professional also needs to pay adequate attention in maintaining good mental and physical health which becomes catalyst in beating time-cheaters, absence of good health drains a professional on three fronts, first loss of interest in profession, financial loses and above all loss of time in the form of taking leave from office, which ultimately puts bad impression on seniors and put extra burden on rest of the team members as they have to share responsibilities to manage task in your absence.

We must spend ten minutes before sleep to prepare for activities going to take place next day, what to wear, what to eat, mode of transportation to be used. Because our **tomorrow begins today**. Our nation loses billions of rupees due to ill health of citizens. Adequate sleep of approximately 7-8 hours, Regular sleep pattern i.e., going to bed and getting up at same time until unless there is a special occasion.

Managing stress and learning some relaxation techniques. good reading habits, deep breathing techniques, Yoga etc. All of us are humans and it is very natural for us to fall ill due to one reason or the other, but make sure it does not become regular practice, it has one more effect which very few professionals understand. When we regularly take leave due to ill health we are not found fit for important assignments and our reputation start deteriorating. However intelligent or hard working one may be, no team will wait after certain time. Secondly, our regular absence due to ill health leaves very little room for us to take leave to celebrate family functions, go out of town with family for vacations or to attend any professional course for career upgradation, it becomes vicious circle, and very difficult to get out of it. So, keeping in view the points mentioned above maintaining good physical and mental health should be one of the top most priorities for a professional.

Essential activities and proper utilisation of available time;
Well begin is half done is applicable not only to start an

assignment or project but it is also applicable to our day, when a professional begin a day on a positive note with the thought of "I CAN DO" motto, s/he fills self with positivity and utilizes time to its best, plan your tomorrow today or in other words 'our tomorrow begins today' and be clear about your intentions.

Key is spending energy in present and planning of next step, if one is feeling low on energy find out the steps to regain it, take a break and recharge self and move again. Action is the key, mere being a thoughtful professional will take you nowhere one has to transformed those thoughts into action to achieve the desired results. End your day with gratitude. Some people start their day on a very positive note getting up at the right time, finding their files, keys, mobile, laptop etc. at the right place. Whereas some students or professionals wake up very disturbed in morning looking for everything required at wrong place resulting in stress leading to unprofessional behaviour.

Seriously look at your daily routine activities and find out if they can be revised, it could be getting ready, having lunch, breakfast or dinner, official meetings, personal commitments or sleep etc. we should observe these activities and adjust the time allocated to them, because habits or the time allocated to above mentioned activities are imbedded since childhood, we will lose all positivity and pleasure if we start looking at time through one lens only which will have adverse impact on health, there should be rational distribution of time for personal and professional use as well. We can also calculate the cost of an hour but not time. For Example, an individual is earning Rs. 50,000/- per month or Rs.1667/- per day or Rs. 69/- per hour. Now we know where we stand.

When I started thinking of writing this book I was really perplexed, but I came across very valuable suggestion from my mentor that a big task must be broken into smaller one and that exactly what happened; If I say to all of you that you have to write a book of 400 pages. What will be your reaction? But if I say, you have to write one page daily for next 400 days how u will feel. Happy. Big projects need to be broken into smaller tasks to be completed.

Correlation of Time, Stress, emotional stability and energy

Stress and time awareness is directly related to each other, negative stress we experience is directly related to wastage of time. If we learn to utilize time well, we will experience less negative stress and resulting in happiness and good health. There is direct correlation between emotional stability and mismanagement of time, because we tend to become restless & irritating for being not able to meet deadlines and take some bad decisions in the sequence. Being in control of emotions helps a lot in utilizing time, especially for students and professionals. For example, if somebody invites you for a movie on Sunday, but you have not finished your project to be submitted on Monday, this is going to test your emotional stability, if you are emotionally strong you will not accept the invitation or vice-versa.

Time awareness is also one of the factors for optimum utilization of energy, assume a condition in which a professional having lot of time but not proportionate energy then what is the use of that available time. Every individual's energy level differs from time to time, some individuals are full of energy during morning hours, some are comfortable during noon and some find their energy level high post lunch. We have to understand our different energy levels and act accordingly. When we understand our personal co-relation between time and energy properly helps us in understanding the meaning of time awareness in a better way

Need: The purpose behind putting these words together is to spread the message and to underline the importance of time awareness with totally different perspective with respect to four pillars of corporate world i.e., Leader (Top Management), Team Leader (Middle Level Management), Team Member (Entry Level Executive) and Student (Future of the nation).

All the individuals mentioned above plays very important and different roles at different point of time, so one blanket theory does not fit for all of them. They must take different steps at different times as per the need of the role and be time aware about actions to be taken thereafter by keeping in view assigned duties and responsibilities, their job will become a lot easier and systematic once they understand different actions with respect to time awareness. When we categorise activities as per our role, we become more efficient, feel contented and produce better results. Categorisation means at one point one thing may sound differently for different persons in the same manner time awareness is different for individuals playing different roles.

Time awareness for Leaders;

A leader can **generate** time by investing in latest technology and in the health of their team members which gives multiplier effect, because at this level, we have to think about time awareness in the perspective of whole organisation. A leader must understand that time is hard cash.

Scenario; If employees are frequently complaining about power cuts, leader will think of providing them proper power backup, a leader will invest in best gazette available in the market, this will serve two purposes, first no space left for an employee to complain, secondly, best gazette will maximise the productivity. A lot depend on leader for time generation, he can introduce power naps of 10-15 minutes during hectic day of work, because many studies have confirmed that power naps improve brain's ability to retain information and recharge it, to gain maximum out of time and avoid exhaustion, same has been recommended by psychologists that energy of a human is finite and needs to be refreshed at specific intervals by taking appropriate steps as per the need arises.

During lockdown I came across very strange incident as most of us were working from home including my son, during a casual chat at dinner table he told us that he had received an official e-mail from Human Resources Department stating that "HR department has noticed that most of the team members have not taken any leave since last three months, in order to maintain productivity and in the interest of 'Trichual', it's mandatory for every team member to take four leaves in a month". This is the right motivator which any leader can practice to increase productivity and efficiency of team.

Time Investment: "Investment" as we all know that spending something during present moments with an intention to reap the benefits in future when the value of invested commodity rises, most of the humans understand the meaning of investment in the form of stocks, fixed deposit or real estate, but in a professional set up it is very important for a professional to invest time to gain that expertise which s/he could not gain during initial stage of career.

For a leader right investment of time could be attaining knowledge about new trends in specialization to be in tune with time, under normal circumstances a professional becomes a leader approximately after 20-25 years of service, if s/he tries to implementing obsolete systems to excel, will not work, a leader cannot solve 21st century problems by applying 20th century solutions, present day problems could be solved only by new solutions, when a leader invest in time for attaining fresh knowledge or process, it serves two purposes, first the leader becomes more confident and independent, secondly, he pass on the message of continuous learning and upgradation at any stage of career and life.

Scenario: Subhash has joined XYZ corporation as CEO, two months back, his previous organisation was developing software for gaming industry, his present organisation is a 'Fintech' company, although there is basic resemblance in modus operandi but knowledge of finance is very much required to command the team, Subhash has done his masters in finance fifteen years back, to bridge this gap and become more efficient leader, he wanted to refresh his knowledge about modern trends in finance, Subhash's intention and efforts of thinking of investing his time wisely and become better professional, as he has to deal with well qualified and diversified team.

There is no better way other than to learn recent advances and researches in the field of finance, not only this he want his team members to be in tune with time as well, for this he has made some special provisions in the budget to purchase & subscribe books, journals and electronic material. He personally takes interest in development of his team members and kept all the hard copies of the reading material in open book shelfs in the cafeteria so as to attract and encourage team members to be abreast with modern and international trends in their respective field.

Time Generation; What is this? We are talking about generating a thing which does not exist physically, have we found a machine through which we can generate it, let us see how we can generate time. Time in an organisation can be generated by using faster mode of operations such as modern gadgets and processors, In current scenario most of the job is done through online or by electronic medium, a leader must provide latest processors and fast internet connection to get the best out of their team members and fill them with confidence.

Team members will give their best output only when they get best input, secondly, as a human nature every team member compares their tools, working conditions and facilities with the organisation of their friends and family members, any plus or minus is enough to push them up or pull them down. If a leader is successful in providing best available tools and gadgets, he has won half of the battle in winning team member's mind and heart.

Time generation can bring wonderful result as it is not only the efficient way of getting the job done but also helps in winning the confidence of team members. When you decided to purchase agronomic furniture for your team members and make sure your team does not suffer from posture related problems, you want them to came back to their work place every morning with a smile on their face, not with a smell of ointment, this again has very positive impact on the overall performance of the team, when team member realises that, organisation is taking care of them by spending extra money on scientifically designed office furniture, they reciprocate by giving their best performance.

Now we have come to know the meaning of time generation in an organisation, time generation in an organisation can be defined as getting more work in same duration by providing better facilities in the form of furniture, gadgets, or equipment. When we give emphasis to time generation our team's productivity and efficiency reaches next level.

Scenario: Subhash has joined ABC. Corporation as leader, soon after joining his new team and to prove himself he wanted every task to be completed in seconds, but it is not possible as every task takes required time. Subhash was really perplexed, and he started looking after every minute detail and check whether everything is going in right direction, his micromanagement was not welcomed by his team members, then what is the way out to free himself of this.

He decided to discuss the matter with senior team members who in turn counselled him to mentor his team members for the process he desired, because personal interaction and mentoring new team members will remove mis-understanding and mis-communication, only with mentoring new team members will come to know about the professional demand Subhash put on them, this will act as double-edged sword, one edge will generate precious time for him and his team members as well and second edge will bring team members come close to leader by becoming more productive by themselves.

Time Utilisation; Time utilisation is the key for any leader for a successful tenure in not only in any organisation but throughout whole career, utilisation of time in this perspective means we are doing more meaningful activities during our free time, a successful leader encourages team members to utilise their free time in a better way, we all know that there is a time slot when we are not doing our professional duties or in other words we are not engaged in executing our routine official task, it utilisation of this free time which can bring positive and constructive results.

For a leader time utilisation should also be one of the aspects to which he must give heed, as he is having same number of hours as other team members and competitors, for a leader, tomorrow starts today as he is supposed to plan, organise, right allocation of work with proper guidance and mentoring, utilises time to the full. When we are discussing about time utilisation there is no better option but to provide better facilities and infrastructure to team members, so that they do not have to spend valuable time to look for petty things, along with above mentioned points good medical facilities also plays major role in utilising time.

Scenario: Free time when utilised in a better way brings remarkable change & result not only for leader but for whole team, in the absence of proper utilisation of free time, team members resort to gossiping, disturbing other team members or roaming out of the office without any reason spreading negativity, resulting in affecting the normal functioning.

Subhash was thinking of utilising his and team member's free time in a better way, during discussion with team members everybody was of the view that we should engage ourselves during free time with something related to health, after taking everybody's consent, team zeroed in on setting up a gym in office premises so that every team member can take advantage of it during free time and after office hours as well. Result of setting up gym in office proved to be a wonderful decision.

It was observed that interpersonal relationship between team members have improved a lot as they gym along and indulge in casual conversation about their families, festivals, recent trends in fashion, sports, international affairs and modern developments in management which ultimately reduces their stress. Subhash was also very happy to see his own BMI maintaining a steady level and fit team members taking fewer medical leaves, above all team members were seen interested in doing the allotted task as soon as possible in order to have more free time to enjoy gym facility, a healthy competition was seen among team members who will finish the daily task and hit the gym first.

Time Matrix for Leader; Time matrix for leader is that protocol if s/he starts following it will solve lot problems and obstacles removed. When a leader learns to allocate task in the four quadrant of time-matrix, s/he truly understand the difference between urgent and important tasks resulting in solution to lot of problems. Secondly, a leader has to maintain the quadrants of time matrix by keeping in view the whole organisation, and get the tasks done by using his power and flexible approach. Biggest advantage a flexible leader can take decisions by replacing urgent with important and important with urgent in the interest of organisation.

Urgent and Important tasks; First quadrant of time matrix shows us to do finish our task on urgent basis as soon as we receive information or instructions about it. In corporate sector every task is considered urgent, but at the end of the day they turn out to be routine task, in order to give urgency it's due importance, a leader must not fake it or in other words only those activity should be marked 'urgent' which are in fact urgent, it has been observed that leaders in order to get the things done quickly labelled those activities as urgent which are actually routine task, this mis-communication defeat the purpose of importance being important.

Scenario; One of the urgent and important tasks in the platter of a leader could be preparing **quarterly report** for board meeting, because in the board meeting a leader has to show the progress made by the organisation under h/her guidance, this report needs to be prepared with utmost care and presented with diligence to maintain and win the confidence of top brass. Quarterly report is not just a set of papers it is communication document which expresses where about of organisation and its next goal i.e., where we are and where we will be, while preparing this report a leader is expected to communicate to management what we have achieved in last quarter and what are our plans to achieve in next quarter.

Not Urgent Yet Important tasks; In this quadrant of time matrix a leader's observing capacity is tested. Being a keen observer helps a leader to observe and correct the faults if there is any, it may be in the process or any faulty policy, when a leader find any fault in the process or want to re-write any policy, s/he cannot do it in a flash, lot of thinking and discussions goes into it so that the outcome is permanent and stamp of 'best' is engraved on it, it could be done only when these activities are cooked on slow flame, which also denotes under the 'not urgent but important' category.

Scenario; One of the most important activities for a leader is to play role of HR custodian, although there is a human resource department in every organisation, but being leader of the organisation s/he is ultimately responsible for everything good or bad, hiring activities or making policies about retaining talented manpower must be given due importance, no step or action should be taken in hurry, a leader has to take decisions regarding human assets of the organisation which are most important factor for an organisation, in order to make human assets more valuable any decision or policy about them cannot be taken or made in hurry, as a leader one has to think very carefully for pros & cons of it. Any wrong decision will have long lasting impact on 'Trichual'.

Urgent but not important tasks; There are some activities in the daily routine of a leader which are not important but urgent. It could be a phone call from top management to attending a meeting and give feedback, in this meeting s/he does not has to play the role of decider but onlooker or moderator, as outcome of this meeting will not have any impact on decisions.

A leader has to take decisions which are urgent but not of that much important it may be getting his car insured and serviced, because any mode of conveyance which takes you to place of work has to be fit to fly anytime, any delayed servicing/insurance will lead to wastage of time in case of breakdown or being issued a challan for not showing proper documents will result in financial loss accompanied by wastage of time and undue stress. As an organised professional a leader must take appropriate steps to execute those tasks which may not seem to be important but which needs urgent attention, it could be getting medical insurance cover for family and natural disaster protection insurance (fire, earthquake or flood etc.) for h/her home, these important things in life give huge contentment and is source of peace, when we are contented and are in peaceful state of mind, our efficiency & productivity increases manifold.

Not Urgent Not Important tasks; In any corporate setup there are some activities which are nor urgent neither important for the smooth functioning of organisation, now the question arises why do we indulge in this type of activity which is not of any help in enhancing the efficiency or productivity of our organisation, the answer is that we all are human beings and cannot function like machines, our action and mind keep on drifting to unproductive arena, but there is fine line between wasteful and unproductiveness, wasteful activity is totally useless, whereas unproductive activity combined with thoughts can be turned into productive use.

Scenario; For a leader of an organisation not urgent nor important activity could be worrying about a new product coming from its competitor, worrying we all know is totally unproductive activity as a matured professional leader must turn it's worry into thinking, in place of worrying or being bogged down by the information of new product launch by its competitor one should fasten seat belt and put on his boots to counter it and strengthen the current position in market with full zeal by aligning strategy & energy.

Apart from professional responsibilities, a leader is responsible for wellbeing and happiness of family as well, but it has been observed that leader always put family responsibility in the nor urgent neither important quadrant of time matrix, although as commander of the troop, leader's self-interest comes last and everything else comes before, but as a human and above all a social animal, a leader must have schedule for quality family time, which is in the interest of leader and as well as team, an activity which should not take last seat, is taking annual leaves to take his family for a vacation, this can be put into category of not urgent and not important.

Time awareness for Team Leader.

For a team leader time awareness is totally different from Leader, s/he has to be aware of the time keeping in view team's and self strength & weaknesses, only then time awareness will be understood by team, because there is very thin line between various aspects of time awareness. It is very necessary for team leader to take appropriate steps to make best use of time for self and team. Let us discuss and understand those aspects one by one and take our team ahead.

Time Investment; Understanding and mastering time investment will help a team leader to get maximum return on time if invested wisely, can turn out to be a big boon for a team leader. As we all know that investment means spending a particular thing where you get maximum return, investment is not only related to money, it could be timely help, encouraging & positive words or expert advice etc., all this helps in spending now and expecting the best return when we need it, it could be helping a team member in distress, or employee going through difficult personal life, we all help each other with the notion that we will get it back when we needed it most, to get the best investment on time a team leader should spend it on the investment tips given above,

Time well and wisely spend with team members brings extra ordinary returns, it could be talking to them informally or helping them solve their personal and professional problems, guiding, coaching and mentoring them for future roles. Telling them few trade tricks, opening up with them so that they share their problems. Time investment can be done by a team leader in the office or it could be in parking lot or in office corridor by giving a pat on the back of a team member, motivating them by telling them s/he remembers good job done. When a leader practice informal motivation s/he is creating conditions where team member is ready to finish one hour job in forty-five minutes, which is the main purpose of time investment.

Scenario: Recognising team members extraordinary efforts in trying circumstances also make good returns on time investment. Subhash, the team leader was parking his car when he saw one of his team members Uday, He remembered how professionally and efficiently Uday had executed the assigned task despite of facing problem on medical front, Subhash could not give him a pat due to his busy schedule, Subhash walked up to him and congratulated for completing given task well in time despite of challenging circumstances.

Subhash specifically mentioned and thank him for spending extra hours in office in spite of medical problems and told Uday that all team members are praising him for his dedication towards his team and organisation. These encouraging words filled Uday with energy due to which he started working with double enthusiasm. In this way Subhash had invested time in the right direction.

Time Generation; Time generation can be done by team leader in many ways, to generate time a team leader must be flexible in his approach, time generation is basically accepting and following flexible approach by relaxing certain norms & regulations for team members who are executing given task sincerely, when a norm is relaxed for a sincere team member it results in generating time, Team leader can generate time by recognising and facilitating team-members by using authority by delegating important tasks or by allowing them to leave office before time for personal reasons if requested by a team member or providing them movie tickets or refreshment coupons in recognition for a good job done, when team leader practices above mentioned , then s/he is generating time and will never have any problem in asking team members to stay back for an extra hour for professional reasons if a need arises.

Scenario: A team leader can generate time by many ways one of it is delegating, delegating serves two purpose one, it provides spare time for the one who delegates allowing to pay attention to more diversified and important assignments, and for who accepts delegated duties gets empowered in decision making process.

Subhash decided to delegate procuring activity to Sam who was very excited to accept this new job responsibility, he was feeling contented that his sincere work has been recognised by team leader and from now onwards he will be fully responsible for fulfilling the material requirement of organisation, he will try to provide them best with in given time frame. This has not only increased the efficiency of the team but relieved Subhash for more important work.

Time Utilisation; Time utilisation as we all know that is known as best utilisation of free time available under the given circumstances, team leader's job is to create such a system where free time can be utilised to create policy and procedures to increase the efficiency of the group or create such an environment where **rate busters** are encouraged, and speed of **chisellers** are pushed to attain the next level, when team leader is able to get the job completed in less time than the allotted time is indication that meaning of time utilisation has been duly understood. Time can be best utilised when all the team members of a team are present to accomplished a project, time utilisation in other words is avoiding time wastage, as discussed, a team leader must be aware and understand the median age of the team members, when it's full of energy, when it needs break when there is a need of recreation, in fact team leader has to optimally utilise energy of team members and recharge it for next task.

Scenario: Time utilisation by a team leader can be done by paying attention to policies and procedures to minimise attrition rate,

A team leader very well understands the adverse impact when a well-trained team member leaving organisation. It takes around two months to fill the vacancy and during this period other team members have to bear the extra burden. When Ashok, one of the experienced and efficient team members put his papers, third resignation in a month kept the alarm bells ringing in board room, leader when called Ashok to enquire about the reason behind who in turn informed the leader that culture and working atmosphere of organisation has not changed since last ten years, whereas other organisation has transformed, we have not moved a bit in forward direction. After listening this team leader immediately called the HR head to resolve the issue and frame policies which are in tune with modern and advance practices of management & time.

Time matrix for team leader. A team leader's correct approach towards time matrix will help to get the task executed by team members efficiently, a team leader must mention while assigning the task, the category of time-matrix quadrant, this will make the procedure and job easier for team members. It has been observed that when assigning of task is accompanied by categorization of urgent, important, not so urgent or not so important improves the efficiency by resulting in removing the confusion. Whereas on the other hand most of the inefficiency happens due to lack of clarity about category in which the assigned task falls, in the absence of clear instructions team members executes the important task on urgent and urgent tasks on not so important basis, resulting in loss of time and resources subsequently putting the team in to trouble. So, a team leader who wants his or her team to move forward in right direction must develop good understanding of time-matrix. As mentioned below category wise. So, it is in the interest of team leader to mention category of urgent, important or not so urgent, important, while assigning the task.

Urgent and Important tasks; For a team leader nothing is more urgent and important than keeping its herd together, a team leader has to create an atmosphere of confidence & understanding and that can be created only by spending time with team members, removing their doubts, communicating with them to take a forward plunge. Last but not the least a group leader must invest time in solving internal strife and conflict among team members.

If a team leader is able to keep his herd together, s/he has won half of the battle without moving an inch or without firing a bullet, it may be visible from outside that team is performing together, but one has to go little deep in to the functioning and actions taken by them as a team, because if a team is performing together but unable to achieve its goal, then something is missing and not coming out, a team leader's most urgent and important task is to find out that missing factor and restore it back in the team, it could be an in-efficient team member, wrong job allocation, negative attitude or an element of dissatisfaction among team members or anything else which is hindering the team's success. Whenever a team leader smells that 'missing' something, it becomes urgent and important task to turn this 'missing' into 'finding'.

Not Urgent Yet Important tasks; When we are trying to find out the activities under not urgent yet important category, we must understand that there are certain activities which can't be done in hurry, they require adequate amount of attention to get the best result to have long-lasting impact on team.

As a team leader one has to involve in activities and take steps which are not very urgent but very important, these activities needs to be cooked on slow flame, it may be following an under-performing team member, when we follow a under-performing team member a lot of care needs to be taken so that team member's performance does not go down further due to small mistake or ignorant handling, any reason for underperformance can be find out only with observation done carefully and with proper attention, which requires serious intervention to be done but with spending proper time.

Example; When a team leader has to do grading of employees for different training programmes, which requires sincere understanding of team members in terms of aptitude and attitude, having understood their and team's requirement, taking it on urgent basis will result in wastage of time and resources. Similarly, there are many activities such as taking any decision regarding shuffling of team members, or sending recommendations/appraisals of team members to higher authority for promotion, demotion or retaining, all these activities mentioned above needs time and cannot be done in hurry as they are related with human assets of organisation which are heart and mind of every team.

Urgent but not important tasks; A team leader has to involve self in many activities which are labelled as urgent only, they are not labelled under important category for their routine tasks. Some activities which come under the category of urgent but not important, it may be a decision to accept an invite to facilitate winner of inter-departmental quiz competition, as CEO is busy in attending board of members who have arrived on very short notice, or attending a meeting on very short notice in which a team leader don't have much say but h/her name is there just for being a senior professional.

But keeping in view that urgent but not important tasks cannot be avoided, they are very much part of an organisation, they keep on cropping up from time to time, a team leader must be mentally prepared to execute those tasks without losing its cool and spoiling relations with top management, as a team leader one cannot refuse to do urgent but not important task as it is directly ordered from seniors.

Not Urgent Not Important tasks; As a team leader sometimes s/he has to involve self in those activities which are nor urgent neither important, but again they crop up uninvited, sometimes these tasks are personal and sometimes they are official, among personal tasks falling in this category could be phone calls from family members and friends which are part of family and social system, but problem starts when it becomes out of control, so in order to maintain the decorum and dignity of position a team leader must create a balance between the two fronts i.e. professional and personal . Secondly, on professional front some activities cropped up which don't need urgent neither important attention but still as a team leader one has to involved self.

Scenario; For a team leader there is no urgency nor important to pay heed to the rumour or false words spread about him or her, it could be a team member whose unjust demands were not considered by team leader, every team member is aware of the past record of a team member who is spreading rumours and false information, a team leader must have foresight to understand the motive behind spoken words, to handle this a team leader must develop thick skin so as not to get disturbed by allegations, on the other hand s/he must start thinking how to handle this awkward situation.

Time awareness for Team Members;

In this time of digitisation and technological advancements gadgets have made our work faster and accurate, we depend a lot on them. Imagine a scenario in which you reach office to finish pending report and your system did not respond to your command, once you start looking for reason behind this you came across an e-mail from system administrator for updating software, not paying heed to this important mail is going to cost you one full day. Even simple habit of not charging your phone or carrying power bank can leave you in the middle of an important conversation. Similar is the case with your mode of travelling that also needs to be well maintained. One has to be well organised to keep up with the time.

Scenario; Akshat is maintenance manager in a production unit, he had scheduled monthly maintenance of machineries and information was sent to all concerned person via e-mail. On the given day when all the team members were about to start maintenance of machines, they found that all important lubricants & oils to be used in maintenance are not available in stores. Resulting in huge loss of time and risk of breakdown while operating ill maintained machines.

If Akshat has proactively understood the time awareness, he would have scheduled the maintenance of machines after checking all the major requirements for it, as a team member of mechanical department he assumed that all the requirement and readiness from his side is complete, he may go ahead with the plan but there are some factors on which he has to depend on others and check the availability of the required factor. In this case procurement of lubricants is responsibility of purchase department, checking the availability and non-availability should be in the checklist of the professional or department who consumes it.

Time Investment; Time investment in terms of a team member may be described as when a team member uses available free time whether in the office or at home to involve self in those activities which are supposed to be of immense benefit in near future.

Free time by any individual team member must be wisely invested, as they are in the beginning of their career and is the right time to understand the need of continuous professional education, in this fast-changing world, one has to be in tune with time, so the best investment in free time for a team member could be an advance course in related field such as machine learning, artificial intelligence, finance or digital marketing etc., Even if there is no clear target is visible, a sincere professional must spend available free time to upgrade self, and indulge in meaningful activity to upskill .

Scenario: Ashok has just joined a multinational organisation after completing his M.Tech. in mechanical engineering, after working around one year in the same position he came to know that his company is going to setup another plant in a nearby district, this new plant will be based on modern machineries which requires expertise in Machine learning and Artificial Intelligence. Ashok discussed the matter with his superior and as suggested he applied for the course and simultaneously requested for official leave to attend the same. Ashok's move puts him in to 'first movers' advantage', as he was able to strengthen his position as important and most useful team member who is known as expert about new machines. In this way Ashok has invested his time wisely by keeping his future in mind.

Time Generation; Individual team member's time generating activity moves around timeliness for self and colleagues, normally at this age a juggle between personal and professional life is imminent as both are very demanding, if we want comfort and advancement of modern life, we must be ready to pay the price for it as both lives are equally important during this period.

A successful professional learns the importance of punctuality, routine, good mental and physical health in order to generate time, when one has good routine and every activity is done with in prescribed time limit or less, it sets example for other team members as well. A decent routine is the key in generating time which helps a professional to achieve set goal and helps a professional to achieve the target in allotted time by avoiding wastage of time and duplicity of task.

Scenario: Time generation by a team member can be done by following a particular routine, when one follows a routine, mind always sounds an alert when any activity is missing in that routine, there should be practice of leaving some space for unexpected or new activity which may be incorporated, As a professional Amit always keep half an hour for any unexpected or additional task in his daily routine it may be unplanned discussion or meeting, uninvited guest or casual conversation lingered on during lunch or coffee, but he make sure that his normal routine is not disturbed.

Time Utilisation; For a team member there is no better way to utilise free available time with team members and strengthening inter-personal relationship for future needs, one has to be proactive in taking interest and be supportive in personal and professional lives of other team members. It is very helpful in giving and getting help in case of any emergency or need.

For a team member best way of utilising time is to listen every instruction very carefully, when an instruction is listened carefully it works for both sides, one for the person who is giving instructions and the recipient of instructions, secondly when an instruction is listened carefully and fully abided, it opens up trust between giver and taker and they started sharing healthy relationship beyond professional arena.

Scenario: Kush was working as administrative officer in a reputed organisation; he was having problem in listening instructions clearly not because of any medical reason. But in order to please his seniors, before any verbal communication takes place, he started saying Yes Sir- Yes Sir. But one incident changed his habit.

Once his boss called him on intercom to apprise him of a hearing scheduled in high court on 10th June and instructed him to prepare all legal documents pertaining to the matter, as usual Kush kept on saying Yes Sir-Yes Sir, he in his note pad jotted down date of hearing as 10th July in place of 10TH June, on 8TH of June his senior called him to bring files related to court matter in his cabin, his face went pale as he had not prepared a single note under the impression that date of hearing is 10th of July. We can easily understand that what would have happened after this.

Time Matrix for Team Member; Team members are those professionals who have just stepped in to corporate sector and currently adjusting themselves to prove their capacity in this world of cut throat competition, to execute the given task in the most proficient way, they must understand the concept of Time-matrix, understanding time matrix will help them remove confusion and pave the way towards better efficiency.

In the absence of knowledge about time-matrix, team members are unable to decide which task is important, which task is urgent or which task is nor urgent neither important, clarity about task falling in which quadrant of time-matrix will help a lot and set priorities regarding assigned task. Secondly, if quadrant of time-matrix is not mentioned while assigning a task a team member must ask very politely and seek clarification about the same from senior while accepting any task, this open communication will always be in the interest of self and team.

Urgent and Important tasks; For a team member one of the most urgent and important thing could be preparing monthly report or any other routine job assigned by senior, every team member should understand the importance of job they are assigned or engaged in, they must do it with sincerity and accountability, benefit of doing the assigned job within given specific time is that you are free for tomorrow.

Scenario; As a young member of family and society you have to execute so many personal and social responsibility as well, which also requires few days off from office, if one has executed most of the assigned tasks, there will not be any problem in getting your leave sanctioned.

Not Urgent but Important tasks; Category of not urgent but important in a time quadrant must be taken very sincerely by a team member, as these important activities require learning and have lifelong impressions, what about giving importance to quality in this quadrant, if we have understood the meaning of quality it will stay with us throughout our career, it could be one of the few activities for an individual team member which are not urgent but important.

Scenario; It may be preparing for monthly meeting of quality circle, as a new entrant in corporate world one should have fair longing for quality and its importance, having understood the concept and implemented in its daily routine will make you stand ahead of other team members who are interested in doing the task in a routine manner and without any enthusiasm whereas a professional with quality concept wanted to execute the task with best result.

Urgent yet not important tasks; Few actions a team member must take which are urgent but not that of much importance, it may be reporting a broken wash basin tap or door lock handle, these activities does not seem to be important but urgent, one has to report to technical department urgently to prevent loss of precious resources. **Scenario;** One more urgent but not important category is organising desk or cabin on urgent basis as during last meeting, a pen drive having very important report went missing, resulted in cancellation of meeting and a stern warning from team leader, so uncluttering and organising desk & cabin is one of the most urgent activities which a team member has to take, it may not of be of utmost importance to organisation.

One more activity which a team member has to take under this category is accepting the casual invitation of group to visit canteen for coffee or tea without any reason or it could be self who wants to have a cup of coffee to rejuvenate self to uplift the mood or for some change and come back on desk to start working with more zeal.

Not urgent nor important tasks; An individual team member should not indulge in activities which are not urgent nor important one of it is gossiping around coffee dispenser, secondly, when he is called to stay back in canteen during lunch hours etc.

Scenario; It is not urgent nor important for a team member to spread negative information about the organisation through which he is earning his bread & butter, fulfilling social and professional responsibilities. A team member may be assigned a task which is neither urgent nor important, but very much an integral part of organisation or department. One of it may be planning for monthly combined celebration of team member's birthday. By performing these tasks for organisation, a team member proves his or her importance

Time awareness for students;

Time awareness for students is perhaps one of the most important concepts which s/he must learn during student life, it could be time investment, time generation or time utilisation. A student must understand that however intelligent s/he is, if not aware of time, life will not move in positive direction and fulfil set goals, by being not aware of time-awareness a student will find it very difficult to lead a successful life, being unaware of time will invite struggle at every step of life and won't be able to accomplish small tasks.

If a student wants to lead a life well lived and fulfil h/her parents dream, mastering time awareness is the first and most important step in this direction. There is an old proverb that 'time is money' but in my opinion **time is life**, if a student is able to understand this concept that life equals time and every second, minute or hour gone is gone and cannot be brought back by the mightiest of human being, s/he has won half of the battle.

Time Investment; Investment of time is that concept if a student is able to understand it fully will help h/her to travel longer distance in shorter time than those counterparts who are ignorant about the concept of time investment, or in other words concept of time investment will motivate a student to indulge in those activities which brings multiple returns and have permanent effect on career and life.

Student must divide their time between study and other co-curricular activities to expose themselves to a more challenging atmosphere which makes them grow, they must invest their time in attaining knowledge besides by getting good grades. A student must understand the meaning of whole personality, investment of time must be in the direction of removing identified shortcoming and adding any new habit which might help in enjoying better future, it may be learning new foreign language or looking for information for further studies to strengthen present qualification, time is not money, it's more precious than money, because lost money can be recovered but not time.

Scenario: During student life Anamika has understood the importance of one thing that is investing time in better planning for all the affairs related to studentship whether it is preparation for examination, any extra curriculum activities or preparing assignment, she always plans in advance to avoid last minute rush, planning become first and foremost activity of her student life after an incident due to which she has to part with her very precious year of life.

During her twelfth standard, she kept on postponing her studies to be done just before exams, as luck would have it, she fell ill and could not perform as per her expectation and decided to repeat the year. Now she keeps regular pace with her subjects by planning well in advance to outsmart any unwanted or untoward incident, she has rightly understood the concept of time investment by planning her activities and scheduling study hours.

Time Generation; Time generation by students can be done by engaging self in those activities for which they have allotted specific time, Students can avoid wastage of time by keeping themselves physically & medically fit, being medically & physically fit gives confidence and develop positive attitude towards studies.

Being medically unfit might cost you a year, if one can calculate the cost of a year in monetary terms which might go into lakhs and amount of pain it gives to self and family. In order to generate time a student must learn to know those factors, which can create a hurdle in h/her schedule, it could be health, distraction or any hidden factor which could prop up due to any family matter, one has to identify and sort it out.

Scenario: Being mentally and physically fit means is their ability to understand constructive criticism in a positive manner, during their duration of academic programme students find it difficult to accept any advice. They think that they know everything, but to come out with flying colours in their studies an individual must take path of maturity along with youth.

Look at the case of Namita, she was given feedback about the submitted assignment, a remark was written on the cover of assignment by evaluator, "specify the reason behind your conclusion". After receiving this feedback, Namita met evaluator and corrected her assignment to the satisfaction of evaluator. Whereas other students just ignored the remarks and continue as usual. Result of a brainstorming with her evaluator gave Namita great deal of confidence and number one position in programme.

Time Utilisation; Students need to utilize their time in terms of studies and must be aware of the time available to complete their semester, for example if their semester is for six months, they must divide all subjects (generally there are five or six subjects and related assignments in a semester), allocating more time for difficult subject and subsequently lesser time for easy subject. Practically speaking a student get less time than the announced by academic calendar.

One more thing a student can do is to utilise spare time by being friendly with their seniors, which will save them from so many problems in terms of guidance and they can ask for previous years question papers, notes and assignments. Time utilisation in a student life is basically directly related to common sense prevailing in an individual, time could be utilised by living near place of study, as travelling is one of the menaces which consumes lot of time, money and energy, if you could not live nearby your place of study, you should choose that time and mode of commuting which takes less time, even if reaches well before start of lectures and leaving college once the classes are over.

Scenario: Best way a student can utilise time is to identify procrastination and how to handle it, procrastination is one menace which eats up lot of time and leaves a student stranded in the middle. As I have mentioned earlier, youth suffer from "knows everything" syndrome and do not want to hear anything from anyone.

A very true and personal example I can share with all of you is about my graduation days, during graduation our annual exams were held in the month of April-May, but fortunately or unfortunately, exams were postponed for a fortnight every year but as a student suffering from procrastination always follow the 'Murphy's Law' in this regard and could not take advantage of those fifteen days for which exams were postponed, after hearing the postponement of examination, I postpone and re-schedule my time table for another fifteen days, but I could not take advantage of the postponement period and my grades remain same irrespective of extra fortnight available for preparation of examination.

Time Matrix for Students; Student life is that part of life which can built strong foundation for our future, as we stepped in this world with eyes full of dreams, we have to involve ourselves in lot of activities to realise those dreams, it is better for all of us to label those activities in different category of time matrix, urgent, important, not so urgent and take action accordingly, not understanding the time matrix will result in lot of confusion and wastage of time.

Students should make their priorities to label every activity coming their way as per time matrix or in which quadrant of time matrix it falls, it could be preparing and submitting an assignment, planning daily schedule, utilisation of extra time, decision about taking part in sports or any other activity, selecting friends, observing spending habits etc. When a student is able to master time-matrix, s/he is able to take clear decision regarding utilising of available time. As this whole chapter is about making best use of available time, student must understand that time cannot be saved or stored it can be used only to benefit ourselves.

Urgent and Important tasks; As we all know that there is nothing more urgent & important for a student but to secure good grades and realise their dreams, s/he must do preparation of exam giving it full importance and urgency. Because it is our marksheet which clearly states that what you did during your time of study or how responsibly you acted when you were assigned the task of completing the course,

Scenario; There is tendency in students having over confidence and ignoring the reality, being a realistic and testing self on the balancing beam to get the best result. Secondly, one of the most important and urgent tasks for student has to find out the crust of life and way of living it to the full, which includes finding out the weaknesses in self and ways to remove it, trying out new hobby and being aware of the new developments in subjects and programme.

Not urgent yet important tasks; In my opinion one of the not so urgent but very important task for a student is to find the right company during educational program, s/he needs to find out the those individuals who are like minded and possess those qualities which can be of help during difficult times and is also ready to help them back, in other words a student must look for true friend who is interested in giving first and taking it later or without thinking of getting anything in return.

If a student looks for a company or want to become friend in a hurried manner or on urgent basis by becoming friend with whoever s/he meet first, might land into big trouble, as friendship at this age (20-25 years) have long lasting impact on life, one might be attracted towards wrong company and practices, derailing the progress of self or become harmful to society, being in the wrong company will shatter dreams of self and family as well. Whereas choosing good company will have very positive impact on a student which will not only of great help during the course of study but in future as well.

Scenario; Students who were part of good company will be professionally well settled and remaining in touch with them through good networking skills will bring success and happiness, in case of any professional help or exploring any career ladder can be done only with the help of good company, another benefit of professionally successful good company is that we are able to create family relation in the form of marriage of our near or dear ones.

Secondly, revision, assignments or home work is perhaps are those tasks which falls under this category, assignment, homework or revision activities for a student may not be urgent but it is time bound and very important, which may be preparing and submitting given assignment on a topic of importance, it's through assignment a teacher evaluates the sincerity and creativity of a student, if we go through the difference between examination and assignments, for exams a student has limited time and has to produce answers without any external help, whereas for assignments there is always a pre-decided period and adequate material available for execution, it's like open book exam. A teacher always gives assignments on the important topics as every teacher want their student to perform well and assignments are the best tools for their development.

Urgent Yet not important tasks; This quadrant of time matrix is basically related with personal need of students or academic related activities such as arranging materials for a project to be submitted with in time frame or arranging finance to be with class during a short trip to a nearby hill station, during student life there are some personal needs as well.

Time Awareness

Scenario; During student life we have to perform some activities which are urgent but not important, this might include ordering food for friends who have made a visit to our house or purchasing a new dress to attend friend's marriage, all these activities which you have given a status of urgency will help a student in long run and other students will also reciprocate in the same manner.

Not Urgent Not Important tasks; During student life there is a tendency to give importance and urgency to activities which are in fact not required at all, Students tend to follow those things which are not going to help them in future and may be put in category of life threatening and utter useless for a student. It may be accepting an invitation from peer group when they say or promise that everybody will experience something new, student must understand the meaning of "something new" is always combination of drugs and alcohol.

Scenario; One of your classmates could not submit his assignment on time and was scolded by teacher, when you asked the reason behind the delay, he said he was binge watching a web series whose name you even don't know, you felt very bad and seems to be out of this world for not knowing the name of that popular web series, suddenly you also start thinking in the same direction of spending more time with OTT platform. Student must avoid herd mentality and start learning to think independently.

Another activity which is neither urgent nor important, but students indulge in it, is their fascination for speed, and using their mode of personal conveyance to impress others, unnecessary exhibition of speed and stunts have left many parents 'orphaned'.

Living in the moment; As a CEO, Team leader, team member or student what we should do to understand the real meaning of time? We must learn to **live in the moment**, which means applying all our abilities to the task we are executing at this point of time by focusing the mind to the present, we will build our future on the basis of what we are doing at present and maximizing all the possibilities being offered by life, problem occurs when we are thinking of our job while eating, while at work we are thinking of holidays, while partying we are thinking about our job, we are never fully present at one place or situation. We feel disturbed as our mind is caught up in the past or by the hope and fear related to the future.

To live in the moment, we have to make conscious effort to focus on the task we have undertaken whether it is doing anything related to job, eating meal, doing laundry, washing dishes, shaving or studying for exams etc. when we pay attention to single activity results in calmness of the mind and bear good fruit. For being present in the moment we have to make our mind still from the thoughts of yesterday and worries of tomorrow by acknowledging that the past is over and **our future depends on how beautifully we live in the present**. When we as a human being started our journey on this planet, we were **natural warriors**, but with all the scientific and material development we have turned ourselves into **natural worriers.** We are always worrying about the future or dwelling in the past robbing ourselves of the present sacred moments.

Conclusion; We have to make 'time' our friend, if we take care of our friend and behave well with it, Time will give us return gift of friendship by always remaining by our side. Time is the most precious invisible metal available on earth which is equally distributed among habitats of this mother earth and the best thing is it is free, but if not respected it has the power to consume anything form careers to individual.

www.ingramcontent.com/pod-product-compliance
Lightning Source LLC
LaVergne TN
LVHW091616070526
838199LV00044B/814